AUTHOR'S NOTES

The stories, the people and the wines in this book reflect an extraordinary time in Cape wine.

I have attempted to moderate the levels of gush. But these wines *are* my kind of wines. They and their back-stories grab me. Some are humble, a few very grand. They are grown and made by old friends and new, colourful people refining traditional ideas and sometimes trying zany ones - and why not? And because I lived among them for 20 years, the book is part self-indulgent memoir too with all the risks - and convenience - of self-exculpatory amnesia.

So it's subjective mostly. I subscribe to Martha Gellhorn's take on reporting. "All this objectivity crap," she said. I try to take my cue from hard-bitten, soft-hearted reporters, once my foreign correspondent colleagues on various frontlines who brought their stories to life through people more than arid analyses.

This is not a systematic — much less a comprehensive - tour of the wine lands. It's a ramble. After an absence of 16 years. Written not for the cognoscenti, whose cellars must already reflect the audacious leaps in quality and variety, but for the not-yet-hooked. An old-fashioned reporting assignment, following my nose. Someone would say: "Oh, you must see so and so, she's made a fantastic Grenache." And we'd go. Then we'd hear about off-the-wall experiments elsewhere. We'd go.

Cape wine is in flamboyant ferment. The range of gorgeous — less fruity but more generously savoury - Chenin Blancs is astounding. The Cape White Blend, anchored around Chenin, is hailed as a phenomenon on the world scene. New cachet for South Africa. Our old vine Grenache is the stuff of goose pimples. A personal weakness for Cabernet Franc is better catered for. Lowly Cinsaut? You have to try the new stand-alone ones. Even long-scorned Clairette Blanche is yielding hidden qualities. A few Chardonnays have been to the gym and shed years; they are less oaky, less flabby — stylishly taut. Cheers to that. And a toast, also, to the irreverent new generation players who are knocking the stuffiness out of wine tasting and drinking.

The scramble for grapes from ancient vineyards on the fringes of traditional wine country is hectic. Remote mountain passes and dry river beds have become new beacons on the national wine map. Everyone, everywhere, seems to be re-calibrating.

Lightness, freshness and informality are set to stay. Alcohols, at long last, are declining — though not by enough nor fast enough. Big grunters — massively dark, compressed reds - are still around though their tannins are finer-grained. There'll always be a place for them. But the drift to easier, less worked-over wines - both light and weighty - truer to their vineyard origins, is irreversible. Organic and even biodynamic principles are widely appreciated, if still not as widely practised. And ecology-conscious protocols are less frequently breached too.

This has been a fascinating, palate-stretching story to cover. Not as logistically testing as travels through the vineyards of Africa for our last wine book, *Africa Uncorked*. Maybe not quite as adrenalin-pumping as interviewing Uganda's General Idi Amin the day after he seized power in a coup, his bloodshot eyes slowly scouring the room for trouble. But quizzing as complex a bunch as the Cape's wine people has its moments. The rewards are in their bottles.

Of course I wouldn't suggest the wines described here are the best in South Africa. Can there be 'best' in matters of taste? Wine is free-style art-form. Critics come ready-made and aplenty. Your own palate is the true compass. But do I think you'll drink happily and adventurously among these wines? And the people who make them? And that they will inspire more of your own explorations? I hope so.

JOHN PLATTER

For Lily Rose and Samuela

ON
THE
ROAD

CONTENTS

CABERNET FRANC

They did it, probably, somewhere in hilly Basque country several centuries ago. Cabernet Franc, a black grape, and Sauvignon Blanc, a white, consummated a relationship that changed the face of wine: they begat Cabernet Sauvignon. An unlikely match with an unintended outcome – but aren't many? The progeny is certainly much louder than the black grape parent – louder in tannin, colour and general intensity. And now it dominates the world of red wine. But who, trying a few – and the problem is the few - of the great Cabernet Francs of the world, isn't charmed by the gentler, lighter, more reserved and urbane black grape parent?

Why not more Cab Franc sooner in the Cape? A mystery, really. A difficult grape, yes. But not impossible, in the right location, and with some extra care to aerate the vine canopy. Have South African consumers – and growers - been blind-sided by Cabernet Sauvignon - and Cab S-dominated Bordeaux-style blends - as the zenith of reds? And yet, a few of the very grandest French clarets include heavy proportions of Cabernet Franc; and among the most celebrated is Ch. Cheval Blanc, which contains about two-thirds of the grape. Chris Williams, the studious winemaker at Meerlust, recently told me: "Cabernet Franc is always my favourite wine in this cellar – before we blend it to add complexity to the Rubicon." I don't think I persuaded him, but I did suggest reserving a barrel or two for a Meerlust Cabernet Franc. Imagine.

I love these wines. They often have a dry, chalky quality - my mind sees white limestone cliffs. Those I've tried to describe below are variable, but each is a moderating respite from the booming, bold qualities of Cabernet Sauvignon, especially in its youth. Happily, the choice of Cabernet Franc labels is widening interestingly. There was even an inaugural Cab Franc 'Carnival' in 2015. Good news for me, and others looking to explore different red avenues.

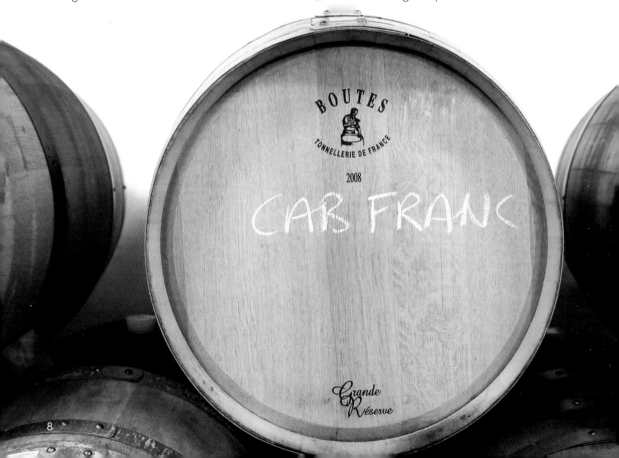

NORMA'S GRAPE

Warwick Estate's winemaker is Nic van Aarde, whose international CV includes an adventurous, curry-fired, two-year stint at Zampa Winery in Nashik, India's Napa Valley. "Challenging doesn't begin to describe working there," he says. "Exploding bottles, water contaminated with insecticide, child labour... I've seen it all!" He made Chenin, Sauvignon, Cabernet Sauvignon, a red blend, a pink from Shiraz and a Méthode Champenoise bubbly. His after-life, at Mulderbosch, and now Warwick, is tame and restful by comparison. Though not short of challenges. Burnishing the reputation of Warwick founder and first winemaker Norma Ratcliffe's favourite wine is one of them. "Cabernet Franc is my grape," Canadian-born Norma has always said. She was a pioneer of letting it stand, and shine, on its own, making her first in 1988.

Nic van Aarde also loves Norma's grape. Why? "It's a grown-up, more restrained version of Cabernet Sauvignon," he says. So we taste. The grapes for the **Warwick Cabernet Franc 2012** come from a mature 18-year-old vineyard. Strict berry sorting. No fining. Just over two years in oak, 25% new. It's what I look for, juicy, minerally but quiet. Even a little of what I call (and like) dry chalkiness, to off-set the sappy, dark-cherry fruit. Just writing this has me salivating. A relief from big, assertive Cabernet Sauvignons. A fabulous change of pace.

Son Mike Ratcliffe is now the boss here. Leading a team is in his genes. He's confident and adventurous, very well-travelled and not short of firm opinions. A sample: "There are too many one-barrel wonders in the Cape! Too many flagships. And we drink wines far too early." He is on the board of every local wine organisation imaginable, several international ones, and has founded a couple, like Rootstock, a forum for the younger generation in the wine industry. He is also the MD of US-Cape premium producer Vilafonté, one of my all-stars, whose global viticultural guru, Phil Freese, keeps a beady eye on Warwick's vineyards, too.

Out-of-the-box thinking and modern marketing are Ratcliffe's strengths, and include the indefatigable use of social media - Warwick's online Wine Club has more than 1000 members. The food and wine events and family-friendly grounds - the whole relaxed vibe of the place - have won Warwick a string of tourism awards. Off the farm, he's driven the raising of millions at annual Cape Wine Auctions, in aid of local charities. "Rats gets things done," even his critics acknowledge. "My Dad always told me to follow the enthusiasts, and I do," he says.

BABOONS, BIRDS, PONIES

There's a war in these hills and we can put our money on Keermont Vineyards proprietor Mark Wraith. "The big machines will be here soon to dig those out," he says, pointing accusingly at tiny wattles trying to make a come-back after his regular sweeps to clean the farm of alien invaders, and restore its wild fynbos glory. This 160ha property is a treasure of variable terroirs. Hillsides reach 340m above sea level. Vineyards plunge down gorges into the river that separates the Stellenbosch and Helderberg mountains. We're driving on steep granite tracks zigzagging up the hills. "Oh, and that too," he exclaims as we swerve around another corner, tyres sliding loudly on the loose pebbles, when he sees a pine peeping out of the floral kingdom. Just 30ha is reserved for vines. This is not easy farming. Baboons and birds – starlings especially – gorge at harvest time. He is equally focused on developing official Single Vineyards on these wild uplands, as well as preserving some older plantings. Like 'Riverside', with knotty, old-vine Chenin Blanc planted in 1971, yielding a barely sustainable 1,5 tons a year: about a quarter of what would be considered viable. It's survived repeated grubbing-up schemes – including a family plea to turn it into a pony paddock.

Taking the winding, narrow road into this gorge outside Stellenbosch is rewarded by expressive wines with clearly delineated pedigrees, linked to their immediate, individual environments. To be sampled in a quiet and understated tasting room. Wine-making is by Alex Starey, who grew up here and qualified at Stellenbosch University. He is equally respectful of the grapes in the modern way: within practical limits, try not to get between the vineyard and the bottle. All of which finds favour among hands-off-winemaking punters. Export markets take 80%.

Watch for the next Single Vineyard label: **Keermont High Road Cabernet Franc 2014**. Unequivocal evidence for a serious place in Cape wine for this grape, mostly unsung and buried in blends. The barrel sample was just gorgeous: a Bordeaux quality, deep raspberry flavours.

PICKING THE EYES

Bruwer Raats says: "I don't have a legacy." There's no family estate, no long wine dynasty. Perhaps that's why this determined, confident, articulate man is so intent on creating one. Not in big real estate (yet?) but in reputation. As Mr Cabernet Franc of South Africa, he finds the niche swelling beyond niche – a legacy itself perhaps? "I welcome the competition," he says. "Let's make the pie bigger."

Raats' operation is a methodical juggling act, in French negociant tradition: not only identifying scattered, selected, usually old vineyards but picking the eyes - only the best sections and rows of them, in collaboration with growers. He's been honing his game for more than a decade. He handles the grapes – and blends - at Mont Destin, just outside Stellenbosch, where he consults too. Red vinification is geared to "soft fruit extraction mirroring Burgundian Pinot Noir techniques"; to sparing use of new oak, limited to 30% new but often less; to maximising reflections of climate and soil identities in wines. He believes the magnesium and calcium in weathered Table Mountain Sandstone, the soils of elevated Cape mountain sides, fix the signature qualities of Cabernet Franc – a lighter, mineral-inky-iron-like quality. The grape's awkward tendency to show a green leafiness can be minimised, even obliterated, either by more vineyard attention or targeted oak-integration, preferably both. Is all this TMI (too much information) or shooting a line? I don't think so. His distinctive wines answer the question.

His fruit sources include two very old, very high-lying vineyards – one surprisingly unvirused - evidently key to the characteristics of his wine. Loyalty to Stellenbosch is total. Not a grape from outside its boundaries. Few know the profusion of terroirs better. His years as winemaker at Delaire gave him insights into the higher and often lesser known, sometimes even hidden, upper regions. But he ranges wide; have a look at the sources for his Chenin. And watch for the new B Vintners Heritage range in collaboration with Gavin Bruwer, a younger cousin: to "promote the renaissance of Stellenbosch".

The **Raats Family Cabernet Franc** is the big hitter, the 2013 a burly, broad-shouldered, emphatic (bit like its maker), dark wine. Still with tannic dryness when tasted in 2015. Expensive. **The Dolomite** more retiring, lighter. My favourite is the middle-of-the-road **Raats Family Red Jasper**, named after Bruwer Raats' dad, the viticulturalist in the family. A completely charming Cabernet Franc-led - 85% - blend, with a blackcurrant quality, touch of liquorice, fluid light texture. A taste worth acquiring! Effortlessly washes down meaty-gamey dishes.

THE DISCIPLINE OF MODERATION

A contemplative gentleman, a working architect, free of airs or the strutting that his uniquely fine wines warrant. That's David Trafford. After a quarter century, turning a hobby into a sideline into a business – often in the headlines for the best award- winning reasons – this remains a one-family, owner-grower-winemaker- marketer affair.

Trafford is unapologetic about the consistently high alcohols of his wines, 15% and more not uncommon. The usual – producer - line says this is okay provided the wine is "in balance" and the hot-burn alcohol doesn't stand apart, if it doesn't "disfigure" the wine, if the consumer "doesn't notice it!" Plausible - up to a point. But the pituitary gland doesn't make such allowances, is not in direct communication with our olfactory senses (which may be enjoying the wine hugely) and is unable to regulate the speed of intake; it has to cope with the rising alcohol level; we impair our balance, vision, bloat our bladders, bulge our livers; they become sluggish at clearing the polluted gridlock. We de-hydrate and wake with splitting craniums.

You have to take modest sips – interspersed with gulps of diluting, re-hydrating water and bites of stomach-lining food - over a couple hours, for a couple of glasses of Trafford's wines. And he'd say: that's right, how wine should be savoured. His are not raucous-occasion, slurping wines. The charm of these efforts is worth the discipline of moderation. The winemaker hasn't designed these levels, nature has. He's definite about that.

The De Trafford establishment, home and winery, function under a thick canopy of ancient oaks amidst luxuriantly unfussy gardens sloping to a river, out of the way, casually signposted, at the dead-end of a secluded valley south-east of Stellenbosch. Many busy architects seem to leave their own places to last (undisguised add-ons, subtractions), almost as monuments to organic and unselfconscious living. Ditto Trafford. The winery is reassuringly real, casually unkempt on the outside, like many in the deep French countryside, where they are concerned about what's in the barrel not the extrinsics. No superficiality. As Trafford's knowledgeable assistant, Xenia van der Meulen, says (the boss was in Spain, boning up on Priorat): "We're so out of the way here, if people find us, they usually know our wines well enough not to need a sales talk." Very small, at 5ha; decomposed granite soils. Selected vineyard parcels are bought in from long-standing growers, including neighbour Keermont. Unfined, unfiltered, wild yeast ferment.

De Trafford Cabernet Franc 2012 is a recent addition to the range. Like a Cabernet Sauvignon but with the emphatic parts toned down, the smile brighter. There's lusciousness, lightness – perhaps a little less power and gravitas than in a Cab S, but it's graceful, with a dry, mineral quality and supple, cushy texture. I'd have it with steak tartare. To bounce along with the oniony, salty, raw beef, without muscling in; Cab Sauvignon can be an elbowy queue-jumper.

AND

Anthonij Rupert Cabernet Franc 2009 A wine with clout, serious, big occasion stuff. At the more emphatic end of the Cab Franc spectrum, with chalky individuality (seen in St Emilion sometimes), dense but softening tannins for massive width on palate. Exclusive – only a score or so barrels; all new oak for 18-24 months. Unfiltered.

Cape Chamonix doesn't do Cab Sauvignon. As former winemaker Gottfried Mocke said "We can't ripen it here. Cab Franc ripens much earlier, works a treat." The **2012 Cabernet Franc** is a mildly dishevelled old gent, taking a morning stroll around the village square, smiling, nodding, settling down to read the newspaper (not on an iPad) at a café and chuckling here and there at a cartoon as he rustles the pages. This gentle red is without airs, smooth and juicy, balanced and kindly. Without bitterness – but not without something to say. There's some grip and an occasional whiff of savoury cigar smoke. It's closed with a screwcap: down to earth in that, too.

Oldenburg Cabernet Franc 2011 The variety in uncomplicated, comfortable mood. Gentle mulberry flavours, easy to like. The experienced Philip Costandius in vineyards and cellar here.

Rainbow's End Cabernet Franc 2013 from Banghoek, vineyards high above the Helshoogte Pass between Stellenbosch and Pniel – terroir which this variety seems to enjoy. A stunning find. Altogether gorgeous. Ripe, deep. Hands-off winemaking: gentle basket press, no filtration or fining. The Malans, Jacques, Anton and Francois also produce a single-vineyard Reserve.

Stellenrust Cabernet Franc 2012 This cellar's modern approach – unfussy, clean and fresh - drew me to this charming, quite low-key, light-textured red. Subtle and supple, sweet cherry fruit. Easy drinking.

No wine takes charge with the authority of a fine Cabernet Sauvignon. Wherever a red wine fits, it can do duty. It was what I called for in hospital not long ago, when the doc, perhaps afraid of withdrawal symptoms, gave me the wine all-clear.

The grapes are small, dark, thick-skinned and reliably deliver the hallmark blackcurrant, silky rich intensity and, improbably, simultaneously, the generosity of minerally tannic power. Cabernet Sauvignon has reach, delicious oomph and longevity. As a vine, it is forgiving, amenable to a wide spread of soils and climates, though it can sometimes run out of summertime and struggle to ripen its grapes fully, especially in cooler sites and in wet, cold vintages. Its vigour and brio are then easily reduced to miserable harshness.

However, Cabernet's numbers, the acreages planted, the worldwide spread, volumes consumed, prices paid, show it's the world's favourite fine-quality red, the most respected, dependable wine on earth. Its centres of excellence, where it fetches its highest prices, are Bordeaux, France, its home; and Napa, California, where its top labels enjoy unbelievable cult status and stratospheric tags. In South Africa we grow and make respectable, world-class Cabs, most of them in and around Stellenbosch. Constantia probably deserves more recognition.

Not everyone will agree of course, but I believe that of the great classic wines from classic grapes – Chardonnay, Pinot Noir, Riesling, Cabernet - only Cabernet improves with help from blending partners. Chardonnay and Pinot are diminished when mingled (except with each other in Champagne); Riesling is all about its own penetrating purity. Oak barrelling? It's a befuddling jumble of myth and science, but huge in the make-up of many wines, especially Cab. Thank God it's exempted from the "additive" charge. The anti-pleasure police would love to pounce. It's what centuries of use does, absolving Quercus, European oak, from any wine-doctoring stigma, conferring integral part-of-the-wine status. The dazzling array of flavours and spicy compounds that suffuse a wine resting in barrels, leached from the staves (and the forests of France!) are legion and life-altering in a wine's evolution. So powerful that minor slips – a few weeks too long in a new barrel – are easily magnified. Winemakers need their wits - as well as luck, and a wily way with French coopers, keepers of the secrets of their forest sources.

CABERNET SAUVIGNON

One cautionary note: Cape wine's most serious drag on quality, especially among reds, the leaf-roll virus in vines, is less common now. But many vineyards are still affected: their grapes don't ripen properly or evenly. There are exceptions, but they then can't offer the lusciousness that transmutes into generous, balanced wines. Unripe tartness, however, should not be confused with normal and healthy, youthful tannic astringency. If you're getting tinny, mean, thin harshness in a 5 year-old plus Cabernet, don't waste your time. Your palate isn't lying to you. Move on.

Cab can stand magnificently on its own, but because it is sometimes so powerful – in colour, flavour, tannin – it can be successfully teamed with and tamed by compatible grape varieties. But it nearly always remains the senior partner. (See my kind of Red Blends.)

THE ZEN ZONE

As you turn the corner into the Jonkershoek valley, the mountains, the leafy oaks, enclose you. It's quiet in this secluded glade, a zen-zone. Instinctively, you feel the wines here at Stark-Condé have to be different, and they are. It's cool and wet; harvest season ripening proceeds relatively steadily, sensitive flavours are not burned out of the grapes.

Marie Condé drives us up and up; the vineyards cling onto rugged, vertiginous slopes; forests, nature reserve and Stellenbosch town lie far below. High on a crest, looking down on the winery, are the towering trees after which the **Stark-Condé Three Pines Cabernet Sauvignon** is named. There were four; one was struck by lightning. Had it not been naturally taken out, Marie's Japanese mother might have chopped it down herself. Four would have been bad fortune…

So, no surprises, this is a beautiful wine. For its sheer intensity and focus, you wouldn't leave it out of the Cape A team most vintages. A great tribute to the touch and feel of self-taught winemaker José Condé, once a New York ad agency designer. The lofty vineyard's red granite soils add to a sense of strength, seriousness and minerality in the wine. The berry concentration – propelled by an inky-irony infusion of Petit Verdot - justifies the long (20 months and more) oak barrelling in quality oak, a high proportion of it new. It's a virtual single-vineyard wine (just dashes of Petit Verdot and Merlot); so collectors can expect a distinctive consistency within the vintage emphases. Ages majestically - after initial tightness. The 2009 an emphatic example. Fine dining, please.

RIPE TANNINS MURMURING

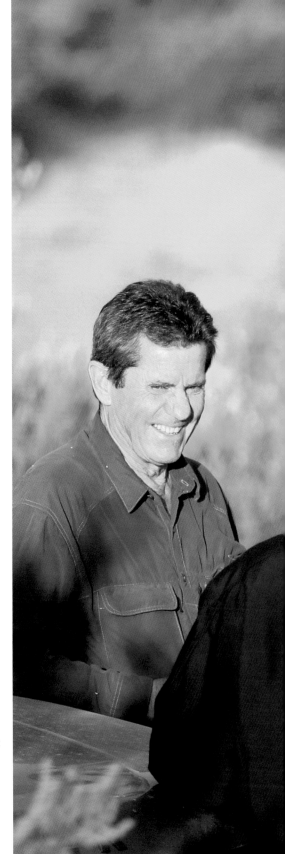

Could there be a more reassuring brand philosophy in a wine world rampant with hyped prices than Gyles Webb's founding dictum at Thelema: never to charge more than he would pay for a bottle of similar quality? He's widely acknowledged to possess one of the sharper palates and memories so it's not an idle promise.

To step back a moment and visit the Webbs at home. The wines - often a fine Burgundy or two – have been dealt with at dinner. Time for music. Quite loud. A move to the lounge, where Webb seats me in his luxurious Eames chair. His generous Michaelhouse manners. He begins to shuffle among his CDs, adjusting and re-adjusting his specs.

Not for the first time, I suggest digital. "Do you want to see a grown man cry? I LIKE rummaging. Some people like vinyl for heaven's sake." 'Yes," I say. "Because of the inconvenience." We proceed like that. He's opposite, dwarfed between two gigantic speakers. West African Kora. A Maria Callas. Geoffrey Yunupingu. The Bendabili from Kinshasa. A connoisseur of the unusual too. His wife Barbara has fled upstairs out of earshot. Erica has retired to the guest bedroom and deployed her earplugs.

The malts are out. Conversation – in the rummaging shuffling intervals – progresses discursively. Occasionally even productively. Once, probably past midnight – have lost count of the evenings I've enjoyed the Webb hospitality on fleeting visits back to the Cape - we fashioned a blend in our heads, from a few rows here and there of his Cabernet, in one barrel. The Webb Platter Private Cab is, obviously, unique. We began with a 2006. By 2015, we're on a 2010. Not reserved for momentous occasions; opened to turn them so.

The tireless reveller and raconteur in Webb masks the competitive stickler. Detail in the winery – and even more visibly in the vineyards - has always been fearsome. The Webbs were new to the business when, in 1983, they and their families bought this fruit-farm on the Helshoogte Pass above Stellenbosch. Gyles made his first wines in our cellar over the road, at Delaire, while they were building theirs. Ever since, Thelema has been a Cape vineyard showcase, winning every viticultural award going. Says Robertson winegrower Abrie Bruwer, who often flies rather than drives: "The best vineyards in Stellenbosch; it is clear from the air." The winery, its layout and equipment, are models of clean functionality, all the more striking against glitzy neighbours.

Barbara Webb's sister, Jennifer, is the in-house architect. It's always been a family-owned and run business. The wines shot into the front local and international ranks almost immediately in the late 1980s. And they've remained there - in an increasingly crowded field of rising quality.

My bias is obvious so let's defer to an articulate, thinking man's wine critic, Tim James, author of an authoritative tome on the Cape scene: *Wines of the New South Africa, Tradition and Revolution.*

In *Grape*, his online publication, he's been conducting a valuable – though, as he says, "hardly scientific" - poll with some frequency since 2001. It's tracked winery rankings, as determined by the ballots of 25-30 critics and journalists, including British MWs, local sommeliers and retailers – a decent spread of cognoscenti. Though not strictly comparable obviously, it's probably the closest South Africa has to a French-style Bordeaux classification, a useful if imprecise pecking order of general acclaim factoring in critical stuff like wine trade buzz, peer respect, prices achieved. These are not the fleeting results of wine show contests for single bottlings, or the necessarily subjective opinions of individual writers (like this one!) or one-off panels.

Thelema is one of only seven which made Grape's first Top 20 list in 2001 and still won a place in 2014 at 12th spot. Some track record.

We've served **Thelema Cabernet Sauvignon** at home for years. It goes down a treat – for its consistently juicy-ripe, approachable, balanced charm. It doesn't lose the grape - in the overpowering way that showy blockbusters can. It is finely oaked – and has been wild-yeast fermented for 'sense of place' individuality since about 2000. And it says all the other right things: mulberries, chocolate wrapped in spice, ripe tannins murmuring in the background. Earlier vintages displayed a sweet mintiness – loved by many, intriguing to some, disliked by others. Webb himself recognised it was an authentic quirk of nature - especially in one old vineyard fringed by gum trees. But he was always ambivalent, believing it detracted from classic Cabernet quality. So he eventually bottled a separate label - The Mint Cabernet. The standard Thelema Cabs acquired more typicity thereafter. And the minty vines? No more. They've made outstanding braai wood.

THE AXE

"Okay, it's time. We must sharpen the axe. Make Cabernet Sauvignon the signature variety of Stellenbosch," says Johan Malan of Simonsig, one of those rare beasts in the cut-throat, self-promoting wine business – a self-effacing winemaker. And not easily roused. It's astonishing to find him so animated when I broach the subject of Stellenbosch's place in the Cape's 21st century wine 'revolution'. New regions and scores of new producers from far-flung outposts claim the market buzz and editorial space, where once Stellenbosch was South Africa's wine epicentre.

"It's time we reasserted ourselves as THE great Cabernet region of the Cape, like Napa in California, only with more topographical variety," says Johan. There are some plausible viticultural – late ripening etc - reasons for the claim. And he's showing the spirit of his late father, Frans, always a bundle of excitement and an inveterate innovator, which kept Simonsig in the quality stakes and – after the end of sanctions – gave the label a pole position in the export scramble. It's still one of the most widely exported brands. The kaleidoscopic list of varieties and styles is Frans Malan's feverish legacy. Johan and his brother Francois, in charge of the extensive vineyards for more than three decades " keep trying to tidy up and slim down" says Malan. "But then a new idea and a new wine always seems to pop up."

The landmark pop-up of 2015 underscores his new mission – to assert not only Simonsig's but Stellenbosch's Cabernet primacy. It is the inaugural **Simonsig The Garland 2008**. A seriously cassis-rich and deep-coloured, distinctive, penetrating **Single-Vineyard Cabernet Sauvignon**, from old vines on a farm over the road in the deep granite soils of Knorhoek. This vineyard on the Simonsberg is owned by Johan's mother's family. It has yielded a statement and collector's wine, priced accordingly, for long keeping. Quite unlike any other Simonsig Cabernet. The final make-up established after a tasting with Cabernet colleagues including Etienne le Riche.

THEY LEAVE ME ALONE

The international jeweller Laurence Graff – diamonds his calling-card - has had long business associations with South Africa. He lives abroad, but bought Delaire, perched high on the Helshoogte Pass, in 2003. Everything is spectacularly sumptuous – the in-your-face views of the craggy Draken-stein ranges, the towering Simonsberg, the rich array of modern art – his private collection includes Picassos – the well-guarded jewellery shop beside a running indoor brook, the gourmet restaurants, the bespoke butlers at the private, fully saunaed, chalets with views to Cape Town. If this sounds like a travel brochure, well yes, this is far from your average wine farm: Graff has turned it into a glittering tourist destination.

Winemaker Morné Frey, inseparable from a red baseball cap and a quizzical smile, seems suitably unmoved by the hushed glamour and the starchily uniformed staff gliding by – as he sees them from his glassed off, all bells-and-whistles cellar looking into the restaurant. "They leave me alone here," he says. A good idea. His style cleverly mixes the modern and traditional. "I like the purity of fruit to show in my wines." He's up with the Swartland Revolution ideas but adapts them, encouraging fruitier, fresher accents, especially in the Chenin Blanc he buys in from those regions. His latest home-grown Chardonnays offer a distinctly less heavy style, suited to the fine-dining next door.

It is all almost unrecognisable from the distant days when Erica and I owned Delaire, in 1984. She dreamed up the name – playing on the French word for an eyrie; we called them 'vineyards in the sky'. We often seemed to float above the mists and clouds and the Stellenbosch and Groot Drakenstein vineyards below. We loved our five years there, but I am a gypsy. We converted a fruit shed to a basic winery. Visitors who came to taste – occasionally buy – wines, would picnic (no charge) under the pin oaks, roughly where the diamond vaults now tempt impulse buyers. And where the jewel of the range is **Delaire Laurence Graff Reserve Cabernet Sauvignon**, which is not quite priced 'for the rest of us' – at R2000 the bottle.

 It is a sensational beauty – so tightly wound up, concen-trated, you want to fast-forward its maturation - to see how it unfurls. The very dark colour, dark-fruit minerality, black chocolate, spicy, mulberry substance suggest patient, long meditative intervals between sips. Tasted the 2011. Tempting luxury.

MOCK CHARGE

Vergelegen's André Van Rensburg is iconoclast-in-chief of the winelands. A huge man, with a formidably lucid wine brain, his vigilant eyes analyse your every inflection. He's easily roused to verbal combat - and bombast. I'm not in the mood for a joust this morning, besides I haven't seen my friend for years. I'd suggested a brief, leisurely catch-up and philosophic meander around a couple of his current talking-point wines. And here at 8.30 in the morning he's lined up 20 bottles.

"Get on with it," he orders. "We're here to work." Exactly what I feared. He starts pouring — into tall Riedel glasses, the beads of condensation forming quickly. And can't help himself. He's immediately off on his beefs of the day: first, wine critics — "clueless and biased", not the best of starts and, not altogether convincingly, he adds with a glower, "nothing personal of course". It's a common refrain around the winelands. The critics are doing their job, evidently. Consumers, not producers, should be their first concern.

Second beef: the Swartland Wine Revolution - the youngsters from the warm wheatlands region out west hogging so much attention — away from his beloved Vergelegen, where ("I'm going nowhere") he's on his 18th vintage. "They've already finished the harvest," he exclaims, throwing his arms wide. Shock, horror. "Can you believe it?"

"I can, André." Not going there...

This is in the third week of February 2015, the earliest and quickest vintage in recent memory. Elsewhere, they haven't even started picking the reds. "How can they call themselves a serious wine region?" He bursts into mocking

laughter. Not a fan, to put it politely, of the home-bred grape Pinotage, he once incensed its growers by suggesting they devote their energies to vegetables instead. Their outrage delighted him. But like an irritated elephant, his ire is usually spent with a mock charge, dissolving into bonhomie.

The tasting proceeds in fits, with wines and science pouring out together. Abstruse quotes from the American Journal of Enology and Viticulture on containing leaf-roll virus: "It shouldn't be the scourge it is; we've got on top of it here at Vergelegen." Detours on why he's hired a world guru, Michel Rolland, from Bordeaux, to advise (some would say to 'advise and consent') on freshening things up in vineyard and cellar. "We've had vigorous exchanges." I can imagine. What can Rolland think of Van Rensburg's provocative claim that the initials GVB (grown, vinified, bottled on Vergelen) signify "Grand Vin de Bordeaux – without the Brett"… a reference to the bacterial spoilage that can mar even some famous French reds.

For decades Vergelegen seemed invincible at wine shows. They've been quieter in recent years. "I don't enter local contests now," he says. His record abroad, however, remains impressive. Nine international gold awards in 2014. The Flagship range **Vergelegen V** is positioned as leader of their 100% Cabernet pack, and I do like the **2009** and the **2011** (drink around 2020). Fine, stern, firm, proper wines from an ardent Bordeaux man. But I find at least as much pleasure in the less ambitiously priced, supposedly lowlier **Reserve Cabernet Sauvignon 2006** – a cooler vintage - with tiny dashes of Merlot and Cabernet Franc. It has a quite sensational array of perfumes and a French claret-like, still youthful, intensity on the palate in 2015. Inky minerals, penetrating structure. Just marvellous. Scythes magnificently through the crispy crackling of a braaied pork belly, André's preferred food partner.

RESTRAINT AND GRACE

Etienne le Riche's wines have the poise his ballet teacher wife Marcelle imparted to aspiring dancers for many years in Stellenbosch. And the correct technical intrinsics: Etienne was a Nietvoorbij research scientist before he joined Rustenberg in 1974, only the third winemaker in the estate's century of continuous wine bottling. A glorious 1982 Cabernet still stands out - though fading now - as do successive vintages of juicy, classy Dry Red - a blend of Cabernet and Cinsaut, a grape on the verge of a Cape comeback. Leading the revival here is daughter and marketer Yvonne Le Riche, whose Cape Wine Master thesis was on Cinsaut. Watch out for this sort of wine in future from Le Riche - an updated rendition of an historic Stellenbosch blend.

Son Christo is now winemaker (heavy lifter?) and his father 'cellarmaster', with time off to play golf. Leaving Rustenberg after two decades - replaced by a New World, new-generation winemaker – seemed to galvanise Etienne. He launched his own wines in 1996: quiet but confident, and classy, much like their maker. They have been on everyone's must-have lists from day one. Though not made for shows, they keep winning contests. And probably will do so even more as tastes - and even competition judges – continue to veer back to restraint and grace.

A swift sweep around the compact winery, his own space after many years in rented quarters, reveals a familiar, slightly battered inflatable bag-press. A German Wilmes, the kind some places display in their vintage sections with ancient corkscrews. He pressed that remarkable '82 Rustenberg Cab in it. "Still going strong," he says. "Leaves you in complete charge." It's a press I once owned: bought around 1990 for our vineyard Clos du Ciel from Rustenberg! Le Riche snapped it up when we sold the Clos. A moment of nostalgia – a beautifully functioning antique in the best hands.

His scope as a winemaker broadened dramatically when he was able to draw Stellenbosch grapes selectively from distinct climates and differentiated soils: gravelly, looser valley floor dirt for fruity richness, softer mouth-feel; mountain-granite for minerally structure. Juggling these variables with at least five different coopers, combining modern with some traditional cellar techniques and equipment, the Le Riches blend with a relentless focus on their trademark: juicy drinkability.

Serious punters will go for the **Le Riche Cabernet Reserve** – packed with cassis and cigar-box flavours - two years in mostly new oak. A special-occasion wine, always a couple of octaves more concentrated and recently even more emphatic than the **Le Riche Cabernet**, with its cherries and mulberries, plus some lighter cedary-oaky tones – from shorter, lighter new oaking. That's my go-to Le Riche; the Reserve my birthday wine. For this quality, both excellently priced. **Le Richesse** – with some Merlot - is a fine everyday option.

AND

Anthonij Rupert Cabernet Sauvignon 2009 A great year and a correspondingly imposing wine, fine, penetrating, balanced. Inviting, clove-scented introduction. Suffused with plush mulberry fruit and spices. Will keep but drinking well in 2015. Earned 93 - "Outstanding" - from US Wine Spectator.

Experienced winemaker Ronell Wiid can look down on most of her peers from **Bartinney Private Cellar**, perched above the Helshoogte Pass, where she consults. These distinctive, steep vineyards produce very individual wines; the **Cabernet Sauvignon** speaks appealingly quietly, doesn't shout. Lovely savoury undertones to the fruit.

Boekenhoutskloof Cabernet Sauvignon No critic has left this out of their top Cape selections for years now. Long-time winemaker - and partner - in the Franschhoek property, Marc Kent, achieves the difficult feat of producing finely perfumed reds of real depth, delicacy and length. With regularity. A Bordeaux quality to it. Fine oaking. 2011 outstanding.

Jordan Cabernet Sauvignon always shines in competitions. Understandably. It features a bit more spice than many Cabs, which adds to its charm. Though plenty of muscle, too. A fine food wine.

Leopard's Leap Cabernet Sauvignon 2013 Here's a completely unpretentious, juicy, tasty, mildly firm, don't-think-about-it-too-much, everyday red, with just enough Cabernet character — some spine, hint of blackcurrant. Friendly price. The great Hugh Johnson — constantly plied with the world's grandest wines — once wandered down the list at one of our regular haunts in Stellenbosch, De Cameron, and stopped at a very ordinarily priced Corvo Rosso, from Sicily, a modest commercial wine. "That's it," he said. He waxed enthusiastic about its gutsy simplicity. We'd had a long day of serious tasting. We could now quaff and relax. This Leopard's Leap does that job.

Meerlust Cabernet Sauvignon So unfailingly elegant it's sometimes drowned out by louder, brasher fanfares. A pity, because this is real class in a glass. A star at table.

The single-vineyard **Rustenberg Peter Barlow Cabernet Sauvignon** keeps the flag flying as the Barlow family celebrates more than eight decades of ownership at this historic estate, where wine was first made in 1682. Elegant, finely oaked, the 2009 has been a major competition-winner. Most lately the International judges' Trophy at the Old Mutual Wine Show. Where the estate also took the trophy for Most Successful Producer Overall (its Five Soldiers won the Chardonnay class). Owner Simon Barlow is now taking more charge in the vineyards, son Murray directs the cellar, since returning from the University of Adelaide in Australia with a Masters in Oenology. In the 1980s, I described Rustenberg as the Margaux of the Cape, because of the wonderful suppleness of the reds.

Springfield Whole Berry Cabernet Sauvignon Friendly, juicy, fine-textured. 2012 very good.

Warwick Blue Lady is not the estate's leading lady; they place their First Lady Cab a rung higher. But for my taste, Blue, only the top barrels from a single vineyard, has a more engaging personality. It regularly wins over Cabernet taste-off judges too. Loads of plums and cassis. Good with meaty, wintery food. However, given a choice, I'd always go for their Cabernet Franc.

Waterford Cabernet Sauvignon Cab in a very well-cut suit. Consistently smart, elegant, complete. Comfortably in Cape's top league. Delivers the lot: integrated, not too obtrusive tannins, well-ripened black currant fruit, an overall limpid juiciness. Specially excellent in 2011.

The French have priorities. They wrote their exclusive worldwide use for the designation Champagne – get this – into the articles of the Treaty of Versailles in 1919! That was about war and peace, you thought, and to re-order a new world, after World War One…

South African bubbly producers had to find another name for their Champagne-style wines: *Méthode Cap Classique* it is. Chardonnay and Pinot Noir, the same grapes used in France, are widely used for our MCC. Some producers, while following all the traditional Champagne rules, including the classic second-fermentation in bottle, vary the grapes: local heroes Chenin Blanc and Pinotage have been made into fine bubblies.

The Americans are less particular – not as easily bullied? - about the nomenclature; 'Champagne' appears on fizz labels made in the USA. But only by wineries which used the designation before 2006, and they must add California, or wherever, to distinguish their bubbly from the French. No such dispensation for the Cape.

Important – if you want to keep up: you should know that the long, slender Champagne flute is out. Yes! We've all been comfortable for decades with the sensible successor to the wide-bowled glass shaped for Marie Antoinette's breast (Champagne overflows with such tall stories). The old-fashioned *coupe* allowed the bubble to waft into the ether instead of containing it, and funnelling the aromas to our noses. Now, we are told, we should abandon our flutes and return to wider bowls: like conventional white wine glasses, curving inward at the top. "Not long before we'll be drinking still Champagne!" said one producer.

It remains a commonly held view – among those who drink Champagne Champagne here - that the top Cape bubbles have yet to match the *Grandes Marques* of France. We don't find here – not yet anyway – the ethereal, biscuit-toastiness of mature Champagne which its devotees so admire. A winemaker groping for that in our warmer climate risks losing finesse. But I believe the examples that follow show we're doing just fine. There is certainly no call for any local political parties and dignitaries to toast themselves, as they do, in foreign fizz.

Graham Beck's celebrated bubbly master **Pieter "Bubbles" Ferreira** put together a solo, virtuoso sideshow — on a small, exclusive scale - for the first time in 2015. He was the one, inevitably, to pull us up on how out-of-date we are to be drinking from Champagne flutes! "It's back to wide, at the base," he announces with a grin. "But with a taller, narrowing rim still — to capture the vapours, but off a wider base." And, be careful, the rim must be sheer, not flanged — so the wine doesn't hop over the front, sweet-spot sensors of our tongues. He demonstrates his new, R1000-plus glass, with a stem so stylishly slim it's unlikely to survive a couple of washes, let alone toasts. What next? "People apparently also want less active bubbles." His first-born own-label is a **Pinot Noir Cap Classique** so fine, light — incredible for a straight Pinot bubbly - and penetrating, it dissolves all resistance, any quibbles about this and that. The sheer minerally finesse and precise, arresting acidity places this in the top league. Irresistible.

CAP CLASSIQUE

BUBBLES-INSPIRED

Pieter Ferreira is as life-enhancing as his finely crafted bubbles. And he makes a dizzying range of them. After a quarter of a century, he's the go-to sparkling eminence for newcomers and old hands alike in the world of Cape fizz. And he's as generous with his – sometimes impish, bubbles-inspired – advice and time as his wines are classically fresh, lively and penetrating. His top *Méthode Cap Classiques* (MCCs) make it increasingly unnecessary to stretch the wallet for Champagne.

He has an extraordinary facility – a rare gift – to craft blends from hundreds of options of wine samples – the base wines, which are utterly unrecognisable from the final, desired versions. Imagine the long rows of sample bottles. Paring them down, culling again and then down again. You and your team come to – preliminary - conclusions. Some for the Brut Rosé, others to the Brut Zero, others to Blanc de Blancs. Others relegated to Demi Sec. An eye out at the start for the Cuvée Clive flagship. Then, all over again a few days later. And again. Then, finally, fatefully, thousands of litres diverted different ways into individual bottles for their second fermentations – and long resting on yeast-lees before the specialised tricky business of disgorgement, bottling and further maturation. It's all intuition and experience - and long-distance palate endurance. And that's alongside the formidable string of still wines, red and white and pink, and dessert, that he also directs in the Graham Beck range.

No surprise Ferreira has been appointed to oversee a prestigious new Californian Champagne joint-venture. It's between the Jackson family and Clive Beck, whose father, the late Graham Beck, a coal miner, kept his coal-face licence long after he'd made his own fortune, branching into fine art and thoroughbred horses – a stud in Kentucky - and then wine. The Beck wine enterprises include the Robertson estates – lime-rich soils for strong-boned horseflesh, cantering alongside the vineyards – and the smart Steenberg estate in Constantia.

Beck hired Ferreira, Durban-born, as a youngster after he'd completed a chemistry degree in Pretoria and cut his teeth with the colourful Mr Bubbles of his time, Achim von Arnim, of Haute Cabriere and Pierre Jourdan in Franschhoek. Which is where he met his effervescent wife Anne – her parents got Franschhoek rocking to an elevated gastronomy in the early 1980s at Le Quartier Francais restaurant.

It was rugby legend and winemaker Jan Boland Coetzee who recommended Ferreira to Graham Beck, and vice-versa. An inspired pick. "I had the time of my life with Graham Beck," says Ferreira. "Wouldn't change it for anything. I miss him. He was so witty and kind, brusque often, but always kind." A visit to either Graham Beck in Robertson or to Steenberg provides an immediate impression of the old patron's expansive, and expensive, tastes. And the wines continue to prove that Beck's crazy pursuit- or so many believed - of fine bubblies in traditional soetwyn (sweet wine) country was equally inspired.

Graham Beck Blanc de Blancs All-Robertson Chardonnay vineyards, of Champagne vine clones. Delicate sweet nose and a whoosh of citrus and oranges on the palate in 2010. Racy lightness, vigorous bubbles. A regime of 4 years on yeast lees provide palate oomph.

Graham Beck Cuvée Clive is the Wow-wine of the range. Only made in finest years. Aspirationally priced for smart occasions – but cheaper than Champagne. An assemblage of outstanding 'outliers' – up to 72 different components of selected base wines. Creamy-smooth amid fireworks of long-repressed bubbles (5 years on lees). Chardonnay (70%) and Pinot Noir 2009. Some barrel-fermentation.

Frans Malan of Simonsig pioneered the first Méthode Champenoise bottle-fermented sparkling wine in South Africa in 1971. **Kaapse Vonkel** is still going strong. In the same year he launched the Stellenbosch Wine Route. And in 1973 was a mover and shaper of the Wine of Origin (WO) Certification system. I tasted occasionally with him and others at the Wine and Spirit Board in Stellenbosch for WO certifications, 9 sharp on a Monday morning, so our palates were still fresh. (But was I always hangover-free after a weekend? Too late now.) We sat in isolated cubicles and judged about 60-70 wines blind, about a minute per wine – pressing a green light for a pass, red for a doubt. Then we'd chat for a while over (very bad) coffee. Frans would tell me about his frequent overseas missions. "I was such a crook," he laughed. "I stole with my eyes all the time." The estate's bubbly was part of his swag. Decades later, they've had more practice than anyone in this business; their trio of sparklers exudes competence and confidence.

For my taste, the pinnacle of piercing, feathery purity is delivered by the **Simonsig Cuvée Royale Blanc de Blancs**, 100% Chardonnay. Most recently tasted, the 2010. A 2004 shows grace and excitement can last. "A ballerina on her toes," says Johan Malan. It's bone, bone dry – and vividly demonstrates how, in classic Methode Champenoise, the inclusion of Pinot Noir – often with dulling malolactic fermentation – while providing fullness and complexity, sometimes detracts from a Champagne's – or in this case Methode Cap Classique's (MCC) - lightness and elegance. Another huge bonus: it provides intense delight with nary an effect afterwards.

STREET THEATRE

The handsome, tanned guy in a well-cut blue jacket, buttoned at the waist, wearing pointy, shiny brown shoes, strides into a busy street in the Cape Town city centre with a sword in one hand. In the other hand, there's a bottle of bubbly. No he isn't, yes, he is … going to decapitate it! Wait, he must decide whether to cover himself first, with a waterproof jacket. No? Yes. Then he puts the bottle to the sword. It fizzes into the road, spraying parked cars, including his own vintage, topless, nearly exhaustless 1973 yellow Citroen Mehari. Jean-Vincent Ridon pours a few glasses and we repair to the raised pavement outside the HQ of his tiny Signal Hill winery. It's off a busy corridor – lined with his portable mini-bottling line - behind Bizerca Restaurant at Heritage Square. We raise our glasses to this irrepressible display of French panache, this one-off in the Cape winelands, inveterate experimenter – and gulp his captivating **Signal Hill MCC Pinot Noir 08**. "Disgorged on demand" it says on the price list. Encore!

THE HAND-CRAFTED BUBBLE

Tall, slim, rakishly debonair, Jean-Philippe Colmant was a tombstone-maker in Belgium. His move from heavy marble to feather-light bubbles – he gives a 'nothing-to-it' shrug - includes designing and constructing himself – "builders are too expensive and get it wrong all the time" – the most efficient, original, frills-free fizz facility I've seen. With very powerful refrigeration, so he never has to rush things. All on a tiny Franschhoek property, next to the Huguenot Monument, with rows of Chardonnay and Pinot Noir vines, and horses for himself and his five children.

He's promised himself and **Colmant** devotees never to grow beyond 45000 bottles a year. So he can perform all the essentials virtually himself, making this, in a very nearly literal sense, a hand-crafted bubble. With the requisite fine mousse and substance, from long lees-in-bottle maturation. If he goes bigger, "I lose some control", smaller, and the numbers and economies of scale don't work.

Why bubbly only? "It wasn't as if I was unfamiliar with Champagne," he says. Just over the border from his Belgian home lay the vineyards of Reims and Epernay and the august houses of Krug, Bollinger and Roederer. JP was a frequent visitor, got to know the high-bar settings. And grew up, like most Belgians (moules-frites baby food?), with a fervent interest in what to eat with what you drink. No one made us hungrier when discussing wine-food matches...

The trickiest part of champagne-making (OK, MCC, the rose by another name) is the blending, the 'assemblage' or the second, in-bottle fermentation. By now he's familiar enough with the different regional attributes of his grapes – from Robertson, Elgin and his own Franschhoek vines. But finessing the balance and proportions of the base wines is an altogether more elevated skill because of the nearly unknowable trajectories of yeast-driven developments. It's acquired more from intuition, and a knowing palate, than from formulae or study. He's done the obvious: consulted friends – and competitors! The fizz fraternity has welcomed the newcomer. And, though JP's tasting skills are now comfortably up to it (his first bottling was a 2006), the tradition continues. Pieter 'Bubbles' Ferreira sniffs and tinkers here every vintage. You are tasting a fabulous collaboration when you dip into a Colmant.

There are five to choose from, including a pink. My favourite is the (NV – Non Vintage) **Brut Chardonnay**: light, racy, with a searing minerality. A beautiful, resonating, apple-fresh finish. It's 70% home-grown, 30% Robertson grapes. Invariably sells out in six months. Jean-Philippe has been a trailblazer in (speedy, free) door-to-door delivery, appreciated by those of us who do not live nearby. The **NV Brut Reserve** - about half-half Pinot-Chardonnay - is weightier, with greater length, and includes Elgin grapes, too. The **Sec Reserve** shows trademark Colmant raciness but is rounder with a touch more sweet dosage, 21 gms/l.

His food partner suggestions, apart from the usual suspects? Duck with a berry sauce. Blue cheese pizza. Karoo lamb chops. Fresh mussels. A hunk of Parmesan. Fresh fish, under-rather than over-cooked. Mussels (steamed in a splash of bubbly). And a curry with the Sec Reserve.

AND

Silverthorn The Genie It wouldn't be worth my while to remove this Non-Vintage, Methode Cap Classique rosé sparkling wine from the check-out basket: it's a new favourite of my 89-year-old mother-in-law, Rosemary Ladlau, gardener, author and past president of the World Association of Flower Arrangers. The unlikely grape is Shiraz, from the Robertson farm of Steenberg's John Loubser and wife Karen. It's plush, easy, charming. Good even without the queen mum's say-so.

Silverthorn The Green Man Vintaged MCC, a classic, precise sinewy Chardonnay blanc de blanc, the long – three years and more - bottle maturation on its fermentation lees infusing delicate yeasty essences. A fine sparkle, really gripping elegance. Another piece of Steenberg MD John Loubser's careful craftsmanship, from grapes off the family's Robertson vineyards. A hit at our son's wedding.

Steenberg makes a consistently fine **1882 Pinot Noir MCC**. And most recently an irreverent, low-alcohol alternative, too, light and bright, festively-packaged, plausibly Prosecco-like: **Steenberg Sauvignon Blanc Sparkling**. It's flying.

31

A raw deal – that's been Chardonnay's fate in South Africa. It's been unfair on the grape. When made well, its wines are magnificent, classical strokes of natural and man-made genius. In the soaring upper reaches of dry white quality its only rival is Riesling. But so many have been saying: "Ugh, Chardonnay, it's too heavy, all that oakiness." Some even claim it makes them nauseous. The Cape's growers need to blame themselves – and a few do - for the damning acronym ABC, Anything But Chardonnay. The grape behaves in the vineyard. It submits willingly in the cellar. However, Chardonnay has to be crafted, few wines more so, and the options and techniques are many and tricky.

Chardonnay fatigue isn't a domestic problem: a global avalanche of indifferent labels has swung opinion against the grape over the past few decades; ever since it breached, in a big way, its original confines of Burgundy and Chablis – and Champagne. It's probably still the most planted white wine grape in the world but in the tumult of trying to emulate Burgundy's revered peaks of quality, the Montrachets, we, and before us California, Australia, Chile and a host of other Chardonnay-inexperienced wine countries, produced too much vapid or flabby, or blunderingly heavy or planky Chardonnay – a travesty of its pedigree.

That hit me one cold afternoon in a castle in the hills behind Beaune, Chateau de Posages, where a Bienvenues Bâtard-Montrachet was on the table – I forget the vintage - plus a few red Burgundies. Before we could get to them, the rogueish Roland Remoissenet, long since retired as a negociant and sold out to an international bunch, insisted we visit his dungeons. Sudden bursts of chilling music, agonised screams, flashes of light revealing blood-spattered walls and images of the dying – it was a gruesome medieval museum of torture which seemed to delight Roland, at least in the way it startled me and presumably other guests. He then cooked lunch - truffles in a simple omelette, a dish both sensuous and light. But the Bâtard vapours, and the penetrating purity and opulence on the palate struck me completely dumb, have never left me. A huge handicap, because they set me off on frustrating attempts to recreate them: and I've never – even in the few supposedly superior Le Montrachets I've tasted – met a Chardonnay as mysterious or articulate.

CHARDONNAY

However, Cape styles are changing, improving appreciably. And swiftly. The consumer has spoken. The trend, as for wines in all classes, is lighter, fresher, more pure, less doctored. And in Chardonnay, much less oaky too. A future of Chardonnays unrecognisable from the confusion of mediocrity in the past awaits us here. The salvage operation is gathering pace.

I've chosen several examples, including a few traditional, but not too over-worked ones. No "unoaked" Chardonnays. What's the point? But there are a couple that are decidedly different - unChardonnay Chardonnays - because, I believe, they reflect unusual terroirs and have been relatively unmolested by their makers. Left to reflect their originality, authenticity and presumably their "sense of place". Worth watching. I have also come across a number, not included, in which the pendulum swings too far. My tastes have been changing too – away from toasty and buttery, which I used to enjoy (and still do occasionally with strongly-flavoured dishes). The tauter, leaner wines, if they retain some fruit and grapey quality, are generally more relevant at table.

In its perfect rendition, Chardonnay should excite, above all, with a riveting citrus and minerally quality – which lightens and lengthens, but is generously cushioned, so that balance and charm are retained. There may be some melon, perhaps pineapple, just a hint of marmalade. And in the background a merry-go-round of spices, wafting in and out of focus, teasing out the limey edginess with butterscotch, cinnamon, vanilla, clove – hints and whispers, no blasts, nothing too overt, certainly not overtly sweet.

The fine Chardonnays in these pages originate from very diverse soils - clay, shale, schist, granite. And from far out west and the deep south-east. And the personalities of their makers could hardly be more disparate too. We're not short of choices and they're all doing their damnedest to achieve elegant syntheses in their own ways.

Chardonnay is being trimmed of its flab.

ASSURANCE AND ELOQUENCE

"Wines must have soul," says Chris Williams, who set out to study law, changed courses for more scientific and jovial wine pursuits, and now stewards venerable Meerlust. With assurance and eloquence. A tutored Williams tasting is a delight. 'Linearity' in wine pertains to its 'depth' not its 'breadth'… Listening to him, tasting with him, wines come alive, show their personalities. The estate's closeness to False Bay is a huge factor in the finesse of all its wines. 2015 was Williams' 11th vintage at Meerlust. He's not yet quite as part-of-the-furniture as his predecessor, but then Friuli-born Giorgio Dalla Cia, hired by the present owner's father, Nico Myburgh, presided here for a quarter of a century. "A great tutor and mentor," says Chris, whose changes in wine style have been gradual though unequivocal - and with never an inelegant suggestion that he might have 'improved' on his predecessor's legacy.

The **2013 Meerlust Chardonnay** marks a slight tacking in direction; first Williams modified Dalla Cia's sturdier and oakier approach. Now the wine is tighter, fresher, more classic — with a citrus quality and a leaner, more elegant feel. More age-worthy too.

NONE OF THIS SNIFFING AND SPITTING

I've known Newton Johnson Chardonnay intimately for so long it's almost my own. When we left the Cape and retired from wine-guide writing, the Johnson family let me into their cellar to make up a barrel or two each year with Gordon and Nadia Johnson, then, and still, a brilliant young husband-and-wife winemaking team. There are quite a few of these super-couples accelerating quality across the winelands. Elder brother Bevan Johnson, a broad-shouldered surfer, takes charge of much else with his keen, calm business mind, including marketing and travelling furiously. Founding father Dave Johnson, one of the first Cape Wine Masters, claims a hands-off role while poking his nose into everything. Felicity Johnson née Newton, is the architect of all seven of the houses the family has lived in, and their two wineries. Slight and gentle, she speaks in a smiling whisper; she is often the Final Palate when wines are being blended. This is an engaging, all-hands-to-the-wheel show.

Before their own Chardonnay vineyards came on stream commercially, they bought in grapes from then uniquely (now fashionable) cool, exceptionally high-altitude Villiersdorp vineyards. Gordon and Nadia cut their teeth on these generally sound - though sometimes over-cropped - grapes, from densely foliated vines. They were also honing their cooperage selections, barrel-fermenting and battonage and oaking skills, progressively moving from partial to full natural yeast-ferments, judging the fine line between hands-off winemaking and sensible interventions. The wines became classier, finer – by a process which the most venerable of French vignerons, Henri Jayer, called 'the principle of limiting sloppiness'.

We drank riveting NJ Chards – and still have the results of hours of blending back and forth, cursing one cooper, toasting another. The older vintages are a bit frail now but still venerable *grandes dames.* Now their own vineyards are on stream, their cellar precision is matched by complete control of their own fruit. Gordon and Nadia can harvest at exactly the right moment, limit the crop for concentrated fruit, sort for only the healthiest, ripest bunches. There's been a perceptible upward shift in finesse and balance; more crisp penetrating freshness – citrus zest, some spiciness. The **NJ Family Vineyards Chardonnays** deserve a place in the New World front row. And their price-quality ratio is brilliant. Their lower-priced second-string **Newton Johnson Southend Chardonnay** is a favourite sundowner and casual summer lunch wine.

We're drinking - none of this sipping and spitting stuff – both, on Dave's gleaming yellowwood table. He's handmade every wooden piece in the house, from pepper grinders to salad bowls to all the kitchen cabinets. He's also a famous diver and seashore forager. The table is piled with great bowls of crayfish and mussels (from Grotto Beach nearby), and samphire from the Bot River lagoon. Onrus is his source of sea urchins and alikreukels. We feast for hours; all the children and grandchildren pop in, the room rocks with laughter and toasts. The Restaurant at Newton Johnson, at the winery down the hill, is a South African Top Tenner. But here in the Johnsons' wood and glass house, set in a wilderness of flowering fynbos overlooking mountains and sea, we could not be more charmed.

LIME AND MANDARIN

There's a dated Burgundian conviction that always merited questioning: one and the same grower-wine-maker cannot excel at both Chardonnay and Pinot Noir. In the Cape, the 'Burgundy specialist' estates, or virtual estates with their own vineyards, whose Chardonnays and Pinots I enjoy, Newton-Johnson, Hamilton-Russell, Meerlust, Chamonix and Iona, all challenge that old belief.

Gottfried Mocke, until late 2015 at Cape Chamonix, now at Boekenhoutskloof, was the most versatile of the bunch in his stylistic spread, unashamedly not Burgundy-only; and he had the most complex viticultural obstacles to manage. No maritime moderation in the enclosed, inland Franschhoek valley. For all its chi-chi pretty-village allure, Franschhoek is hardly a perfect cool climate vineyard area. (Ditto in-vogue Swartland.) It stacks up quite poorly against many other Cape wine regions, though we should exclude the valley's dedicated MCC producers who crop much earlier anyway.

But Chamonix lies on a reasonably shaded side of the Franschhoek mountains, reaching a useful height of 520m above sea level, and harvests two weeks later than the valley floor – viticulturally a significant quality gauge, grapes benefiting from more leisurely ripening and extended hang- time. Provided there's no late-season heat wave to sap flavour and shorten wine keepability.

No surprise that the self-effacing and smart Mocke was head-hunted by his friend and mentor Marc Kent. He's a practical, hands-on soil scientist who under-stands the limitations of his vineyards and amelio-rates them. For more than a decade he re-arranged the Chamonix vineyards to align varieties with soils and aspects. It's paid off in Chamonix's steady climb into the Cape's 1st division. I wonder how he'll influence Boekenhoutskloof's many and farflung vineyards?

Cape Chamonix Chardonnay 2013 smells of lime and mandarin. On palate it's generous without flab; a lively core of spicy-fruity acidity keeps it fresh. The oaking (which puts so many off lesser Chards) is contained, near flawless. This is not one of those inelegantly loud wines. Up to the smartest cuisine. But not too grand to look down on simpler dishes.

BODY AND SOUL

The Platter Guide is Wendy and Hylton Appelbaum's favourite book, says their winemaker at DeMorgenzon, Carl van der Merwe. Understandable, if your wines have twice won the guide's White Wine of the Year award. A remarkable accolade for these relatively recent Joburg immigrants. They could have set up anywhere, a pad in Monte Carlo, on Central Park, their own island. Stellenbosch is lucky to have them. They're not absentee landlords, owning a trophy vineyard, farming by phone; they live at the shop and breathe body and soul into these wines.

When Wendy Appelbaum is on a mission, things happen. On a golf course (once scratch, her handicap is still in single figures); striking business deals, revving up the judiciary to put the squeeze on outrageous money-lenders abusing our (feeble) usury laws; and turning an obscure vineyard into a new Cape great.

For the past few years, with Mike Ratcliffe of Warwick, she's spearheaded the Cape Wine Auction, leaning on producers to donate lots of smart wines. In three hours in 2015, either side of a balmy, sunny, wine-flowing, wallet-loosening lunch, they raised more than R10 million. For winelands charities, mostly education-related, from crèche to university. Wendy is following family tradition: her father Donald Gordon of Liberty Life was a heavyweight philanthropist whose trusts still fund the Wits University Medical School.

DeMorgenzon Chardonnay Reserve 2013 was both a Decanter and Platter Guide 5-star. Neither shabby laurels. Delicious Cape classicism here: all the requisite citrusy width and poised freshness in concert. Carl van der Merwe has shown reverence for a much-abused noble grape.

THE MAKINGS OF GREATNESS

Anthony Hamilton Russell arrives from over the hill on his motorbike, a satchel slung over his shoulder. He's wearing a wide-brimmed farmer's hat. We're at the HRV Hermanus winery early, before breakfast. "I'm just an old farmer," he announces, rubbing his cold cheeks. Yes, and the jacket is Jermyn Street, the cigars Cuban, the accent and university Oxford. And the language is wine-honed. Readily adjustable for anywhere: America, the UK, Europe, Far East.

I've listened to him on song. Here's one of the agile brains of Cape wine. I conjure with an idle, silent thought. What if he'd been in charge – might the Cape wine industry have made light of its manifold export, and other, difficulties? We'd certainly have had more fun – and entertained the world more - without the grim lot who ran the show.

Anthony is quite like his father, Tim, the founder of HRV, who died in 2013. The bright lively eyes, the quick, some-times cutting, humour. Anthony's side-splitting take on the newly assertive youngsters stirring excitement and headlines with off-beat wines had better remain off the record.

Tim was good to listen to – a man of broad-stroke analyses who could swoop into telling minutiae. He was unflinch-ing in his quest – nearly everyone thought it quixotic at the time - to prove Burgundy was possible in this southern tip of Africa, until then known for its cattle, wheat and fruit farms. He stumbled initially – trying Cabernet, which didn't ripen – but made steady progress in this then wine wilderness in the mid-1980s with respectable Pinots and Chardonnays fashioned by his winemaker, Peter Finlayson. He quickly became a free-thinking pioneer too, quite Burgundian in outlook, visiting France frequently.

Two things might have felled lesser men. The first was an inexplicably obstructionist attitude from wine officialdom. Invoking the letter rather than the spirit of the law they began prosecuting HRV for laughably minor infractions (which they ignored elsewhere). Tim's courageous adventurism was exposing them for the misguided, blinkered dullards they were. The only time I saw him lose his cool was after one of these court judgements went against him and a gloating official came up to shake his hand. "No," said Tim, looking him in the eye. "You don't deserve my respect, nor a handshake." Incredible. Government functionaries were effectively trying to block what soon was to become – and could have been even sooner - one of South Africa's few and early wine export success stories. That "heavy-duty evangelism" as Tim called it, soon withered.

The other obstacle remains, a more intractable one. Leaf-roll virus. Tim and Anthony re-planted, and re-planted. But new plantings of "virus free" vines slowly succumb again. The crops become smaller and smaller – 2,5 tons a hectare, financially borderline, even at HRV prices. "I've re-planted the entire farm one and half times," says Anthony. He's becoming philosophical. Yes, they perform the preventative protocols (pruners must not take their shears from infected vineyards to uninfected one, and so on) but "I think rather than beating up our vineyards and terroir, we should massage them, handling better the grapes we do get". Is this nature's way of limiting the crop – and improving flavour, he wonders? Not many other takers for that view. However, The HRV wines continue to shine, perhaps even more so in the most recent vintages. The re-planted vineyards coming into their stride?

We begin to sniff and spit and he wants to know, have we heard about the lunar calendar and how it affects wine tasting? Here we go I think. "Perhaps not entirely hocus pocus," he says. "British supermarkets are using it." In brief: the calendar designates four kinds of days - leaf, root, flower and fruit. The former two not conducive, the latter two propitious, for selling and tasting. So Marks and Spencer et al schedule their promotion and sales days accordingly. And have been pleased by the results evidently. The more cynical - and realistic – view is that most of us will go on buying and drinking wine every day of the week.

"So, is today propitious?" I ask. He twiddles his phone. The www.bunkahle.com site isn't coming up fast enough with the lunar business. But he texts me soon after we've left: "It's a fruit day!" I puzzle. Should one adjust tasting notes downwards? What if the wines are drunk on root or leaf days? Or shall we just conclude there's a fault in reality? Again.

Hamilton Russell Chardonnay 2012 was a top 20 wine of the year in 2014– worldwide - in the hugely influential American Wine Spectator. Yes, it's right to be cautious sometimes, of such 'competitions' – fashion parades, fleeting snapshots, judged by one set of palates which would probably change its collective decision a day later – but this was a breath-taking achievement nonetheless. The top 20 are selected from thousands of the world's finest. No other local wines made this shortlist. The HRV has earned its stripes over more than 30 years. During which there have been many small zigzags and a few large vineyard and cellar management swerves; more barrel racking introduced, sterile filtration abandoned in 2010, and so on.

It is defined by a kind of fresh elegance. There's limey bounce which tempers, balances the oaky richness – well short of any creamy cellulite – lifted by snatches of spice. Fit for serious dining at Michelin-starred restaurants. Or one of Olive Hamilton Russell's own extraordinary lunches. Though it can last longer, especially if you're after a softer, more evolved mouthful, I prefer these youngish, with tighter poise; up to about 7-8 years. The 2015 has the makings of greatness.

WOW OH WOW!

It's a balmy Caledon wheatlands midday, in the veranda courtyard of the Gabrielskloof tasting and wedding venue. Green lawns, two long, narrow parallel ponds, a few visitors' hounds sniffily getting to know each other, tots rolling giant red and blue balls into the water, the occasional gusts from the coast rustling leaves and unsettling dozens of tasting glasses on flapping table cloths. Noises off: the echoing clangings of a modern winery. This is the domain of Peter-Allan Finlayson. He shares the space with a few like-minded colleagues and rivals in the 'modernist minimalist Cape wine movement'.

Lanky and laid-back, Peter-Allan is, he reveals almost with pride, "a failed philosophy student!" He is also "Dad-trained", an heir to a family reputation steeped in wine. The Finlaysons once owned Hartenberg in Stellenbosch; his uncle Walter revived Blaauwklippen before founding Glen Carlou, now in the global Hesse empire; several cousins are in wine and in competition. His father, Peter (also in competition at Bouchard-Finlayson) helped restore Boschendal before becoming the first wine-maker in the Hemel-en-Aarde Valley for Tim Hamilton Russell (HRV). A couple of adventurers and pipe-dreamers many thought at the time – the first bottling was in 1981. We applauded how they thumbed their noses at blinkered officialdom, of course, but rolled our eyes a bit. Look at the valley now, a thriving, high-earning patchwork of vineyards, the Cape's Burgundy corner: a decisive vindication.

I've dipped my nose into thousands of glasses, hoping for surprises. And hallelujah, here's one of those. You want to end the tasting right there, take the day off, grab the bottle and dash to the nearest decent fresh fish place. And "'Wow, oh, wow!" away. It was so pure and direct – these are 'feelings' as much as specific aromas and tastes, and almost impossible to convey. A wine in such perfect balance that it stuns you into a speechless trance. Like the glimpse of an unforgettable profile you'll never see again.

And there's one of the troubles about great wine. It's so rarely the same the next time. Because our churning minds infatuate, conflate, blur and inflate future expectations. First time encounters can never be perfectly replicated. Perhaps because, as his father used to like saying, wine-making is part science, part alchemy, "and probably mostly art". As wine legend André Simon noted: "There are no great wines, only great bottles of wine."

But I fancy Peter-Allan's **Crystallum Clay Shales Chardonnay 2013** (and 2012) will not disappoint in future. Truly fine Chardonnay is so rare outside (and even inside) Burgundy. This one reeks of subtlety, of limey freshness, gorgeous silky sustaining acidity and a minerally centre that seems to engage and orchestrate other elements of the wine into harmony. Those parts include a few quiet spices – toasty cinnamon, nutmeg - from barrel fermentation. From a single vineyard, outside Walker Bay, of particular clay and shale soils. And the usual 'minimalist' handling, wild yeast ferment etc. Fabulous. Sensational.

BOFFIN JUICE

Richard Kershaw is probably the most persuasive Chardonnay winemaker in the Cape and anyone in search of a masterclass – drill as deeply as you can – should seek him out. A good starting point would be his website. Clones are his thing. It's all in the genetics.

You'll get the idea from the way he's detailed the three clones he blends to make his terrific **Richard Kershaw Elgin Chardonnay**. Clone CY 96 - nervous, aromatic, elegant and sharp; CY 95 - fuller bodied and rich yet tightly structured: CY 76 – floral, minerally, with the following too: melons, figs, stone fruit, lemons, nuts, cashews. We're going geeky now, but if you need to know, these are all low-yielding Dijon clones and collectively they produce at least 25 structural and aromatic elements.

But we must simplify, for myself and others daunted by these levels of boffinry. The 2013 is a modern Chardonnay, taut, and, yes, gripping, minerally, complex and thrillingly fresh and citrusy, offset by melon. And I do get a bit of that nutty tang. Not much more needed for excitement. No buttery chubbiness to blur definition. All modern wine-making mantras ticked, including gentle handling. Barrel fermented, minor proportion in new oak. The wine-making phrase Kershaw likes – and applies especially to his equally charismatic Elgin Syrah, is: "I do bugger all." Well, yes and no… but another time.

He made his debut with 2012, establishing his operations, and grape sources, in Elgin, the Cape's coolest area, he says, with, he says again, South Africa's finest Chardonnay sites. He's a British Master of Wine (MW) the only one in South Africa producing wine. "Not bad," someone said, "for a lad from Sheffield." A huge teddy bear, bustling with enthusiasm, he arrived here in 1998 to work at Mulderbosch-Kanu and fell for a Cape girl. They're raising their daughters in Elgin.

He has one big message for Cape wine: unimpressed by the well-worn catch phrase about our diversity in one country, he wonders if that is an effective marketing strategy. Each wine region should identify its best-performing varieties and styles, its unique strengths, go flat out to grow and promote those. A second supporting grape or style, fine. But fewer befuddling, diluting messages.

Swartland obviously is already acquiring renown for Syrah-based, Rhône blends and old vine Chenin. So Klein Karoo for Port? And then what? "Elgin for Chardonnay," he says, shoving a fist in the air. Which mightn't tickle the Walker Bay people. And Stellenbosch, mighty, grand Stellenbosch? "Oh, they'll never agree on anything." The idea of emphasising regionalism and specialisation – as the French have done so spectacularly – makes sense. With a couple of exceptions, the outlines of organic coalescing are still barely evident.

Our meeting is too brief, at least for the cascade of inexhaustible Kershawian ideas. One of his strengths – clearly a key to the quality of his wines – is his special relationship with master coopers at small specialist French cooperages, cultivated since his MW researches. Mismatched and heavy-handed, inexperienced oak barrelling of our wines has been a problem. Not at Richard Kershaw's. You get that in the wines – aimed at serious Chardonnay buffs.

PRETTY OKAY

Walking the vineyards along the steeper slopes behind Aloxe-Corton in Burgundy late one evening with the son of a French grower, Michel Voarick, I noticed a few bags of grey-white, lime-rich dirt by the side of the road. "Oh, the owners are replacing some of the soil that's eroded downhill," he explained. "By the morning, you won't see anything. It's allowed. More or less."

There's a lot of 'more or less' in Burgundy, the least fathomable of French wine regions. Its twin glories - Pinot Noir and Chardonnay - come from vineyards on the 'least altered' mid-slopes, not the silted valley floors nor the weathered steeper valley sides.

Poor soil can inhibit growth, reduce the crop, concentrate the berries and wine flavours; rich soils, do the opposite. At the vineyard on the Helderberg which we once owned, and named Clos du Ciel, with sweeping views of False Bay and Table Mountain, the soil was both fabulous (deep, rich, moisture-retentive, decomposed, granitic) and lousy (low pH, a precursor for spineless wines requiring unfortunate acid adjustments).

Seduced, along with generations of impressionable young who've slushed down oysters with penetrating Chablis - together they become one fabulous sea-winey taste - I was determined to grow and make a Chardonnay with balance, or what Remington Norman calls 'active harmony… in dynamic equilibrium'. That meant first fixing our soils, so as not to have to fix up the wine later. Early intervention usually trumps late.

Which, on that tiny patch of vineyard, to accommodate about 7500 vines, called for heaving in, by deep-ripping more than a metre, 80 tons of lime! Before planting - you can't get in with the big rippers afterwards. Laying the foundations for decades of what you hope will be pH neutral soils, 'more or less'. Burgundian friends then advised: single-vineyard wine, yes, but don't put all your eggs in a single-clone vineyard. So, there are nine clones in that one tiny vineyard, an unusual practice now, and (we believe) unique then. The soil may have become fairly uniform, but the vineyard's micro-climate and the DNA of those clones set it apart.

We launched our maiden bottling in 1990 and made under a bottle per vine. But how gratifying to share it with friends, with the vines looking through the window. And useful to understanding the challenges of growers and winemakers – and appreciating their skill when they pull things off.

In our ramshackle house – a huge fireplace dominating the kitchen, always tinkling glasses, and popping corks - the wine was exhaustively tested. By, among others, Joe Slovo, watchful, squinty eyes, surprising confidences; Martha Gellhorn; Cecil Skotnes, who wood-cut our first label; Christiane Amanpour popped in, once. When Jancis Robinson came to stay, she and I tasted from a few barrels and she told her *Financial Times* readers it was pretty okay, or something.

Some 27 years after we planted the vines (having long left the farm), Longridge's Jasper Raats, just down the hill, made his first vintage from the vineyard, from those same vines. So we visited our old place on a balmy afternoon for the re-launch of **Clos du Ciel,** a **2013**.

Supple, elegant, a little frail but not shy, so together and composed and finely balanced. Subdued nuttiness and marmalade, lime blossom flavours and gentle oak spices. Silky texture. Just beautiful. And at 12,5% alc. You can drink a few glasses! For R500 a bottle. Which, even adjusted for compound interest on prevailing annual inflations, outstrips our price of R20.

Christian Eedes, of the required-reading *Winemag* website, organises an annual Top 10 Cape Chardonnay review, among other such events (Cabernet, Syrah for example). He has predicted "cult status" for this Clos du Ciel. So good luck to Jasper. It's a rare little vineyard and he's stewarding it with feeling.

John Platter, Giorgio Dalla Cia, Jasper Raats

AND

Ataraxia Chardonnay Kevin Grant's long experience, specialising in Chardonnay ever since his tenure as winemaker at Hamilton Russell, shows in this 2013, and even more so in the 2014, vinified further north at his Upper Hemel en Aarde Valley cellar. A massing of classic citrus flavours on the palate finishes with steeliness. Plenty of mid-palate volume. Always a fine, confident choice for a broad array of seafood dishes, the intensity sufficient to dispense with a Sauvignon.

Bouchard Finlayson Kaaimansgat Chardonnay There's only a handful of must-have South African Chardonnays. This one's been around so long, and so understatedly marketed, it's sometimes taken for granted. Not by aficionados though. Peter Finlayson is a pioneer Burgundy master in the Cape. He was the first Tim Hamilton Russell winemaker back in the mid-1980s. The first, a couple of decades ago, to source the outstanding high-altitude vineyard in a secluded bowl behind Villiersdorp that defines this wine. It's a lovely, nervous, firm and recently more lightly oaked example. Classy. A style it's reached from a fuller, more buttery and toasty incarnation in earlier vintages. Finlayson also has a strong following of knowledgeable Pinotphiles.

Capensis New, grand, sophisticated, expensive Chardonnay - R900 a bottle in 2015. Shooting for the stars. Inspired by an intriguing concept – and limitless resources of two international wine high flyers, a Cape-Californian collaboration between Anthony Beck, of Graham Beck, with Barbara Banke of Jackson Wines. Three very disparate sites: a high Banghoek-Stellenbosch one is a recent Jackson purchase; with a lime-rich Robertson block; and an extra-cool, lofty Kaaimansgat vineyard near Villiersdorp. Blended to make this striking wine at the Graham Beck winery near Robertson by Graham Weerts – a local boy, now the Jackson wine supremo in California, flying winemaker for this project. The vineyards are managed – fastidiously curated might be the term – by Rosa Kruger, the internationally celebrated South African viticulturalist. Launched with a 2013. The 2014 has lime-lemony purity, spicy-mandarin trim. Barrel-finished, for some width, tightened by a mineral core. Splendid. As it should be at the price.

Cape of Good Hope Anthonij Rupert Serruria Chardonnay Really drinkable 2013, with mouth-filling freshness, lightest of oaking. Sustaining, edgy acidity, some citrusy elements too.

Delaire Graff Chardonnay A pull-back from previous buttery-toastiness from 2013. Striking fresher, modern style – for the table, seafoods especially, emphasising citrusy, lean length, just touch of spice. Lovely. No softening malolactic fermentation, no battonage. Lightly toasted barrels.

De Wetshof The Site Seven labels of Chardonnay come from this one winery, and bold, ambitious pioneer, now Chard veteran, Danie De Wet, winemaker since 1973, producer of all three 'classic' whites, Chardonnay, Rhine Riesling, Sauvignon Blanc since the early 1980s. The Site vineyards are about 30 years old. Recent 2013 shows restrained dry, taut elegance and freshness. Pleasingly moderate 12% alc! Barrel-fermented, just a hint of oak. I prefer this to the weightier, leesy, more biscuity Bateleur or Finesse.

Hartenberg The Eleanor Chardonnay Always among the Cape's finest. But a stylistic shift in recent vintages from 2012, to a modern, taut, fine, alert and beautifully sleek wine. All the arresting citrus qualities intact, a much less distractingly toasty example, especially in latest-tasted 2013. Secondary complexity may develop as it ages, some tangy marmalade perhaps. But its brighter state is irresistible. A lot less new oak, gentler battonage. The style to lure back people who've drifted away from this classic grape.

Iona Chardonnay 2014 is complex but fresh and light-textured, gorgeous, in the modern restrained style. Up at this farm, the air is cool — and it's here in the wine. A far cry from buttery fatness. Some barrel-ageing, 25% new. (Geek-alert: softening malolactic fermentation is slowed, curtailed, but not prevented.) A partner for the finest fish dishes, salmon, dorado etc, preferably with lighter sauces.

"Chardonnay doesn't go with tomato," says Gary Jordan. Tomatoes and Chardonnays are both presented in such splendid variety that most of us aren't daring enough to be that sweeping. But perhaps to be on the safe side, team **Jordan Barrel Fermented Chardonnay** with something else. A lighter touch with oak from 2014. A delicious, tense, classic citrus core provides balance and length. Frequent award winner.

Neil Ellis Elgin Chardonnay The Ellis Chardonnays have never been blowsy pushovers. As fashions have swung to more classic, held-back tastes, they've met the long-established house style already in place here. 'We'll never go buttery," says Warren Ellis. Wild yeast-fermented, just 25% new oak. For firming grip and spice. 2014 tasted, excellent.

Paserene Chardonnay This 2013, featuring Elgin grapes, represents a contemporary grape-not-oak approach, quite unlike the heavy-handed old style which had everyone rushing to the exits. Does it go too far in the other direction? I will certainly look forward to the next vintages. Made by Martin Smith whose day job is assisting Zelma Long at Vilafonté. His label says: 'Pure, Fragile, Restraint'. One to watch.

Thelema Ed's Reserve Dry White is a 'discovery' wine — inimitable by definition. A Chardonnay with attitude. From an unusual muscat-flavoured clone that insinuates its spiciness into the marmalade, citrus and peachy qualities of this variety. Oaked, it is broad and generous and lively, rolling out more essences as you work your way down the glass. The spiciness probably is the reason this wine "does well in Viognier tastings" reveals mischievous Gyles Webb. Ed presided over Thelema front office sales for many years; there's never been a prouder mother-in-law. A whisper of doubt about a house wine and you risked being booted out of the door — with a ripe re-evaluation of your palate. Ed was not reserved. She did have a robust sense of humour. The regular **Thelema Chardonnay** remains a frequent guest at our table, but our new everyday favourite from this stable comes from Gyles Webb's Elgin vineyard, his **Sutherland Chardonnay**. It has remarkable finesse for its affordable price, and fresh limey-flowery fruit salad flavours.

Tierhoek Chardonnay A discussion-wine: unconventional, un-Chardonnay-like Chardonnay, with bramble, ripe pineapple, hint of clove and spice; light barrel toasting; wild yeast ferment, minimal handling. 2014. If this is typical Piekenierskloof Chard, and if winemaker and her vineyard deliver recognisable vintage consistency, there'll be a following. I'm going to keep tabs.

Waterford Chardonnay Not always mentioned with bated breath by Chardonnistas. But lately a beauty. Respectable fresh minerality, highlighting zippy citrus flavours, has crept in. It has a grippy, Chablis-like crispness. Manageable 13% alc.

CHENIN BLANC

What took us so long? There it was, about one-third of the national crop, and for decades it was consigned to ho-hum wine status. Though acknowledged, patronisingly – I plead guilty, too – as a handy all-rounder, a work-horse, for sparkles, for anything from dry to sweet, for sherry, for port and especially for brandy, and that national drink *dop-en-dam* (brandy and water). We called it Steen, and did not realise what a treasure we were downgrading, ignoring, and eventually, pulling out. As the end of the sanctions era drew near, the local wine industry wanted to catch up with the rest of the New World – and Europe. Familiar old Chenin was abandoned in favour of those more fashionable foreigners Chardonnay and Sauvignon Blanc. Soon, Chenin's share of the national vineyard had been slashed to just 18%.

A common 'failing' was its tendency, certainly as a dry wine, to bottle-age after a couple of years, often sooner. Because it could be delightful young, with an estery fermentation appeal, our disappointment at its apparent evanescence simply encouraged us to drink up, and wait for the next fresh vintage. We should have been more patient.

Then we thought we might rescue Chenin with oak – that filled it out a bit, but also put consumers off, when the oaking, as with Chardonnay, was too enthusiastic. Happily, some braver souls stuck to the task, sensing potential, exploring different winemaking approaches to raise its profile (and price). One of these experiments resulted in Ken Forrester's and Martin Meinert's FMC (Forrester Meinert Chenin) – a modern standard bearer for "luxury whites".

Now we're inundated with fine, dry Chenins of many styles, the most interesting from very old – half century and older – vineyards of scraggly, low-slung bush vines delivering concentrated flavours, reflecting their soils and the depths of their ancient roots. Cape Master of Wine Irina von Holdt, first chair of the Chenin Blanc Association, which actively promotes the variety (Ken Forrester its chief later), was a pioneer of the new wines from old vines concept. She named her winemaking operation Old Vines, and continues to source fruit from venerable vineyards.

The Cape's new-age Chenins have both a delicacy of texture and a depth of savoury substance on the palate – and are often quite reserved on the nose. Pushy aromas are not obligatory for wine. Flavours range widely from peach, both white and red, to nectarine and pear. Ideally, there's a savoury, minerally spine.

At international shows, Chenin has lately shone for South Africa. Many believe we make the best Chenin in the world. And the variety is often the centrepiece of South Africa's now internationally-recognised Dry White blends. We still have the world's largest plantings; some talk of it as our "heritage" variety.

ICON? OH HELL YES!

I was a late convert to Chenin Blanc, I'm ashamed to admit. I still come across three blah versions, sugared up or awkwardly oaked, for every charming one. But the **Ken Forrester Old Vine Chenin Blanc Reserve** is one of the charmers. Ken is Mr Chenin, unflaggingly extolling the variety's virtues round the world. The US is a favourite beat, not only because his eldest daughter is a rising-star lawyer in New York. And Augusta is a new stamping ground. No, he wasn't golfing, though he does hit an enviably long ball. He was pouring this Chenin: it was served by Tiffany & Co at the 2015 Masters. It is serious and delightful, among the loveliest of dry Cape examples, the fruit harmonised and softened by a brush with oak for a few months. Snatches of cinnamon and other barrel spices synthesise with peachy-lime notes, and a generous fleshiness provides a broad, resonant finish.

But the best from this grape is, for me, The FMC, a South African icon. A term to be used sparingly. It was Ken's long-time wine muse, friend and business partner, Martin Meinert - of Meinert Wines and previously Vergelegen - a thinker, strong on wine chemistry, who conjured this wine from Forrester's churning mind. "I wanted to locate some botrytis in a dryish wine so seamlessly you'd hardly notice," says Ken. Difficult. Botrytis is the 'rotten sweet' fungus that turns grapes into an over-ripe, dark, shrivelled mess; and then miraculously can convert itself into delectable, pungently sweet spiciness in the bottle. Whereafter it can develop erratically, sometimes overwhelmingly. So you ferment Chenin, with wild yeast, in new barrels, and toss in botrytised grapes — plenty of assertive ingredients - and hope.

Bingo! **The Forrester-Meinert Chenin**, **The FMC**. A show-stopping double-act now mentioned as one of the world's great Chenins by international wine writers. A terrific, assertive, complex, many-layered white with twists of citrusy marmalade, fresh fruits and a faint toasty sweet nuttiness. For reflective sipping, mainly. Surprisingly good with a range of food, including sushi and sashimi.

A personal disclosure: years ago, having tasted this wine in its infancy in Meinert's cellar, I asked the friends to do a private bottling of one barrel. We called it White Mischief (after memories of my Kenyan youth), our son made a label, we drank it, very cold, among friends. In the bush and overlooking the Indian Ocean. Our kind of wine.

Ken Forrester and (right) Martin Meinert at their 96 Winery Road restaurant

TWO TO WATCH

Few are more focused than David and Nadia Sadie after their wine world adventures, in their case distinctly more on quality-based fame than, it seems, fortune. For that they say they're ready to wait. The lanky David – no relation to his close neighbour, the more famous Eben Sadie of Sadie family – is a native Swartlander and sensibly targeted the equally warm Rhône as his and Nadia's main training ground. But he's also worked the vineyards and wineries of Stellenbosch (Waterford – where Kevin Arnold is a Rhône nut too) and Tulbagh (Saronsberg and Lemberg). Nadia, also pretty lanky, is a viticulturalist and soil scientist. An ideal combo.

The couple's tidy list of David wines, is one to watch; they're in a fast-evolving wine style environment with modern wine philosophies – but surrounded by ancient vineyards. Still landless, they have comfortable tenancy at Paardebosch, with their own cellar equipment, centrally situated among a variety of soil and climate types they're mixing and matching. They're fully subscribed members of the Swartland Revolution – temporarily fairly house-bound with two babies – but David is keen to return to his bowling duties in the Revolution's cricket team.

Here they are on Chenin: "We're after linear wines with freshness and length. Like the Loire. Not big bold fat short wines." The Sadies' plans include an interesting take on old bush vine Pinotage.

David Chenin Blanc De rigueur Swartland Revolutionary minimalist wine-making (no inoculated yeast, no enzymes etc) from several parcels of old Chenin bush vines. "We like to mix soil types in sourcing our grapes." Several scents in play in the 2013, from heathery to stony; partly matured in old oak, stainless steel. Palate is firm, solid; tasty, savoury. Grapes picked relatively early to check alcohols, encourage freshness.

OH HELL NO!

"But then again I could be talking absolute crap," says Chris Alheit with a grin. He has been waxing on a bit, entwining chemistry with philosophy in the way that's almost obligatory these days about the importance of the light touch in wine-making. Let nature present her own wines. Don't gild the lily. That's the route to 'authenticity'. And decent boutique prices. Man's manipulations in vineyard and cellar can get in the way, distort. It's a line not all buy without reservation. Chris seems to be allowing room for a longer discussion.

He has another problem. "Riesling is my unicorn," he announces in the middle of tasting his 'authentic' Chenins. "Maybe South Africa is too warm." The 'maybe' leaves things dangling. But I wouldn't be surprised – and many would be thrilled – if he turned his single-minded skills to the German genius grape. He should trademark the name now: My Unicorn Riesling.

He and his wife Suzaan have worked in many of the world's important vineyard regions. They're yet another of the young, up-to-speed, real-deal couples electrifying the modern Cape wine scene. Back home, they kicked off in rented premises, an olive 'shed' in an olive grove in the Hemel en Aarde Valley. Then the vast Gabrielskloof winery near Bot River, sharing space with a bunch of other "young guns". Not far from their home at the beach in Vermont. Their focus is on wines from rare pockets of old vineyards that reflect soil, climate, vintage, grape variety. And it's whizzed their new label to sudden heights. Locally, internationally, these wines are generating excitement. The Cartology is most frequently mentioned, a full Chenin-Semillon beauty. But **Chris Alheit Magnetic North Mountain Makstok 2014** caught my fancy. Sheer originality here. From aged (40 years old) and, even more rare, ungrafted Chenin Blanc vines. Growing far up the West Coast near the Olifants River. The requisite terroir wine, with authenticity boxes ticked: wild yeast ferment; no acid adjustments ("Oh, hell no"); no new oak, neither for ferment nor ageing; malolactic fermentation for generous , silky palate.

As in other Alheits, there's quiet but substantive restraint, no showy flamboyance on the nose – just a faint tickle of honey, signalling the work of natural yeast. But expansive on the palate, with a dry minerally core that lingers. No fancy oak diversions, no edgy fruit, no tricksy winemaking. A grown-up food wine. Chris suggests drinking with braaied kabeljou. Chicken with a tarragon cream sauce. Steak and tuna tartare.

THE FRENCH INSPECTOR

Gary and Kathy Jordan might well be South Africa's bravest winemakers. Who else would have opened a high-end restaurant in London, in the City, and made a shining success of it? High Timber it is called. Haunt of bankers and lawyers, with a wine list which is 65% Cape. This while not taking their eye off the ball back home at Jordan's own SA Top 10 restaurant, headed by star chef George Jardine, and its adjoining café, The Bakery. The Jordans, former geologist Gary and former economist Kathy, both trained in winemaking theory and practice at the University of California-Davis, are surprised we are surprised. Doesn't everyone multi-task like this? Doesn't everyone see the inevitable synergy between wine and food? Well, no. Few are as good on wine-food matching as these two. Their wines seem made for the table: casual suppers or multi-course banquets.

With the plump, juicy quail I ordered at lunchtime, they recommended Jordan The Prospector Syrah, the 2013, a rich, quite soft, savoury-black chocolaty complement. I stole a few sips of Gary's Jordan Cobbler's Hill Bordeaux blend 2009. He was having a steak. A pretty grand pair. Across the table, Erica was loving a fish starter, and the **Jordan Inspector Peringuey Chenin Blanc**. It is named after a French schoolmaster who became Inspector General of vineyards in the Cape. He not only led the Cape wine industry's struggle against the scourge of phylloxera but also unearthed pre-San, stone-age implements which predated the earliest found in Europe. Gary has found some on the farm, too. This is an elegant, classy French-oaked Chenin. From a vineyard planted in 1982.

THE UNDERDOG

"We have looked outside for so long for inspiration," says Jacques de Klerk. "We have tried to make copies of Bordeaux blends and New Zealand Sauvignons. Only now are we looking to our own land, and our own wines. Now South Africa has an opportunity to find its voice internationally." Chenin Blanc, "the underdog" as he dubs it, is his focus in the label he makes outside his day job at The Winery of Good Hope. "It is as South African as a variety can be," he says. "Our heritage. Most of the oldest vines here are Chenin."

His aim is elegance and restraint. And he has achieved this in his **Reverie Chenin Blanc 2014**, from a single bush-vineyard in the Swartland. Somewhere along the N7. Can he be more precise? He would rather not: "Someone stole one of my previous vineyards; I would risk losing this one if its identity was revealed."

It is fermented in old oak, but otherwise free of vinification additions. Result: appetising purity. And it meets a defining criterion – perhaps the key one - of new-age wine-making: low alcohol. Just 12%. "So you not only want to keep on drinking it, you can!" says De Klerk.

NO EYELINER

I know DeMorgenzon's show-stopper, 5-star labels. So when we visit winemaker Carl van der Merwe at the farm, I ask: "How well do you do a boiled egg?" He catches the ball deftly; opens a utility-priced **DMZ Chenin 2014**. And there's a niggling pebble in his shoe. "Chenin is a sleeping giant in Stellenbosch, we've got loads of old vineyards here, we don't exploit them enough, don't shout about them." Other Cape regions trumpet their old vines under new labels. Staid, secure Stellenbosch doesn't. Or hardly. But a new regional rivalry is awakening. And in Van der Merwe it's aroused a competitive edginess. He sounds a bit like a Burgundian turning up his nose at Bordeaux. (A French speaker, he's worked in both regions, including at Ch. Chasse-Spleen for an entire vintage).

This Chenin's spot-on at the price, honest, fleshy, faintly fruity, clean. No make-up, no eyeliner. But so good. The chef and his honest, simple boiled egg. And then he opens a **DeMorgenzon Chenin Reserve 2014**, from a 43-year-old vineyard. Pow! All power and silky grace. Dry, partly fermented in oak. "I'm really scared of too much oak," he says. If only that were the norm.

SERIOUS

She was a delicate, elegant flower, unruffled through the roughest patches of a chaotic swing through Brazil a few years ago, trying to popularise Cape wine among doubtful Brazilieros more attuned to European and American exports, and on account of regional rivalry, more reluctantly, their neighbour Argentina's Malbecs. Delayed planes at sweaty airports, shambles at scheduled wine shows, diverted or lost tasting samples … but nothing seemed to destabilise Yngvild Steytler, in these far-flung fields of strutting maledom.

We survived a hectic circus of stops at Brazilia, Belo Horizonte - another delay, President Lula da Silva was holding court on the runway - Curitiba, Sao Paulo, Rio, reasonably unshattered, but none with more composure than Ingvild. She's been that kind of anchor for more than 35 years at Kaapzicht, one of the Cape's steadiest, quality family estates. Everything here is unpretentious, as the undemonstrative, contemplative Danie Steytler wants it. But he did bestir himself when he met Yngvild, a young lass from Germany hitch-hiking around the world, at the local tennis club. She was on her way to Australia, via Malawi. Danie urgently pursued her to central Africa, proposed, and brought his catch home.

Kaapzicht made its name as a red wine estate. But things are changing. Danie Jnr is taking over and his first big splash is with a serious, up-to-date Chenin, from a seriously old – planted in 1947 – vineyard, second oldest in Stellenbosch. Not much of it, just one hectare of dryland bush vines. And it hit the critical spot, with a Platter guide 5 stars, almost immediately for **Kaapzicht The 1947 Chenin Blanc**. A barrel-fermented 2014. Full and completely dry. Faint blossom fragrance with honey in the distance. More savoury than fruity. Weighty core, balanced palate, serious length.

AND

AA Badenhorst Family Secateurs Chenin Blanc One of those mellifluous, substantive Chenins suited to the table rather than indiscriminate swigging; 2014 has weight – though isn't bulky – and whiffs of honey and blossom with a generally savoury palate. From Adi Badenhorst's own Kalmoesfontein vineyards and a next-door one, all respectably ancient, half-century-old, dryland bush vines. Fermentation and vinification studiedly casual – and extended. The purist's ticket. Only old oak. "Sprinkling of Palomino and another secret grape," says Badenhorst – in the next breath insisting: "I am always an open book." Well-priced.

Beaumont Hope Marguerite Chenin Blanc has kept its enduring place among the most expressive Chenin Blancs. Old vines planted in 1970s, and the ripe sweetness combine for complexity and fullness. Satisfying – and versatile. Lovely before a meal, with it (spicy chicken dishes?) and even with cheese. Sebastian Beaumont has a feel for this grape.

Botanica Mary Delany Collection 2013 with distinctive, delightful, honeyed delicacy and penetration. Ample-bodied. 14% alc. Gently oaked. Grapes from Skurfberg, up the West coast, old vineyards which provide highly sought-after fruit. Lots of stars in the Platter guide for entrepreneurial winemaker Ginny Povall, an American who has bought a flower farm and opened a guest house in Devon Valley, Stellenbosch. And rustled up a few classy wines on the side, too.

Cape of Good Hope Anthonij Rupert Wyne Chenin Blanc An individual, new and rather good, restrained, fruity-nutty dry and full Chenin Blanc – tasted the 2013.

Cederberg Private Cellar Chenin Blanc Has always been a family favourite. Fruity-fresh and clean as the mountain streams in the dramatic wilderness the David Niewoudts call home.

Dorrance Kama Chenin Blanc Don't think I enjoyed many 2013 (dry) Chenins more. So much quiet class, full, deep, complete palate – of balanced, salty, umami acidity. Old Swartland bush vines, no wonder. From a vineyard just above Eben Sadie's winery. Whole-bunch pressed. Chistophe Durand may be French, but his wife Sabrina is of South African-Indian heritage. All his wines team beautifully with curries, she says, "because they have to!" We had this one with a Durban prawn curry; a brilliant match. But this Kama, Sanskrit for 'sensual pleasure' would be good with almost anything.

Fairview Darling Chenin Blanc A thrilling, refreshing mouthful, the 2015. One of my new top hits. All bracing charm. Darling's maritime attributes on display.

FRAM Chenin Blanc Fine, bold label and stirring back label story. All buzzy young winemakers want grapes from far-out Citrusdal mountains. So, high expectations for this 2014 – and they're met. A fleshy, savoury dry Chenin, cagey nose but instant gratification where it counts – on the palate. Wild ferment. Old oak. High alcohol, take it slowly. Thinus Kruger earned his spurs at Fleur du Cap. A man to watch. Platter guide 5-star for the first-release 2013, of which he mystifyingly says: "The only wine of mine I've ever really liked."

Joostenberg Kaalgat Steen is an organic wine, named for lack of adornments or fiddly winemaking. A very different Chenin, with a honeysuckle, Muscat edge from winemaker Tyrell Myburgh. Good choice for lunch at rustic Joostenberg Bistro on the Stellenbosch-Paarl border – or with a takeaway of their own superb charcuterie from the adjoining Deli.

Keermont Riverside Single Vineyard Chenin Blanc Mouth-filling, mouth-watering. Quiet, stone-flint aroma, gently dry-fruity flavours – hints of apricot – and a mineral quality. Layers of substance on palate. A serious dining companion. Old barrel-matured about a year, on lees. 2014 tasted.

Kleine Zalze Family Reserve Chenin Blanc 2013 Magnificent. Rounded, complete, full, dry, long-lasting palate, minerally substance. Fit for smart dining, perhaps at the estate's own award-winning Terroir Restaurant. Smart wine-making. Old barrel-fermented. Blended from several vineyards. Too many accolades, many of them international, to list! Respect for this 300-year-old estate that's kept very abreast of recent hectic times, and continues to up its game. Leading exporter, successful in hard-to-crack China. It's a family business, led by Kobus Basson; winemaker Alastair Rimmer shepherds five ranges in all, good value everywhere.

Land of Hope Chenin Blanc Reserve Very individual and classy. Ancient - 40 years plus – low-yielding Stellenbosch bush vines, oak-aged; succulent, rich creamy texture and citrusy flavours - orange, lemon, lime - especially in finish. 2013 best yet, by some margin.

Leeuwenkuil Family Vineyards Chenin Blanc 2014 Tried this at a Japanese restaurant. But sufficiently hooked to buy it again. Has the Swartland elements – quiet melon-and-savoury core to the palate. The drama is in the lack of (fruity, flamboyant) drama. Matched the saltiness of the soya-powered cuisine with unintrusive poise.

Perdeberg Dryland Collection Chenin Blanc In our 20 years with the Platter Guide, there was always one sure bet: this former co-op, now owned by 30 member-growers, would turn out a superb, and superb-value Chenin. Nothing has changed. The 2013 was judged one of SA's top 10, and it is a winner: lovely acid and balance, a whole fruit salad of flavours.

The quite superb **Raats Old Vine Chenin Blanc** includes fruit from three separate Stellenbosch sites, average age of 45 years, including Bottelary Hills and the Polkadraai, where the clay sub-soils, in Bruwer Raats' view, provide the ideal combination of yellow fruit (pineapple and apple) and white fruit (pear and quince). Minimally oak-finished.

Remhoogte Reserve Honeybunch Chenin Blanc 2013 I am still not sure about this one, a single vineyard Chenin. Suffused with honey scents and flavours, and powerful at 14% alc. Not to be taken lightly. And yet rather fascinating and certainly unusual. I kept going back for more…

Rave-reviews, all over the place, including mine – "lovely" - for **Reyneke Chenin Blanc**, 45 year-old vines, organically farmed for 15 years. With enough natural intensity not be overwhelmed by oaking. All Reyneke barrels lightly toasted.

Sadie Family Old Vine Series Skurfberg Chenin Blanc A talking-point Chenin, the Skurfberg in the Olifants River region now assuming legendary status for the grape, thanks largely to the explorations of viticulturalist Rosa Kruger, long-time Sadie supporter. The 2013 shows a beautiful peachy-dry charm. Pure, refreshing and lithe, flows down mellifluously. Absolutely delicious.

Stellenrust Chenin Blanc 2014 Lovely. Rich but fresh. Zesty naartjie and peach flavours, from Stellenbosch grapes. A Top Tenner in the Standard Bank Chenin Challenge, and I can taste why.

The Blacksmith Vin Blanc 2014 The very bearded Tremayne Smith would have been hauled away by the culture censors and/or wine police in the old days, if he'd disrobed the way he does at tastings now to show off his tattoos, however appropriate they might be: secateurs, gnarly old bush vines, and bunches of grapes, each of the berries a little skull. This Chenin, his first, one of the gentlest, softest, most savoury-flavoured of the vintage. And at 11,5% alc. so invitingly quaffable. Fermented 100% on skins, as more or less obligatory in the modern-day Swartland.

Tierhoek Chenin Blanc 2012 From vines planted in 1980 on the Piekenierskloof farm of Shelley Sandell; though vines are old, the style is modern, hands-off, no pampering of vines by irrigation, no oaking. Result is good body and quiet, reserved flavours: faint green-melon, a slight hint of sea-saltiness. Different, modern, appealing.

Swerwer Chenin Blanc 2014 "Jeez – isn't Chenin the star of the Swartland?" asks JC (Jasper) Wickens. Substance without airs – a holy grail of the new, fresh movement in wine - on display here. From 45-year-old Swartland vines. Their impact not on the nose but in the taste and substantial feel on the palate: generous, dry – slightly nutty, straw and fynbos. Wickens (above) is Adi Baden-horst's co-winemaker, and makes Swerwer wines in his down-time. He has worked in Spain, France and the US, but is now a committed Swartland guerilla.

Villiera Barrel-Fermented Chenin Blanc 2014 Not a little lunchtime wine, at 14,5% alc. But I like this sumptuous style of Chenin, too. Bring it out at a dinner-party and enjoy its soft, rounded, almost peachy richness, perhaps with roast pork or butter chicken.

Wine Cellar Chenin Blanc 2014 A genteel Swartland Chenin – 12,5% alc. - showing well-rounded, filled out but light-feel elegance can be done in the region. Palate grounded in subtle savoury notes. Minimal wine-making by Ryan Mostert, no oak.

A revival in the offing for this quiet grape – its moderating role in red blends blossoming into new respect for its stand-alone qualities, including its freshness in youth. No need to age them. The three wines below are intended to encourage further exploration as new labels appear.

Neil Ellis Groenekloof Cinsaut A real delight. Another discovery wine from the Ellis cellars, this single vineyard old vine red. Pure, silkily soft and unique sweet-dusty wafts, enough tannin to hold itself; cautiously oaked in lightly toasted (25% new) French barrels. A triumph of discreet elegance to buttress ocean-facing Darling's higher ground as one the Cape's finest vineyard sites.

Mount Abora Saffraan Cinsaut A fresh, bright, light red 'undistorted' by oak, or commercial yeast, or filtration: this 2013 ticks the modern boxes. Clean, lively, berry purity. Lovely simplicity. A credit to Swartland Revolution idea.

Stellenrust Old Bushvine Cinsaut We're only lately appreciating how this humble grape, unfussily treated, can offer such easy sweet-ripe charm. This Stellenbosch 2012 is fine, fresh but restful, and despite its unfussiness finishes round and complete.

Terra Cura Silwervis Cinsaut 2014 Zimbabwean Ryan Mostert is an Italian-trained agriculturalist well versed in bio-dynamic tendencies (hence the 'handle the earth with care' label). Natural winemaking tendencies too. He gave up oenology at Stellenbosch University because his tutors didn't "quite gel with my ideas – they didn't understand that real wine is about site not science". A departure Cinsaut this: trenchantly herb-garden-fresh palate after compellingly sweet-scented Cinsaut bouquet. No oak. "Simple and immense at the same time," says Mostert, always charmingly keen to reveal his agri-philosophies. "We should be drinking sites, not grape varieties." Apart from his own labels, Mostert also makes a white and a red in partnership with hot young on-line wine merchants Wine Cellar, originator of the Young Guns new-wave winemaking grouping.

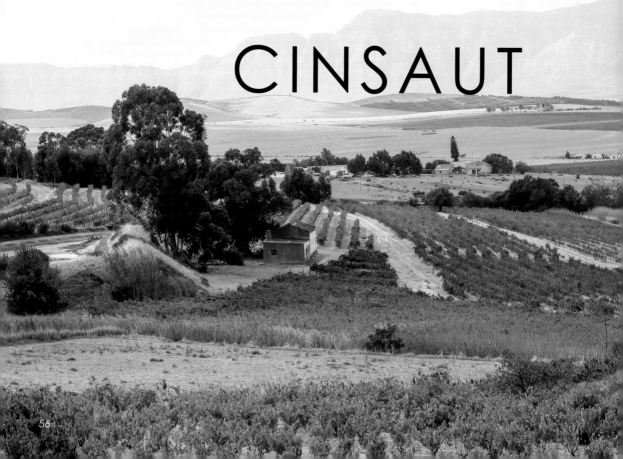

CINSAUT

You hear it often – "we want to make wines we can drink ourselves" – but Jeanine and Mick Craven seem determined to get beyond the cliché, be adventurous and out-there. And with a huge, immediate plus. Theirs are seriously, comfortably, low-alcohol wines – down around the 11% mark. Which is not the only reason buyers from Japan are hunting down their labels: the wines are tasty, bright and fresh, and fit well with clean, precise – and fresh of course – Sushi-Sashimi dishes. The Cravens' friends in the Young Guns group of winemakers like to tease them about these alcohols. Peer-envy? Less heady wines are goals for modern winemakers everywhere. Wine drinkers cheer.

Jeanine is a Faure, so they can draw on family fruit from emphatically maritime False Bay vineyards. Formerly winemaker at Dornier in Stellenbosch, she resigned in 2015 to take fulltime care of the growing Craven business. Mick, a tall, athletic surfing Aussie dude, qualified at Roseworthy, works at Mulderbosch. They met in the States – and that was that, says Jeanine. "And I hope we'll have tall kids," she says, casting a glance at Mick.

"We're not making natural wines, as such," Mick says, avoiding the subject. "We don't want to hang on to the coat-tails of revolutionaries in other regions. We're very Stellenbosch." Nonetheless, the couple is in the vanguard of the new, young, free-thinking winemaking camp that likes low sulphur, light, whole-bunch pressing, zip filtration, fining – a kind of 'what you see in the vineyard is what you get in the bottle' philosophy.

Craven Clairette 2014 From 34 year-old Stellenbosch vineyards. A departure wine, from a grape usually considered fit just for brandy! Friendly low-acid, low alcohol (11%) dry white, light, so easily glugged, faintly grippy, faintly succulent. The Cravens say the cloudiness – which might discourage traditional drinkers – "is not an issue, not at all" – among those with palates attuned to modern tastes. We agree.

CLAIRETTE BLANCHE

South Africa is historically strong (and this writer weak, another failing) on dessert wines. As anyone who knows our wine story appreciates only too well, to the point of boredom, the desserts, red and white, of Hendrik Cloete's Constantia in the 18th Century wowed the world – or rather the royal houses that could afford it.

Will any modern Cape wine ever command such universal acclaim? After a visit to Cloete, a European guest wrote home to say it was "curious to hear an obscure African farmer talk of the monarchs of Europe as his eager customers".

Jane Austen had her aristocratic English characters sip it for its "healing powers on a disappointed heart". That would have included Napoleon, in exile in St Helena, limited to a quarterly allocation of 90-92 bottles. One a day. The stingy British. And they were half bottles – 500 ml. The victor of Waterloo, the Duke of Wellington, also a dessert fan, doubtless imbibed a more liberal allocation. Only Hungarian Tokaj Aszu dessert matched Constantia at the royal courts of Europe, which then included the Tsars of Russia.

A favourite wine note of all time comes from a Swedish botanist, Anders Sparrman, who sailed round the world with Captain Cook. In 1772, after several visits to Constantia, Sparrman declared it "...a very delicate dessert wine which has something peculiarly agreeable in the aroma of it."

Then long decades in the dark for Constantia. Multiple vineyard hazards (including, later, the universal vine killer, phyllloxera) and devastating trade treaties – the British and French, unfortunately reaching harmony and lowering adversarial customs tariffs, so the Brits started buying from across the channel rather than across the Equator. And Lord Nelson had dismissed Cape Town's naval strategic value anyway, declaring it just a "wine tavern". (Nothing's changed, Admiral.)

In 1986, Klein Constantia, once a part of the old Constantia, burst on the scene after much research and experiment with a revivalist idea and called it Vin de Constance. The winemaker then, Ross Gower, a shrewd practitioner of disguising serious work in a shroud of bonhomie, made it sound like all in a day's work when he replicated the magnificent wine – made from the same Muscat de Frontignan grape variety Cloete grew. Gower's wine though was not, as is often thought, made from botrytis fungus-shrivelled grapes, like Sauternes and Noble Late Harvests. Botrytis hit South Africa much later. These grapes are dried on the vine without the fungus. Today, the wine sails on as a Cape icon; for once the word is appropriate. It still has 'something peculiarly agreeable" about it.

South Africa is replete with other fine dessert wines, some botrytised, some fortified – Muscadels, white and red, made from Muscat de Frontignan. But I don't have a sweet tooth, and hardly ever eat puddings of any sort. So these are not really my kind of wine! However, when I do weaken, it is likely to be if the following are offered. Desserts in themselves.

DESSERTS

Klein Constantia Vin de Constance A fantastic concentration of spicy sweet essences, including nuts and dried apricots, survives whirling, bullying fermentation and inevitable cellar battering. A shining, golden-hued gem appears, packaged in squiggly – perfectly hand-fitting - black bottles, like the originals. Fabulous backstory, gorgeous sipping.

Miles Mossop Kika Noble Late Harvest Plush, stylish, apricot-lined botrytis dessert, fermented and finished in-barrel. 2014 tasted. Will last years. Named after Tokara winemaker Mossop's daughter.

Nederburg Noble Late Harvest is my favourite from a cellar bulging with desserts. Many of them sold only on the Nederburg Auction. This is available to those of us who don't have access to official paddles or corporate buying funds. Off the shelf. It is botrytised Chenin and Muscat de Frontignan, and reliably delicious. Small glasses of this at the end of a dinner and you don't need to offer – or make – a pudding. Serve very cold.

The **Paul Cluver Noble Late Harvest** is unmitigatedly brilliant, vintage to vintage, with a riveting Riesling intensity. Leaves 99% of Chenin- and Muscat-based botrytis dessert wines in the dust.

Nuy White Muscadel Sentiment creeping in here: this has been one of our go-to traditional, fortified dessert preferences since 1980. Most of that time Nuy, owned by a handful of growers in a valley en route to Robertson, was in the charge of Wilhelm Linde, now retired. There's an irresistible unctuousness, a luxurious, unashamed, perfumed Muscat blowsiness; velvety, rich, charming, warming perfection in the glistening golden hues. Okay, it's not subtle and it's a plentiful genre, reasonably priced, but this one has always been among the cleanest and, like its custodian for so many years, classiest. As fine today as it's ever been.

GRENACHE

If in wine, as in most things, power with lightness, ease and grace is class, then Grenache is sheer class. And under-rated no more. It is a new cult red. South Africa has around 200ha.of this variety . France has 95 000ha! But only about 13 ha.(according to viticulturalist Rosa Kruger) of our Grenache vineyards are older than 35 years. They are at Piekenierskloof near Citrusdal, in the Olifants River region, just outside the official borders of the Swartland. And they are gold – and pots of honey. Winemakers are swarming in from everywhere.

At a presentation of Grenache wines from around the world in London early in 2015, the British wine merchants Berkmann Wine Cellars invited Rotem Saouma, a Pinot Noir authority, who said: "For those of us specialised in Pinot Noir, the universe of Grenache is completely familiar. The capacity of this variety is stunning. It's accessible but it can age; you have power but lightness too…there is a lot of expression but it is not heavy."

Its traditional role has been a bit-player in the 'Mediterranean' blend, now sometimes referred to as GSM, for Grenache, Syrah, Mourvèdre. Syrah supplies the perfume, pepper and spice, Mourvèdre the dark density and Grenache, which is very light-hued, fills the wine out with its fleshy, smooth, ripe fruit. Other Southern French blends, like Chateauneuf du Pape, have a much wider spread of varieties, but there too Grenache is important, though it always has played junior fiddle to Syrah.

Wine drinkers are now thirsting for it as a stand-alone label. Cabernet is grandeur and more tannin, Pinot Noir is predicated on fresh acidity, Grenache is all easy grapey warmth – capable of freshness too. And, with its translucent sunset tint, a natural for rosé.

No also-ran now. The grape delivers in the bottle, and in the vineyard its performance is remarkable. It thrives in dry lands, in hot lands. It's fairly resistant to many diseases, withstands wind well. It will be critical as the Cape becomes progressively warmer. We'll see a spurt in its vineyard expansion.

Interestingly, three more mature Stellenbosch producers, Neil Ellis, Ken Forrester and Jan Boland Coetzee were early birds onto the Grenache bandwagon. Jan Boland was born at Piketberg; he has a proprietorial view toward nearby Piekenierskloof and its now priceless vineyards. His Grenache 2013 is a wine of great eloquence; never have I heard such universal praise for a single wine from both young revolutionaries and old campaigners.

I AM SPEECHLESS

I have a good book and an hour to kill. Some melba toast to swipe off bits from a softish camembert. The establishment is offering wines by the glass – and the one with the deep orange sunset glow sets off my thirst buds. A couple is enjoying it at a nearby table and the condensation beads are sliding down nicely, like in every drink ad.

I ask the somm: it's a **Vriesenhof Piekenierskloof Grenache 2013**. The grapes are from Piekenierskloof, up the West Coast. Wine wastelands no longer. And Grenache, a humble southern French grape, historically overshadowed by Syrah, is like a suddenly rediscovered, still fascinating, old flame. Worldwide. If you haven't headed off into the wild West to kick up the dust that grows this ancient Grenache, sorry, your locus standi in Cape wine is below par. I am getting there… But in the meantime, let me see what the fuss is about.

I order the wine – even if a glass costs what I'd expect to pay for a bottle - and bury myself in the book. I signal for another glass, and more cheese. I am speechless.

Vriesenhof is now an expensive piece – suburb - of Stellenbosch real estate, though it wasn't back in 1980 when Jan Boland Coetzee bought the farm, soon after he ended a long tour at Kanonkop – and took himself and his bemused wife and kids – none of them had a word of French – off to Burgundy to work six months in the vineyards and cellars of Joseph Drouhin. The Drouhins are rugby freaks. And Jan Boland – who came back a Burgundian at heart - is the Cape's most famous Springbok wine-rugby legend.

For years and years I'd tasted his wines. I respect them as much as I like him, which is a lot. A more honest, earthier, friendlier, more irreverent – more warmly, saltily expletive-prone - man you're unlikely to meet. But his reds were as taut and tight as he is open and approachable. I would despair, and he would admonish: "You must just wait, wait to drink them, you ignorant #@**# bliksem!"

Now in my glass is this absolutely friendly, see-through, limpid, juicy, huggable wine. I am overcome. As the colour implies, it's delicate. But it's also sophisticated, with enough freshening tannins. It's holding the cheese – and me - perfectly.

In his winery – a Burgundian by now, he excavated immediately under the home to house his barrel cellar, accessed by an internal stairway – there used to hang a gruesome rugby action pic of Jan screaming in excruciating pain. Under the scrum, a huge hand is squeezing the life out of his balls; his arms are helplessly bound up somewhere in the scrum.

I'm sorry I never saw those Springbok matches. But it's part of the legend: there never was, never will be, a doughtier warrior than Jan Boland, the Springbok loose forward.

I ordered a ton of Vriesenhof Piekenierskloof Grenache.

THE WIZARDRY

The call came late one night in 1997. From Charles Back. "I think we may have struck gold," he said, almost in a whisper, for emphasis. "There's something very unusual going on here, the Merlot is so different, incredible. Flavours I haven't come across before." He'd had a hunch but couldn't believe it might happen so quickly. Our first vintage, midway into a couple of exhilarating, exhausting years as a founding partner of Spice Route, with Back, Gyles Webb of Thelema and Jabulani Ntshangase. Just as Erica and I prepared to retire from wine writing.

Back had bought a neglected Swartland farm, with a tobacco shed and a few old vineyards, Pinotage and Sauvignon Blanc. Webb had spotted and then hired Eben Sadie, an assistant at rural Romansrivier Co-op. The young man who will be remembered as one of most remarkable winemakers of his generation turned out a beautiful maiden – and a few subsequent - vintages for Spice Route. In the old shed, converted by Back in three months, just like that, to a 30 000-cases-a-year winery at less than 20% of the cost of a new, conventional one. It was the wizardry of make-doism.

The farm was near Kalbas (Calabash) Kraal railway station outside Malmesbury. We wanted to call the venture Calabash. The army of Distell's backroom lawyers had registered the name. Never used it but declined to negotiate. Erica got thinking. If you climbed the hills, she wondered, could you glimpse the Atlantic? Probably, I said. Got it, she said. The old mariners rounding the Cape en route to the East. "Call it Spice Route."

Merlot never became the emphasis. But Shiraz and Rhône varieties and Chenin did. Until then, in the vast, hot, Swartland wheatfields, most farmers treated their grapes as little more than by-products to be shipped in bulk to one large co-operative winery. Back, and then Sadie, changed that emphatically and wondrously for Cape wine. Much later, others called it the Swartland Revolution – and Sadie became its patron saint. Back, of course, as he does, had moved on. He was buying up Darling vineyards – "even better, just as interesting soils, more maritime" - and taking over a whole co-operative at Citrusdal to catch and ride a global wave. The world's newest-trending red grape, Grenache, has grown here, in remote obscurity, for generations. These bush vineyards, especially those around the rugged Piekenierskloof Pass, have become famous almost overnight, and Back is right there, staking his claim.

Spice Route's 'front of house' has now moved, in one of his constant buy-ups and consolidations, to Fairview's neighbouring farm Seidelberg, bought by him a few years ago, and converted into a multi-themed Cape winelands destination. It houses his R70m Cape Brewing Company operation: an artisanal brewery making a hugely popular beer named Jack Black; the uniquely fine De Villiers chocolate-making enterprise importing beans directly from three continents; a specialist distillery with a range of fine grappas; a trio of completely different restaurants; a home décor shop and art gallery … and so on and on.

We catch up with Charles and his artist wife Di on the wide shady stoep of TV chef Bertus Basson's "modern South African" restaurant, under leafy oaks, looking over vineyards towards the mountains. We first sample the new 2015 Darling Chenin. Approvingly in my case. "Now," he said, "if you want to mess this up, make it into a 'new wave' wine, all you have to do is pour it into a barrel and forget to put a bung in it. You'll have your cloudy, orange-brown wine soon enough. But we're not Sherry makers." He laughs. These wars of the winelands are waged in fine spirit. The regional gamesmanship, we all seem to agree, is pushing Cape wine as a whole to new heights.

We dip into the **Spice Route Grenache**: silky tannins do the trick here, and they're ever-present; 2013 is in the vanguard of the 'new-age, old-vines ' style of Grenache from the Swartland. An absolute triumph of charming drinkability – a sappy thirst-quencher uncluttered by fancy winemaking or oakiness.

He promises to get me some other Grenache samples. They do not arrive. He emails a confession: "I had them specially sent down from Piekenierskloof, but a buyer arrived and true to form, I used them to make a sale! Sorry..." That's Charles Back.

THE ORIGINAL
REVOLUTIONARY

Neil Ellis is one of the non-landed gentry's giants of Cape wine. He's parleyed gumption, daring and a very independent streak into building a formidable household name. From zip. Oh, and with brilliant technical competence. And bank managers who've understood, or been made to understand – as Neil Ellis's great confidante, Jan Boland Coetzee, has always advised – "leverage is the bank's problem, not ours".

His early career in the duller, establishment, government side of the industry, from the KWV in Paarl to chief winemaker at government-run Groot Constantia in Cape Town, ended after a decade and he went private first at Zevenwacht, then at Jonkershoek with Hans-Peter Schröder at what was Oude Nektar, now Stark-Condé. The Neil Ellis brand, beginning with a Chardonnay, Sauvignon Blanc and Cabernet in the mid-1980s, grew steadily, with a widening list of Vineyard Selection labels until today's settled, modern, family-owned facility above Stellenbosch. It has taken 30 years and his daughter and two sons are all in the business. Recently he's launched a new red – Cab-Shiraz, like he used to make at Groot Constantia - named Webb-Ellis, a dynastic label linking his and his wife Stephanie's maiden name.

It's routine in South Africa now - had been for centuries in much of the wine world - but in the 1980s, government quotas on vine growing and other restrictions still made it almost impossible to buy in grapes privately from distant vineyards and vinify elsewhere. Ellis's initial forays, the bold strokes that unleashed a modern revolution in Cape wine, showed that a vineyard from Whitehall in Elgin – without its own cellar and far from a co-operative winery – could grow sensational Sauvignon, under a Neil Ellis banner, produced in Stellenbosch. It went against the estate idea – grown, made and bottled on one property – but it honoured the equally important and intellectually neat notion for consumers, drinking and following the fortunes of an identifiable, single vineyard's grapes, handled by a recognised winemaker.

His stroke of genius was to spot the loopholes, widen them, overcome them; for several years he had the ideas virtually to himself. He's remained ahead of the game; he was a leader of the recent stampede to Piekenierskloof in the Olifants River area up the West coast; his espousal of Darling was pioneering too. It has now led to a first foray into land ownership: "Except I can't afford to plant it," he says – we hope jokingly.

'You may think you'll be able to get away with it, after a late night, in the winery," he once told me, fixing me with an unblinking stare. "Don't," he said, "ever. When you stuff the bung into the barrel, there must be no air, not a millimetre. Nothing! You'll never make decent wine otherwise." He was giving me some fundamentals. I never closed a barrel without imagining him looking over my shoulder.

His elder son Warren, a Stellenbosch University graduate, is in charge of Neil Ellis wines now: the odd shift in emphasis has been gradual. Neil's acids were bold, for keeping. Warren's – while still fresh – are a tad easier in the reds; almost dangerously gluggable in the Cinsaut and Grenache. The Chardonnay has the precision and perfect balance his Dad didn't always achieve! A Stellenbosch young Turk more than ready to take on the revolutionaries of other competing districts.

Neil Ellis Vineyard Selection Grenache is among the first labels of this in-fashion grape in highly appealing, easy-drinking, gently-serious mode; from the far west Piekenierskloof, high slopes, old, very distinctive bush vines. And therefore, alas, not a bargain. The 2012 has the allure of a deceptively simple, perfumed sweet aroma, then drenches the palate with dry-ripe juiciness. Bit of a twang in the finish, signals some tannin resilience. Fairly unintrusive winemaking. Only old wood.

AND

Tierhoek Grenache Don't be discouraged by the reticent nose, a generous, tasty mouthful awaits on palate. Great spread from savoury heather to ripened red berries on 2012. Grenache's gentle texture too. Just knowing these are 60-year-old ungrafted vines talking raises an eyebrow. Incredible. Also from Piekenierskloof.

MALBEC

A French grape, appropriated by Argentina for its national signature wine. "Reaching celestial heights" there, decided Robert Parker, the world's most powerful wine critic after the "grape failed miserably in France" in his view. Malbec with Argentinian beef (mostly Angus) is carnivore heaven.

Annex Kloof Malbec 2014 I came upon this Swartland gem almost by chance, on the way to someone else. And asked Hugo Basson if I could taste from his barrels. It turned out he's a Malbec fanatic, has planted five clones, probably uniquely in South Africa. "Making this wine is in my blood", he says. He loves Argentina, has travelled there often, admires its beef too. The wine: beautiful, easy tannins around pure, ripe raspberry juiciness, gluggable, uncomplicated. Only used barrels. Unblended. A must-have in our home. Braai or more serious dining. "It's such a wonderful grape," he says. "I didn't want to blend it with any others. I want a completely South African Malbec. During fermentation it smells musky, just like the pink lucky-packet sweeties my mother used to buy for us."

MERLOT

Something not quite right here – yet. The world over, Merlot is the grape that's meant to improve and enhance Cabernet Sauvignon in a blend, tempering Cabernet's firmer tannic structure and backbone with its fleshy softness and loads of red berry and mulberry flavours. The public loves it – the name is easy, its reputation says it's a restaurant-ready wine, swiggable sooner than Cabernet… and so on. In France, in California, that's more demonstrably so than in our climate. Ours by and large have exhibited a harder, less yielding edge than Merlot's international reputation suggests. (Though that took a bit of a beating in the movie Sideways, which extolled Pinot Noir while scorning Merlot.) So why have we not done more, and better, with it in South Africa? A few growers who've produced stunners in some vintages often don't keep it up. "I think we're still finding the right clones for our climate," says one old stager with long experience. There are plenty of labels around, and the wines are often pleasant. But I so rarely come across one that fits my image of an outstanding stand-alone red. Hurry on with those clones, someone.

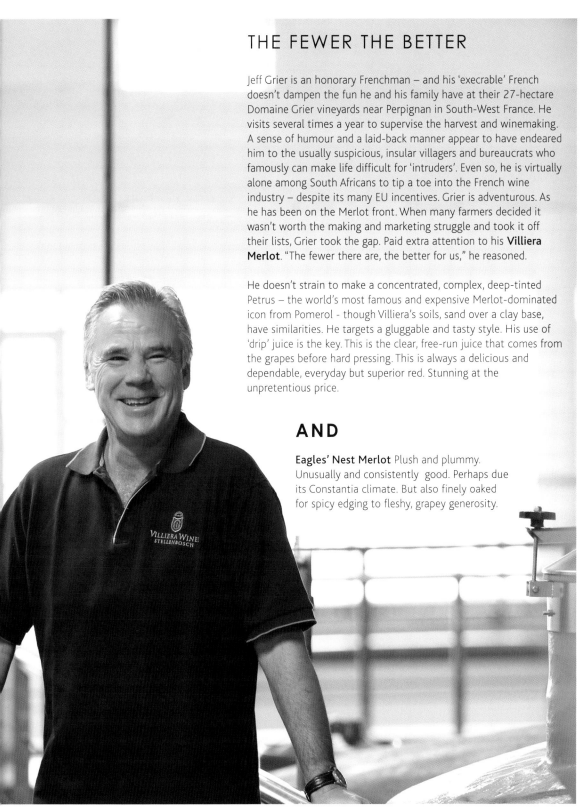

THE FEWER THE BETTER

Jeff Grier is an honorary Frenchman – and his 'execrable' French doesn't dampen the fun he and his family have at their 27-hectare Domaine Grier vineyards near Perpignan in South-West France. He visits several times a year to supervise the harvest and winemaking. A sense of humour and a laid-back manner appear to have endeared him to the usually suspicious, insular villagers and bureaucrats who famously can make life difficult for 'intruders'. Even so, he is virtually alone among South Africans to tip a toe into the French wine industry – despite its many EU incentives. Grier is adventurous. As he has been on the Merlot front. When many farmers decided it wasn't worth the making and marketing struggle and took it off their lists, Grier took the gap. Paid extra attention to his **Villiera Merlot**. "The fewer there are, the better for us," he reasoned.

He doesn't strain to make a concentrated, complex, deep-tinted Petrus – the world's most famous and expensive Merlot-dominated icon from Pomerol - though Villiera's soils, sand over a clay base, have similarities. He targets a gluggable and tasty style. His use of 'drip' juice is the key. This is the clear, free-run juice that comes from the grapes before hard pressing. This is always a delicious and dependable, everyday but superior red. Stunning at the unpretentious price.

AND

Eagles' Nest Merlot Plush and plummy. Unusually and consistently good. Perhaps due its Constantia climate. But also finely oaked for spicy edging to fleshy, grapey generosity.

Craig Hawkins revels in his enfant terrible status. **El Bandito** is one label in his **Testalonga** brand, an export success – in six European countries, though on a small scale - 800 cases a year. A woman's plump bare bottom features on another label. The 'naked' wine idea, not homogenised, commercial, generic, but wine made "naturally" – is a loaded one, now dividing the wine world. He's worked at Lammershoek in the Swartland, understudied Eben Sadie of Sadie Family; began reading Forestry at Stelllenbosch University, then started Oenology; there he ran into trouble because, as he says, his tutors disagreed with him. He wandered Europe playing hockey (having played the piano as a boy), worked as a groundsman - and then discovered off-beat wines, and far-out wine-making, from the Loire to Friuli. And then to the Swartland.

He calls his wines "expressive and creative" centred on two key elements, among others: organic vineyards and "skin-contact - natural winemaking."

Listening, you realise his greatest dread: acquiring mainstream status. For now, little danger of that. Mention Hawkins and 'mainstream' wine retailers take a deep breath: "Oh, give me a break" they say. Hip young wine merchants are excited: Roland Peens of Wine Cellar promoted Hawkins as one of his Young Guns for 3 years, from 2011. Peers hold divergent views. "We tried a few of his wines, undrinkable, all of them," said one. "It's when those guys get evangelical that it gets me," said another. But it was an older-guard Stellenbosch wine-man who insisted we seek out Hawkins.

Among the younger wine-making crowd? Hawkins is one of them. They really like him. "But I like him more than his wines," says one; and won't be quoted! He posts pics of himself in back-to-front cap, smoking a huge cigar. Many admire his guts and adventurism, his aversion to bottling "just what the market wants" rather than the wines a vineyard delivers - expressively. His wines are sometimes cloudy, sometimes orange, in the oxidative way, finding favour in "Natural" wine bars and other outlets in Europe and the States. He argues they're real. By that does he mean others aren't? "I'm not dogmatic," he says. "If the vineyard gives me grapes that need sulphuring, I'll do it."

NATURAL WINES

A prophet except in his own country? A crazy iconoclast? Our Wine and Spirit Board has turned down "orange" wines for official certification in the past; but it is believed they will soon relax their rules.

Hawkins is someone to watch, obviously, and we went to meet him, on a hot afternoon at an out-of-the-way farm outside Malmesbury. He'd just got back from a golfing weekend on the Garden Route. He's also a fly fisherman. He'd only recently moved from Lammershoek and was in these quarters temporarily – with his assortment of different-sized and aged barrels – pending an imminent move to a new farm he's bought in northern Swartland, near Pikenierskloof. Until now, he's been buying in grapes from small parcels of assorted (organic) vineyards.

It is a world away from the glossy estates on the traditional wine routes. We are greeted by a low-slung black sow, its massive under-carriage swaying gently; it snuffles amiably outside the cellar, like a family pet. Cattle graze nearby. Not Craig's, but they fit the picture: no self-respecting Swartland revolutionary is without bovines, they're the organic, biodynamic badge (and, for the mystically connected ones, provide the horn tips that must be filled with this and that to be buried in vineyards as guardians against pests). Tall eucalyptus trees provide shade.

To my great shame, I'd never tried the Testalonga wines. As we sampled from barrel to barrel, from Muscat to Harslevelü (the last two to be blended, dry and at low alcohols) to Chenin to Grenache, I formed only a tentative picture. I like disordered barrels in different sizes, the alchemist's kitchen not the commercial factory. I was intrigued by what I tasted. But time passed too swiftly as Hawkins spoke of his Damascene moments in the Loire that "completely changed the way I thought about everything". It was time to go.

I'm resolved to taste more of his – bottled – wines seriously, plug the gap in my knowledge. This is a likeably original young man. Will he be the one to lead South Africa towards greater acceptance and awareness of the oxidative wines made all round the wine world, and gaining traction and fans in hipster wine bars in Europe and the USA? We'll be hearing more from, and about, Craig Hawkins in future.

Barely a stone's throw from one of Nelson Mandela's old residences, Pollsmoor prison, is wine and golf estate Steenberg, now owned by the Graham Beck group. Super-swish tasting quarters, sophisticated fine-dining restaurant, impeccable vineyards and cellar, all are run by Namibian-born, Cape Town-schooled, Stellenbosch-finished John Loubser. He's managed to keep its fine wine ethos alive during various changes of ownership – and after two decades as cellarmaster has now booted himself upstairs to the MD's office. But when I visit, this class act is back on the tasting floor.

I owe John. On a crazy wine trip to Brazil a few years ago, a bunch of South Africans was invited, entirely capriciously it seemed, by a wine importer's daughter, to join wine people from dozens of countries. A wine-fuelled beef-fest of gargantuan portions drew to an overdue close with a surprise challenge, from the Chilean, Argentinian, Italian and Kiwi contingents. We should all perform our versions of the Haka. The Kiwis had put everyone else to shame when our turn came. We were huddling hesitantly when John climbed on the table, flung off his shirt and began a roaring, torso-contorting rendition of Shosholoza. We gyrated along with more pride than finesse. The restaurant was in stitches. John saved the day.

One of his personal favourite food reds, and now lately mine, is the **Steenberg Nebbiolo**. It deserves more attention. The 2012 is an arresting, tangy charmer. Right for several of chef Kerry Kilpin's dishes. Like seared beef carpaccio. Or more adventurously, a cheese course: see in our Food pages, her recipe for Gorgonzola and kumquat with a pear poached in the wine.

NEBBIOLO

PETITE SIRAH

Spice Route Petite Sirah is the kind of curve-ball wine you'd expect from Charles Back, testing, tempting, teasing the market. A black grape regarded dismissively in France, it is known there as Durif. Though used in California, it's hardly known in South Africa. Not to be confused with Shiraz or Syrah – the 'noble' Rhône grape. This Durif/Sirah is certainly worth a try – if only for its newness. Dark, chalky-dry, it's lifted and moderated by cautious new oaking. I tasted the 2012. On probation as one of my braai wines.

PINOTAGE

We have to tread warily here; this is a 'national' grape. Chauvinism can enter what should be a dispassionate fray.

Pinotage arose from Prof A I Perold's crossing of Cinsaut and Pinot Noir, both *vitis vinifera* – this is not a hybrid - in Stellenbosch in 1925. It barely resembles its parents. You can get – or imagine - snatches of ancestry, but this offspring is very much its own thing. Vigorous and well-behaved, it was bred from seeds – but the child was abandoned by Perold after a few years when he moved jobs. Colleagues rescued the plants and propagated them. But it wasn't until the Pinotage from Stellenbosch vineyard, Bellevue, more than 30 years later, won the top prize at South Africa's 1959 Young Wine Show that people took notice. It now represents about 5% of the national vineyard. Why hasn't Pinotage been a much bigger success-story? Its glaringly obvious marketing potential – as countless visitors and experts constantly remind us – is that it's a uniquely South African wine, unavailable, or very nearly so, anywhere else in the world.

The trouble is, while it can be glorious, it usually isn't. Its sharpish estery qualities – acetone, as in nail varnish remover – can be powerful. And it can smell of bubblegum and bananas, a weird and far from wonderful combination. Apart from a handful of growers, led by the eloquently insistent Beyers Truter of Beyerskloof, Pinotage's partisan-in-chief, and by the Kriges and their winemaker, Abrie Beeslaar, at Kanonkop, and lately most convincingly by Francois Naude, much commercial Pinotage is made without enough care, in vineyard and cellar. Taming those frisky, pungent esters begins in the vineyard, and is perfectly possible, but it's time-consuming and expensive and Pinotage's image, and its wines, still need more work to justify higher pricing.

The carefully oak-matured ones listed here are serious examples of what can be done. But watch out for the new-generation styles being made by young winemakers who do not use the crutch of oak. They're an exciting revelation.

GRACELAND

Beyers Truter is a Character with a capital C. Frequently funny, and also amusingly fickle – to the political parties he signs up with, then discards, from the old governing National Party, to the Trekker (Tractor) Party - which he founded, then left for the Democratic Alliance. Presently he appears comfortable within the folds of the governing African National Congress, a fairly adventurous circumnavigation of the political landscape. However, his loyalty to, his infatuation with Pinotage is unwavering. He's Mr. Pinotage. He won't hear a word against the controversial cultivar. At his insistence, the term Cape Blend – still an unofficial designation, but not for long if he has anything to do with it – is taken to mean that Pinotage features significantly in the wine. Obstinate chauvinism? Marketing opportunism? In his formidable winemaking hands, Pinotage has reached unexpected heights.

Take a glass of **Beyerskloof Diesel 2012** - named after a faithful hound - and down it with, say, a garlicky, rosemary-studded shoulder of lamb, crackling with crisp fat: all equivocation dissolves. There's power, oomph, rich grunt – encased in suede, an expensive feel, like a bespoke Italian shoe. The Diesel is expensive, but not outrageously. I buy a few bottles each year, to toast the maestro and show friends Pinotage at its pinnacle. A censure to all the sweet-acid, blowsy, varnishy stuff out there, Pinotage rubbishing itself. The Diesel is a "severe" selection from the vineyard, says Truter – just one bunch per shoot, or only 4 tons/ha harvest. In the cellar, only the best few of 50 barrels are chosen. A generous oaking is critical, an expense many producers are shy to risk.

The sprawling Beyerskloof establishment at Stellenbosch is now a shrine to the grape: coachloads arrive to pay homage and listen to the genial, evangelical spiel and drink Pinotage in its multiple incarnations: Pinotage Rosé, Pinotage Rosé Brut, Pinotage Reserve, Faith – a Pinotage-Cabernet Cape blend, even Chenin Blanc-Pinotage. And to eat: Pinotage Burgers, Pinotage Ice-cream. And so on. The place is adorned with art and installations and alive with music: a Pinotage Graceland. Tourists, especially, seem to love the grape.

Truter also guided venerable Kanonkop in its pinnacle years, where he needed to master the grandest of Cape Cabernets and their blending mates. International accolades poured in. You find echoes of this under the Beyerskloof Field Blend – a vineyard mix of Cabernet and Merlot.

Next? Now that Truter has handed over most of the winemaking duties to son Anri (left), what's keeping him busy? An Angolan general wants to show that his country is really liberated from the old metropolitan power, Portugal; he wants to grow and bottle wines along Angola's beautiful Atlantic coast. Truter has been over there digging holes himself to establish the new vineyards. He flies to Luanda regularly. A new African wine industry? Pinotage will be a centrepiece.

A TOWERING BOUNCER

For Pinotage in overdrive turn off the R44 out of Stellebosch into Kanonkop. Their oldest, scraggiest, most unpampered Pinotage vineyard, the prettiest too, is right there: a well-exposed, south-west-facing hillside, glowing with virus-infected orange and red leaves in autumn. These bush-vines, planted in 1953, ripen and are harvested early in the season; they are pruned to yield small crops - and the virus itself limits the fruit. Result: intense and rich, Pinotage-sweet wine. Here is an example of managing and massaging vineyards to live with, even exploit, the afflictions of nature.

These vineyards made legends of two great Cape winemakers - or did they steward Kanonkop to greatness? A pointless, if enjoyable, debate. Jan Coetzee went off to establish Vriesenhof; his successor, Beyers Truter, after a decade of bagging every known accolade, left to found Beyerskloof. Where? Just across the road. He wasn't abandoning this terroir. Will Abrie Beeslaar, his deputy, the quieter, less visible cellar chief now, introduce any changes? I don't think so, although he has been spending some time with international viticultural guru Phil Freese down the road at Vilafonté.

Kanonkop Black Label Pinotage remains THE big label of this variety, a towering bouncer. Starting in 2006, they set aside 1000 bottles a year – a few specially reserved from the finest barrels of that ancient old vineyard. Sets you back a bit, at R1300 a bottle in 2015. But they cannot make enough.

SMOOTH AS A BABY'S BOTTOM

"If you ask me," said one of the savvier palates of Stellenbosch, "that's the finest Pinotage made in South Africa." He was looking at the dead bottle of **Le Vin de Francois** under my arm. The work of Francois Naudé, the Pretoria pharmacist who turned a wine hobby into a job. "How lucky was I?" He emigrated to the Cape in 1989 with his wife Magda. Never went, nor looked, back. "My science helped," he says. From consulting, he was soon appointed winemaker at L'Avenir, almost instantly turning out wines to wide acclaim. He retired – first time - when L'Avenir was sold to a French Chablis grower, Michel Laroche. Back to consulting. And then this bright idea – as a sideline. "I wanted to make the *crème de la crème* of South African Pinotage."

He'd already made a more than respectable one at L'Avenir but now talked his best-known Stellenbosch Pinotage neighbours, and one from Bot River, into reserving a couple of barrels for him each year. "Made under my personal supervision, from vineyard to cellar. I choose everything, barrels included, they give me the run of wineries." After exhaustive sample testing in his kitchen, "my lab", he culls these to just 10 barrels, from 5-10 producers depending on the vintage, which gives him around 200 cases. The 2013 was a roll-call of the Cape's finest: Kanonkop, Lanzerac, Simonsig, L'Avenir, Delheim, Rhebokskloof, Wildekrans, all in one bottle. Only the last, from Bot River, is not from Stellenbosch. Beyerskloof is usually in the mix. He tells me: "I'm after power and elegance… but I want it smooth as a baby's bottom."

It's a mind-wobbling wine. His notes say: "Typical deep & intense crimson colour….The juicy fruit flavours of black cherries, ripe plums and blackberry are perfectly matched by superb tannins… a wine of opulence and drinkability." Not going to argue.

Large snag. It's not available to you and me. It all goes up for auction at an annual black tie charity event, at a secret venue, changed each year, for some 140 punters, who get to see the young new wine for the first time, after a settling Champagne or two, with their dinner. "They have to be comfortable with its ageing potential, so it's in a fairly assertive, cocky state when they taste it first." He's been doing this annually since 2008. It's all in private collectors' stashes. A very exclusive club. A few bottles sometimes change hands privately. If you spy a chance, don't pass it up.

Francois had recently lost the bubbly, vital Magda, "the finest woman in the world". We toasted her, with Le Vin de Francois, both of us misty-eyed. "I bet she's got a Champagne and Pinotage club going up there, laughing down at us."

AND

B Vintners Liberté Pinotage 2014 Stated aim of the partner-cousins, Gavin Bruwer and Bruwer Raats in this new 2015 venture: to maximise what they call Pinotage's "unrealised" potential, to change its image of brashness "so it can do its thing, emphasise its strawberry and spice fruit, its toned-down Turkish delight flavours". Their Pinotage is a wine "we have to make in the vineyard: restrain vine growth and ripen the grapes properly," says Gavin Bruwer. This maiden vintage, Stellenbosch fruit, achieves assertive freshness, shows smothering oak isn't the only route to curbing Pinotage's excessive acetone urges.

The Pinotage headlines inexplicably sometimes miss out **Simonsig Redhill**. It's a terrific example of reined-in power, with the grape's voluble fruity intensity nicely checked by cellar techniques avoiding excessive extraction. That gives oak-barrel ageing a chance to tame the grape. Lively, flavoursome, very South African.

Steytler Pinotage Respected even by non-Pinotage fans, for its weighty forthrightness, sweet-berry nose, and fruitiness (stops well short of any boiled sweets nonsense) and all-new top-notch Taransaud French barrels. There's some clove and fruit-cake too.

PINOT NOIR

Pinot Noir is a charming extrovert one sip, inexplicably sulky the next – mysterious and fragile. Its admirers turn easily to helpless fanaticism. The grape inspires guff like this. Like other Pinotphiles, you want the charm but it is elusive. So you want it more. Growers tear their hair out but won't tear out the vines.

"Thank God they behaved today," I heard one whisper with relief after a tasting. "They can be so temperamental."

Pinot at its best is sassy, juicy, silky – strawberries and ripe black cherries, a spice or two, cinnamon perhaps, or a whiff of coffee. A play of pure ripe perfumes. As it matures, the lively fresh fruit yields gradually to an earthier, calmer quality: dewy dampness, forest floor, fungi, compost. The transition phases, about four or five years from vintage (little in wine is precise) are the compelling ones, and a stage of personal weakness. The marvellous texture seduces. The grape's lighter garnet tints – Cabernet is darker, more intense, looks more authoritative and substantive – can mislead; pinot can be as powerful as any red, with its soft velvetiness and quietly resolute tannins.

No wine, certainly no red, is as versatile at the dinner table. In our warm climate, it should be chilled a little, to emphasise its lovely freshness.

South Africa has the late Tim Hamilton-Russell, a gritty wine philosopher-intellectual and founder of the eponymous Walker Bay vineyards in the mid-1980s, to thank for persevering with his Burgundy obsessions. (See more under Chardonnay.) There was hardly a vine in the area then. He won eventually but at great financial cost, surviving frequent ridicule, and baffling, even malicious, official obstructionism. A long and gripping story.

But he couldn't have wished for a finer legacy than the Hemel en Aarde Valley behind Hermanus today, a picturesque riot of competing vineyards and wineries turning out pretty fine Pinots.

It doesn't travel well, Pinot, we're often told, beyond its home - and still its benchmark heartland - Burgundy. But the French would say that, wouldn't they? Oregon, in the States, and South Island in New Zealand, specially, and now, cooler parts of the Cape, show the site-fussy, thin-skinned Pinot can be perfectly enticing elsewhere too. We may not have incubated the impossibly transcendent Burgundy Musigny yet, but we can dream on. Tim would have.

With anything so temperamental at every step, in the vineyard (many clones, a myriad terroir aspects), in the cellar, in the barrel, the slightest stumble can be dire – a dried-out dusty, bitter parody of wine. The barrel-science, and winemakers' experience and insights in particular, as Cape growers acknowledge, need improvement.

But they're producing wonderful and varied Pinots already. Ampelographers – vine-scientists - seem to agree we probably haven't yet nailed all the Cape's ideal terroir combinations of soils, climates, aspects for Pinot. One told me not long ago: "Perhaps we never will." Meantime, we consumers should rejoice in what we've got. It is not too shabby.

Easy Gravitas

Gottfried Mocke, now at Boekenhoutskloof but until late 2015 at Chamonix, is forthcoming but hyperbole-free. He and his bottles, reassuringly, speak the same considered language. His restraint with oak allows fresh and ripe fruit – soft black cherries particularly – to shine through in the **Chamonix Pinot Noir**. These wines feel easy, even light to drink, but you are aware of their gravitas. There's spiciness, and, with a bit of time, some damp compost funkiness. Frequent 5-star winners, they are, geographically, 'outliers' among finer Cape Pinots, which are mostly from coastal areas. What were his secrets?

He sides with those in modern Burgundy winemaking who use a proportion of grape stalks in the (spontaneous, naturally!) fermentation process. "The stalkiness blows off in the end, but the wine definitely stays fresher for longer. More than other grapes, Pinot reflects the vineyard's soil and site. And the vintage. What kills us is when we have a few weeks of heat at the end of the harvest. So we were rigorous about selecting fruit, discarding all but the best."

And what about the great "you-cannot-be-serious" criticism of Cape Pinots – that they don't last, compared with grander Burgundies? He's matter-of-fact. These are Cape, not French wines. And he's candid about the life expectancy of these Pinots generally. In 2015, he thought the Chamonix 2005 was still just 'okay'. But the 2006 was past it. While the 2007, a hot year, was already at its peak. A heads-up: the 2015 vintage finished with a beautifully cool flourish, preserving the freshness of the grapes; it promises a fine, stylish wine.

Line up.

WINE SALES

SUCCULENCE IN SILK

"I like that word ethereal. That's what we're after," says Gordon Johnson, of Newton Johnson Vineyards above Hermanus. This is how English writer Andrew Jefford describes the Pinots of Musigny – and Gordon has also noted Jefford's opinion of some Musigny neighbours - "bugle-Burgundies, blasts of fierce, proud red fruit". For NJ, the direction is clear.

In major wine contests, and among international and domestic critics with substantial followings in recent years, none has outdone this winery for gongs and plaudits. The quality climbed steeply as their own granite-over-clay vineyards began to supply the fruit, which they do exclusively in the **Newton Johnson Family Vineyard** label. But this is not the sole secret, and the many variables shift each vintage. Gordon says: "Perhaps it's knowing your vineyards AND your cooper, trusting him, and he understanding our vineyards and the styles we're after." Wine-and-oak chemistry is under-appreciated – as much intuitive nuance as science. Too little or too much, or mismatched oak – this is a minefield for winemakers.

The 2012s were all fine Pinot bottlings here, the culmination of a good run of vintages, epitomising, consolidating, if not "ethereal" qualities, certainly a now increasingly recognisable style – an array of pure, ripe berry flavours. Succulence in silk. A light, translucent look adds to the soft feel. Spices form part of the bobbing aromas and there's a gentle tannin tug. Charming. A 2008 tasted in 2015 was sublime.

The Family Vineyards range is the best Gordon and his co-winemaker wife Nadia can blend from their three vineyards. Then there's a minuscule, Single Vineyard bottling of **WindandSea** (Platter Guide 2012 Red Wine of the Year); **Mrs M** (a personal favourite) and **Block 6**, which has a sweetness to it and apparently is the choice of a majority of Pinotphiles. You can have fun here.

A THREE-GLASS WINE

There are some wines you tire of quickly. Too heavy, or too alcoholic, or too sweet, or too just about anything. Wine is all about balance. My favourites are always three-glass (or more) wines. The bottles that end up empty at a tasting. Because they are clearly drinker-friendly. Balanced. The **Hamilton Russell Vineyards Pinot Noir** is a three-glass wine. The recent 2013 is majestic – a perceptible, upward gear-shift. The nose offers more ripe cherry intensity than before, qualities replicated generously on the palate. It's mouth-filling and even silky. And, within the vintage variations, there's a general stylistic continuity with the HRV Chardonnay - a delicious elegance. I'm both surprised and unsurprised it does well in competition. Elegance is not always a contest winner. The 2013 is brilliant, and the 2015 might even top that. Again, I'm perhaps in a minority, but not for lengthy ageing. I'd drink within 10 – 12 years. Does South African Pinot pioneer Tim Hamilton Russell very proud indeed.

Alex Dale

Edouard Labeye

"Edouardism"

- No. No. No. No. No. No. No... Yes !!!
- It's works anytime from all ze time
- Impossible is not a French word
- I go away, I come back again
- I guestiate it's rocks
- It's daymare
- smatch !

Peter-Allan Finlayson

NO HEAVY ROUGE AND MAKE-UP

"Our wine sales," says Alex Dale, "have risen as our Robert Parker scores have dipped." The American lawyer's scores in *The Wine Advocate*, a powerful wine buyers' bible to thousands of the world's wealthiest wine collectors, have driven a decades-long surge toward bigger, richer, riper wines. Unsubtle fruit bombs, if you want to deride Parker's tastes. Dale is British-born but brought up in the Burgundy wine business, and now Stellenbosch-based, at his Winery of Good Hope. His winemaker since 1997, Edouard Labeye, is from the Rhône. He rolls his eyes and huff-puffs in contempt when discussing Parker's 100-point scoring system. They both wonder how you score sensations in your mouth and up your nose – an intricate olfactory system subject to countless variables and distractions from one minute to the next - as a percentage?

"The serious drinking public, our market, is way in front of all that; they don't need all the heavy rouge and make-up," says Dale, finally.

A joint initiative with workers, the Land of Hope Trust, produces its own three, first-rate Land of Hope wines – now listed in London at M&S and domestically at Woolworths. Serious coups.(A declaration of interest here: I'm honoured to be chairman of the trust.)

For years I have been tasting Labeye's take on Pinot. His consultancies include Burgundian clients. Favourite cru there? Chambolle-Musigny, Les Amoureuses. His Pinots have not been for instant gratification; on the harder, leaner edge of things. Just recently, there's been a shift – without capitulating to luscious softness. The **Radford Dale Freedom Pinot Noir 2013**, from Elgin-grown grapes, signals a new upland: there's a beautiful, still-fresh and tense, food-attuned finish after a light, long palate. More complete than in the past. Complexity, and the more sensual, degenerate, gamey, vegetal heights of Pinot require more time in bottle. But there's early purity and freshness in the glass.

The 2012 vintage of this Pinot is in the Swedish Royal cellar. After a special tasting with his sommelier to choose the wines for his son's wedding banquet in June, 2015, the King personally decided that the Freedom Pinot, and not any of the usual Burgundies, should be served. It accompanied a dish of pike-perch with a cream sauce.

THE BURGUNDY SPELL

Peter-Allan Finlayson is under the Burgundy spell, a father-to-son endowment. His Chardonnay is a cracker. What about his Pinot? He's fully committed to the often contradictory subtleties of handling this most mercurial of all grapes, and it shows in his **Crystallum Cuvée Cinema Pinot Noir 2013**: limpid, poised, with edgy finesse, raspberry-cherry aromas. These merge with subdued spices – black pepper, cloves. Reassuring, unaggressive tannin core. It's an attractive New World Pinot now, with aspirations for Old World (Burgundy) grandeur as the vineyard matures. But don't expect European longevity - give this about 8 years.

Stop right here if you prefer your wines without winemaking details. Continue if you want to know the answer to my next question: is he a disciple of Burgundian guru, Henri Jayer, who would not use grape bunch stems in winemaking? Or does he follow Jeremy Seysses of Domaine Dujac, a gifted young trailblazer high-rolling in the heart of France's Cote d'Or, who uses up to 60% wholebunch fermentation, meaning some stems? And the answer is: about 30% of the grapes are wholebunch-pressed. The wine also has the requisite 'authenticity and boutique' qualifications: natural fermentation, single-vineyard identity. From the Hemel-en-Aarde Valley, 30% new French oak for 10 months.

THE GREATEST FOOD WINE

Of the **Meerlust** reds, the **Pinot Noir** is the most bewitching. On its day, it captivates completely. But it's moody, like most Pinots, much moodier than the Rubicon Bordeaux blend or the Merlot. It teases and puzzles, sometimes disappoints. It can redeem itself. But, true to its DNA, it's fickle. And Pinot partisans are severe. First sightings of shimmering ruby in the glass and we are minutely scrutinising for the smallest imperfections. It's built into our infatuation with the grape. We recall a sublime moment, and long for heights of dreamy mysticism again. Incense waftings and the incantations of angels in an echoing cathedral. Only besotted romantics set themselves up for disappointments in this way. In the Cape, we're back on earth. Such moments don't happen here, do they? To which Meerlust's brilliant winemaker Chris Williams patiently, smilingly says: "Our sites don't have those birth certificates." Get out of your trance, he's saying. The Cape has its own birth certificates.

We're tasting at the long table squeezed into the back of the winery. After a while, trilby-hatted proprietor Hannes Myburgh, and a trio of his large ensemble of mixed hounds lope in. Hannes is tough and funny, a French literature graduate with a season in the Lafite cellar on his CV, and the rare (in the Cape) ability to sell his wine to Frenchmen in France, in French. His father, Nico, who restored Meerlust after a period of neglect, was inordinately proud of his son's language and literary gifts. Hannes is the 8th generation Myburgh to live and farm here; the gabled manor house is in all the national art history books, and has now been personalised inside with his impeccable and subversive eye; his parties are legend (for example, an annual tripe-cooking competition held in the vast kitchen). Princess Diana sat round the great square, 22-seater table here, and when the Press sniffed her out, had to be smuggled away through the vineyards.

Hannes M

Williams has poured a few of the Pinots. We sniff up and back down the row of glasses. Each a blend of several vineyards on the estate, including about a third of a so-called problem clone, BK5, the first one planted in profusion in the Cape and chronically virused, long since phased out by most growers.

"Has this 2012 enough edifice, enough grunt?" I throw out the pompous words of a Pinot freak to get him going. "I think so," he answers calmly. And then adds what few others would: "South African Pinots are not long lasters." So how long would that be? "Seven to 10 years. Depending."

I'd not ordinarily pick a 'winner' but in this line-up I choose the 2013: truth commission – I've always loved young wines. It has youthful bounce, pretty red fruit, a limpid, soft texture, the promise of funkier damp forest floor, some growl in the finish, a good sign in moderation. In a couple of years that will have settled out. A simple dish, a few mushrooms with garlic, butter, parsley will take care of that. Chris Williams: "Pinot is the greatest food wine. Goes with virtually anything. But chill it a bit. It needs to taste fresh."

It's a fine Pinot.

Hannes Myburgh, Lentil, Chris Williams

REALLY COOL

Iona is a quite exceptional property. And the wines increasingly match the exceptionalism. Even down to the small but personal matter of naming Iona – after the islands off the west coast of Scotland settled by Andrew Gunn's ancestors – the story here hangs together believably. Gunn, big, burly, determined and humorous, looks as if, like most Scots, he'd like to be ruling England still. For now, he seems content with this corner of Elgin.

Iona is cool. Really cool, about as cool as Bordeaux remarkably – and without the threat of frost. Gunn's viticulturists say these are the coolest vineyards in the country. Harvesting lags much of the winelands by six to eight weeks. The drawn-out hang time – grapes ripening more slowly on the vine – is a quality factor. Promoting lively freshness in wines and much more. It's blustery up here, in the white rock-strewn heathery fynbos. The soils are suitably poor – vines have to search deeper, good for small berries and wine quality - 'struggle ennobles'. Yes, you could be on the remote Scottish moors. There seem to be no neighbours for miles. The winding, rutted, dirt Highlands Road, either from Kleinmond on the coast or via the inland Elgin Valley, hauls you up to 420 metres above the sea, a swoosh of a swift away, just 3,5 km from the Atlantic breakers below.

A white-gabled Herbert Baker-designed home, a sinewy Rhodesian Ridgeback, and the thoughtful Gunn - a retired engineer - welcome visitors. From the tasting rooms to the bold art – and art installations, Rozy Gunn is a sculptor – to the cellar, to the layout of the vineyards, there's the stamp of dogged originality. There are 9 clones of Sauvignon Blanc! They're planted both north to south and east to west, adding to blending variables and potential wine complexity. Gunn enlisted Stellenbosch University ampelogropher Prof Eben Archer from the start after he bought the rundown orchards in 1997. The over-fertilizing regimens of fruit farming are out of the system. More recently in 2011, he took on Werner Muller, a below-the-radar man – "I don't like all this marketing stuff" - but a graduate of the best practical training school in the Cape, Gottfried Mocke's winemaking team at Chamonix. The Ionas have taken a quantum quality leap.

Now Gunn has added to the team: British Master of Wine Remington Norman, as consultant. He lives in the Cape for much of the year and it's often puzzled me why this learned expert, with a vast fund of international wine knowledge, and fuselages of irony, has not been enlisted more. He and his wife Geraldine took the Gunns and Mullers on a study trip to Burgundy, gaining access to inaccessible doyens and young gurus there. "Life changing," says Gunn. Norman will not be turning valves. Even I wouldn't trust him with that. But he'll be a sounding board at key moments, like blending; and he'll be priceless, for his acute, forthright palate and wise perspectives. I'd hire him just for his genial wit – the essence of wine.

Gunn is on course too on such sensible things as sustainability. Aspects of biodynamic farming are in place. There are cows for home-grown manure – no synthetic fertilizers nor pesticides. Five cows, says Gunn. As a cattleman I am congenitally unwilling to hear a bad word about cows. I'd say Iona needs a few more!

Iona Pinot Noir is a serious example, one to watch – and to begin collecting. Punters, those attuned to fine Burgundies, sometimes complain Cape Pinots lack that essential bracing, fresh acidity (with mature, not green tannin) that promises ageing ability, to go with the fleshy, silky beauty and distinct savoury aromas. South Africa has got better at the fruity parts lately; it's the combined completeness that's often missing. They've been over-oaked, or over-extracted and clumsy, or tartly thin and under-ripe. In the Iona 2013 there are beautiful glimmers of completeness – the vineyards delivered in a bottle. In a Cape context, a knockout for me. Perfect with almost any meal.

STEALTHY HEARTBREAKER

The Drift is Bruce Jack's family farm in the depths of the Overberg at Napier. From the mid-1990s, this entertaining English literature graduate, a wine-maker with Californian and Australian experience, built his company, Flagstone, from scratch so successfully into a world brand that he was made one of those irresistible buy-out offers by Constellation (now Accolade). The international liquor giant has kept him on for his many wine and marketing skills. But his own wines, in tiny quantities, are now grown and made on this small, remote country farm growing organic vegetables, "healing"aromatic herbs, raw honey and extra virgin olive oil. Latest interesting surprise: he's importing Spanish wines – of grapes like Grenache and Carinena with names like Catalan Eagle (Grenache Blanc and Viognier). Jack's wine writing is beguiling. Look out for it. His wine's names, too, have always been original.

The Drift Pinot Noir Jack calls this grape the "stealthy heartbreaker" but nonetheless aims to make Pinots "very soft rounded expressions ... joyful, bright complex and delicious." I make the 2012 stealthy alright. It's light-coloured, light in texture and feel, deep and clean and direct-flavoured, with 14% alc. – and with some decent berry and gamey aromas, which may evolve into magical Pinot spicy funkiness given time. Jack's name for it: **There Are Still Mysteries**!

AND

Creation Pinot Noir Reserve 2014 Classically grippy and direct. A fashionable fresh cleanliness. Glimpses of damp forest notes and spiciness. English writer Andrew Jefford found "dense, almost peaty" qualities in 2013. The regular label richer, less lean. Both admirable lunch and dinner companions. As they should be: the Martins – Jean-Claude and Carolyn - husband and wife team – have taken food-wine matching to a fascinating level at their vineyards in the Cape's Burgundy valley, Hemel-en-Aarde. 2013 a Platter guide 5-star.

Pinotphiles will be watching closely Elim's virtual 'water's edge' red wines. The early, from 2012, vintages of **David Nieuwoudt Ghost Corner Pinot Noir** show whistle-clean fruit clarity and freshness.

De Grendel Pinot Noir 2012 A Pinot you feel has arrived at your lips directly from the vineyard. In this case from the high – 970m – Witzenberg Mountains in Ceres. A European climate. The vineyards often covered in snow in winter. Winemaker Charles Hopkins has treated the grapes with respect; gentle pressing, racking, one-year in mix of old/new oak, the new classily imperceptible if the wine is slightly chilled. A good way to drink this bright, ripe strawberry and sour-cherry lusciousness. Some might plead for more depth and complexity; they might lose the light charm and prettiness.

Storm Range – Moya's Pinot Noir Pinot specialist Hannes Storm picks and buys in fruit from scattered vineyards, in this case from a tiny block in the Upper-Hemel-en-Aarde Valley, behind Hermanus. It's a velvety 2012, with lovely perfume, some promising mushroom whiffs and smooth, soft, sweet-ripe palate. Storm knows the region well; he worked many years at Hamilton Russell. His brother Ernst uses the same 'free-lance' modus in Santa Barbara, California. Comparing notes helps.

RED
BLENDS

We've placed all red blends in this section. This is unconventional. But this is a broad-stroke, not a minute-detail book. And whatever their composition, and history, these reds belong together – all grown in and made on South African soil.

Epiphany moments. Cabernet made its cosmic mind-blowing impression on me in a callow, unremarkably reckless youth. We'd wound up a polo tournament in Nairobi and badly needed to celebrate some more. We splashed out on "French" and ordered a Chateau Paveil de Luze without a clue what to expect – except a swollen restaurant bill. And then more, and more. How could red wine be so bloody wonderful? Coarse Chianti, balloon flagons wrapped in raffia, swigged from the bottle, dribbles escaping down the cheeks, had been our level until then. And Tusker lager. Subsequent enquiry revealed the causes of the De Luze magic: fine oak ageing, grape varieties, blending, centuries of arcane French tradition. I think the name wasn't in the news for all the right reasons some years later; that only heightened my curiosity and love of Bordeaux juice, however supposedly manipulated or blended. It's a Margaux Cru Bourgeois – quite lowly but a bit more than adequate for rowdy events in Kenya, and the mix was and is still Cabernet Sauvignon, Merlot and Cabernet Franc, a Bordeaux blend.

Bordeaux blend or Claret - same thing. Most often with Cabernet Sauvignon – Cab Sauv, or just Cab - in the blending lead, toned up, down, or filled out, by Merlot and Cabernet Franc; and less frequently by Malbec and Petit Verdot, the last a favourite among winemakers, but in small doses. You have to see a few litres of Verdot turn a whole barrel into an inky, tannic bomb to accord this little explosive device proper respect. Add Pinotage and you have what its protagonists would like to see officially labelled as a 'Cape Blend'.

But currently the local red blend spotlight is shining on another set of flavours, from grapes like Grenache, Mourvèdre, Syrah, Cinsaut and Carignan, all at home in the Rhône and Southern France, so naturals for our warm climate. Spanish and Portuguese varieties are surfacing, too. Mixes of these are generally more approachable, earlier, than Bordeaux blends, and rely less on oaking. It's an exciting, and developing wine category.

A note: strictly speaking, some single-variety wines may be blends… but the law says that wines may be labelled as single varieties if 85% or more of that grape constitutes the wine…

BEYOND BOUNDARIES

I have known Eben Sadie since 1996. He was lured from the relative obscurity of Romansrivier Co-op near Tulbagh, where he was assistant winemaker, by one of our founding partners in Spice Route Wines, Thelema's Gyles Webb. It was a masterstroke. As was Spice Route's location in the Swartland, an initiative of Charles Back who bought an old farm near Malmesbury with a few vines and a tobacco shed, and in no time re-purposed it into an attention-grabbing new winery. Sadie provided the flying start with purchased Swartland grapes; the wines, reds especially, were a revelation – of deep intensity and richness. No surprise when he went solo four years later. He'd found the terrain for his restless ideas. It's now a vibrantly contested space.

In all the commotion of the Swartland Revolution – by mid-2015 there were around 30 members of its Independent Winemakers movement – it's often forgotten that the idea of capital-poor entrepreneurs setting up shop in rented spaces, even in garages, and buying grapes from different locations, was pioneered brilliantly in the mid-1980s by Neil Ellis of Stellenbosch as the KWV began loosening its monopoly and industry-wide tentacles and quota pricing controls. Like Sadie, Ellis was landless. He sourced grapes from Elgin and later Darling and elsewhere and turned them into fresh, exciting wines. The Burgundian negociant idea – placing yourself at the heart of a creative wine-making and distribution operation, without owning vineyards - of course dates back rather further. But Sadie and his contemporaries have refined it, widened it, sold it – and how. Wine growers agree the most difficult part of the wine business is selling it. Sadie has made it look easy.

And in the process, all those who've ventured beyond traditional boundaries have made two of the most valuable contributions imaginable to Cape wine. They've saved precious old vineyards, by paying farmers not to rip them out in favour of other activities. And they've captivated drinkers all over the world in search of genuine, new-discovery wines.

In years past, Sadie has made me drive and then trudge up vertical slopes to see his old weed-infested vines – he either buys the grapes or leases vineyards and manages them himself. Conventional farmers would weep and splutter in shame at these bedraggled plants. But they're how the revolutionaries like them. Now we taste some results. And perhaps it does help to have fondled his stragglers in the flesh so to speak, been awed by their views of the endless wheatlands, listened to the joyful, amiable orator in the open air.

His love affairs have always been with the Mediterranean's many grape varieties and their blends. One grape, Carignan, held a near-fatal attraction. In 2001 he'd been over in Priorat, the hottest spot in wine then, in Spain, in the village of Porrera not far from Barcelona, and, with a local partner, made five barrels of Priorat. He was in Carignan heaven. "My wife, my friends said no. Don't do this swallow stuff, moving between hemispheres with the seasons. I didn't listen," he says. "You should listen to your family and friends." The project fizzled after a few vintages when a squabble with resentful locals turned ugly. During one of his absences, they bored holes in the barrels. *Chau* Priorat.

It shook him – but focused the Swartland project. The Carignan affair still smoulders, and he's gradually upping its proportion in the Columella. "Carignan is like a diesel mechanic. You can clean him up, take him to a party in a new suit. But he'll still behave and look and smell like a diesel mechanic." The stream of anthropomorphisms flows. Pinotage is "the brother you love but can't admit to because he's in jail". And our wines should be more like "a traditional Zulu with a belly, rather than some smooth Frenchman".

Sadie Family Columella 2012 A seamless, understated dream, this South African Swartland blend of Syrah, mainly, with Grenache, Mourvèdre, Carignan and others, the Sadie flagship red, and, like its Cape White Blend stablemate, occupying frontrunner status – and pricing – in its genre. Minimal oaking – which is being phased out to emphasise grapier purity. Grapes sourced widely in the Swartland for a composite regional wine synthesising differing soils – schist, iron, granite - and climates in one bottle. Sadie is a leading, closely-watched exponent of hands-off and let-the-vines-speak winemaking. His regimen is broadly unintrusive, almost spiritually so! A chat, however, will reveal the inattention, allowing must and wine some exposure to air, as in traditional winemaking, is well-orchestrated, well-timed, and incorporates sound basic vinification. Enough tannin for gentle grip and freshness; we're not expected to encounter drama – except perhaps in the absence of it - on the palate, nor the nose. 2012 last tasted.

GRAND AND BEAUTIFUL

So polished, so precise, so delicious, the Vilafonté reds.

One is the **Vilafonté C Series** – about 60% Cabernet Sauvignon, with (more) Merlot than Malbec making up the balance; the other, the **Vilafonté M Series**, now with Malbec and Cabernet Sauvignon roughly equal, tweaked with some Merlot. Some have described the wines as 'top- drawer Californian'. Don't ask me to choose between them.

Oregon-born Zelma Long, their maker, is one of the most decorated, respected women (or men for that matter) in US wine. She was lured to Mondavi by its wine chief Robert Grgich before completing her Masters degree at Davis, California, and became chief oenologist there. "I never returned to school." She then became CEO of the prestigious Simi winery at Sonoma. She first visited South Africa with her viticulturalist husband Phil Freese to address a technical conference of Cape growers in 1990, as apartheid finally was crumbling.

She was hosted by Sydney Back of Backsberg Estate, who was smitten by the brains, the quiet charm, and her life beyond wine. She's an art collector, and is working towards a Masters - in performance art. Phil is a viticultural guru, consulting to some of the best names anywhere and everywhere. Very expensive, but his piquant sense of humour is thrown in free. They said to each other: "Gee it would be fun to grow and make wine here!" And they've done it. It's been one of Cape wine's singular benefits to have this distinguished, so completely engaged and delightful pair in its midst for a couple of decades, thanks to Sydney, who encouraged them, helped find their land in the Simonsberg-Paarl area, and initially found them cellar-space. Phil planned and planted the vineyard, named after the ancient Vilafonté soil-type.

"We wanted to be really involved. And it's been incredibly, enormously gratifying!"

They've since moved to a winery in Stellenbosch – very ordered, clean and cool - opposite their apartment, and travel out three times a year for extended visits, to harvest, blend and bottle. Zelma is the most patient blender in the world, I've heard from those who've watched. It's painful, takes days of long hours. For just two wines and three components.

On the catwalk above the winery floor, on the way to the tasting room, she pauses to explain that Phil's just as fastidious about charting a vineyard's progress to ripeness. "To get the phenolics perfect," she explains. She takes my notebook and draws a graph. It's about analysing berries, gathered from scientifically designated vines around a selected vineyard block. They determine a precise picking date to maximise phenolic ripeness overall – improving it to a near-perfect 90%. This leads to a brilliant, only 1-3% 'outsort' - or discard - of questionable berries at the sorting table.

We're nearing my too-much-information threshold - and yours doubtless, reader - so I rescue my notebook before Zelma fills it with more graphs. Her office has enough charts to launch a space mission. All we need to know is: one rotten strawberry in a jar takes over. At Vilafonté they don't do rotten. One last unresolved- question: I mutter about so many Cape wines being too alcoholic, at 15% alc. The Vilafontés are far from Lite. "But so long as the wine is in balance, it's okay," insists Zelma. More than okay. Partner Mike Ratcliffe, of Warwick, handles sales. He has targeted the US market. And, says Phil, with satisfaction: "The smoke has started to come out of people's ears!"

So to the wines. It's very quiet up here and cool. And there's a trenchant Cecil Skotnes artwork for company, dominating one wall. (They bartered wine for it.) Zelma has laid out six filled glasses. Beginning with a 2003 C Series next to a 2009 M Series, the two oldest. Then 2011 and 2012 in both C and M.

On a whim, I decide to score the two younger vintages out of 100, the American Robert Parker way. Haven't done it in years. Many people are more comfortable with a number. I prefer a few words. Parker's 90-95 are 'outstanding' and 96-100 'extraordinary'. These were my scores, followed in brackets by Parker's, which we looked up later.

2011 M 94 (90)   C 95 (95)   2012 M 96 (93)   C 94 (94)

Parker's lowest score was the 90 (merely outstanding!) for the **2011 M**, which I liked – for its purity and directness, more nervous fruit – plus tension. Very classic. **2011** was a tighter year. Just marginally I preferred the **C** Series. The reverse in the **2012**, where the **M** was more open with a lovely fleshiness. The vintage speaking. Lovely black cherries, plums, chocolates. Zelma attributes this generous fleshiness in part to Malbec.

Ex-*Wine Spectator* man James Suckling, in 2015, tasted through scores of South Africa's finer wines. He placed **Vilafonté 2010 C Series** top of the lot, with a 95. "This is incredible. Like tasting a cult Napa Valley," he wrote. The **2010 M Series** was second, with a 94. "Off the charts, incredible black olive, chocolate and tobacco character." This is craftsmanship. And these are grand and beautiful wines.

AS TRUTHFUL AS POSSIBLE

When Adi Badenhorst says he'll bottle a wine knowing it has 'faults', it's a very exceptional admission. Does it single him out as a risky winemaker? Is it ammunition for critics? No, he says. Risky is different from careful risk-taking. But this 40ish, bearded, pony-tailed pundit on what's what in the buzzy Swartland, cohort-in-chief to figurehead Eben Sadie, has always specialised in non-conformity, always been ready to get entertainingly philosophical, and to delight in rationalising the unconventional as worthwhile… almost as an end in itself.

"Simple," he explains. "I'm trying to get out of the way – remove too much human interference - and let my vines speak directly to drinkers of my wines. So when the vintage is ready for blending and if a few of the wines in different tanks – I'm often assembling 10 different varieties, Carignan, Grenache, Syrah, Mourvedrde and others for my Family flagships - are showing some awkward spikiness, I'm not going to leave them out. Wines change in bottle. How do I know those individual components won't change for the better? Anyway, more important, I want the wine to be a truthful statement of its natural origins and my vineyards in that vintage. As truthful as possible anyway."

This is high idealism – and, thanks to him and other spirited pioneers, less rare now. To his growing numbers of followers, it gives his wines purpose. It's the essence of the Swartland Revolution, which he co-instigated and whose ideals he colourfully articulates.Three-letter words are seemingly obligatory here, adding earthy texture to wine and vine philosophies, and to the Revolutionaries' dislike of market-driven wines. "Corporatism in wine!" he exclaims. "F.k!" Such products, he believes, made to commercial recipes, fined and filtered into low common-denominator conformity, distance consumers from the individuality and personality of a wine.

Go to his straggly-chic, gnarled bush vineyards at Kalmoesfontein and you're likely to get side-tracked quickly. To a bunch of non-wine drinks – aperitifs, tonics, beers - and other more way-out experiments beyond the cellar. Not a hardship of course, if there's time – Badenhorst is an African; he 'has the time where Europe has the clock'. But you get to the wines, if at all, circuitously. "Don't know why," he wonders, "but a lot of wine weirdos seem to come here." He likes them.

A visit can begin promisingly enough. In the winery. Its hub is his unsteady perch beside the music system – growly, lugubrious Tom Waits, Led Zeppelin, Indigo Girls. There are a few unwashed tasting glasses, 1960s posters of busty women, Playboy things, stuck on centuries-old skewed walls under cobwebbed rafters. With the exception of an industrial-sized coffee machine and a sack of special African roasts, it's a choreographed up-yours to modernity. Pipes lie around haphazardly on floors among determinedly asymmetrical rows of different wine tanks, some cement ones dating back to the late 1800s. Self-conscious, hygiene-obsessed wineries are perpetually scrubbed for Sunday inspections. No Sunday best here.

'Filters' to separate juice from husks post-ferment – sometimes here at AA Badenhorst Family Wines, in the Swartland heat, a risky and daredevil many months after it's over – are bundles of pruning cuttings shoved over valve outlets. There's a lot of quaint make-do, cost-cutting stuff.

Is it all a contrived, recalcitrant turning back of the clock, this line that the ancients had it more right than wrong, this veneration of old vineyards, the notion that pretence and showy superficiality have taken over in wine and why can't we return to a blissful state of respect for rustic, less expensive , more expressive simplicity? Try the wines and judge for yourself.

AA Badenhorst Family Red Rich, full, smashing wine, so much going on. No new oak "meddling". Brimming with loads of nicely ripened berry fruit, gently worked for a smooth palate feel. Charming. Most recent tasted: 2011. Shiraz 71% with Cinsaut (15%), Tinta (7%) and Mourvèdre (3%). You have to hope another vintage, with similar propor-tions, comes along soon. It probably won't. And Badenhorst will put his chef's blending cap on again.

FLASHES OF BRILLIANCE

Anthonij Rupert was a tall, soft-hearted, deep-voiced, intense wine man. His elder brother, Johann, took over the vast international Rupert empire from his father, its founder, Anton Rupert, after stints in New York and London honing his banking skills. Anthonij was the farmer and lived on L'Ormarins, his Franschhoek vineyards, where he built, in the early 1980s, the most advanced cellar in the Cape at the time. L'Ormarins, and the nearby joint venture, Rupert & Rothschild, on the Simonsberg slopes, with a separate, Bordeaux-inspired ethos, were both doing well in 2001 when, on a rainy night driving home to the farm, Anthonij Rupert crashed and died near Groot Drakenstein. He was 49.

Quite often he'd drop by for a chat when we farmed at Delaire on the Helshoogte Pass – on his way to Stellenbosch, where his parents lived in their impressively modest home, at a guess the most spartan of any billionaire couple's anywhere! The family's grand art collections were housed in or donated to museums.

Anthonij Rupert breathed vines and viticulture and dug deep into the intricacies of wine-making. Of course he was surrounded by the best experts – drawn from, then, Distillers Corporation and Die Bergkelder, and he was always generous in sharing inside technical information. And good gossip. We agreed that the golden rule about experts applied in wine too: they always seemed to disagree. That's when, in analysing the contradictions, he'd display flashes of the family's originality and brilliance. Occasionally we'd differ – especially on wine evaluations, and that could kindle the fiery, red-blooded side of him.

Johann Rupert has taken over, intent obviously on burnishing his brother's legacy – and rather more. Not only have the L'Ormarins and Rupert and Rothschild operations been made over and modernised, vineyards re-located, the whole area has benefited from Rupert's innovations: a 200-car museum on L'Ormarins, spanning a century of fine vintages; a race horse stud, the domain of his wife Gaynor; a determined campaign to protect – restore and extend - the natural environment. Perhaps his most impressive wine venture has been to sponsor research into the Cape's older, threatened and priceless vintage vineyards, many more than a century old, sometimes in the remotest spots, up mountainsides. For this he galvanised the brilliant Rosa Kruger (see her story later in this book): those initiatives have been key to South Africa's extraordinary current wine revival.

Anthonij Rupert 2007 One of those majestic, ripe-berried, fathoms-deep-flavoured classic clarets, with spicy, elegant power that signals pleasure for the next hour or two. Grand occasion stuff. And also one which might not find favour with the taste-police, who decree only light and fresh and 'natural' will do. This is a very crafted specimen. But there is room for both styles. Here the five Bordeaux grapes – Cabernet Merlot, Cabernet Franc and Petit Verdot – are locked in unison; unashamedly aged for about two years in 100% new French oak, etc etc. But unfiltered. And applauded by the US *Wine Spectator* with a 95 ("outstanding") score, one short of "classic, a great wine".

AUTHORITY AND REACH

It seems like yesterday that Kevin Arnold established Waterford and its vineyards on the southern outskirts of Stellenbosch, its sprawling inner courtyard and fountains and terracotta roofs themed to reflect the warm-climate Mediterranean red grape varieties that have anchored the wine range. That was in 1998 when Jeremy Ord purchased the property and roped in Arnold as winemaker and partner to lead a complete makeover. Visiting Waterford now, it has a settled, unstrained, spacious, been-around-for-a-while feel, surrounded by olive and citrus groves and rows of southern European herbs and lavender – wafting with the heathery garrigue scents of the Rhône and Provence.

But Arnold, who was at Delheim and Rust en Vrede – a decade at each - before, is a restless man and hasn't been able to confine the wines or styles to one theme or place. For one, his team's Cabernets keep hauling in big accolades. Their Chardonnay is top notch. They keep at Riesling – and it gets better and better, if not matching classic (inimitable) racy purity and acidity, at least consonant with his 'restrained elegance, less is more' ideas; Erica buys this wine. Arnold encourages his crew, led by Mark le Roux, not to stop tinkering with Pinot Noir and they buy in fine fruit from Elgin, with pretty classy results. They've been edging toward 'natural' wine-making for some time – no acid adjustments at Waterford since 2004, for example; easy on sulphur, only light fining and filtering when necessary. And more. Waterford has an impressive Library Collection for these work-in-progress labels.

The main thrust remains **Waterford The Jem** - named after Ord - which celebrates Arnold's original concept of Cabernet Sauvignon partnered with a long – up to eight in some vintages – list of Mediterranean grape partners, including Mourvèdre, Barbera, Syrah, Sangiovese. It's given the full, new wood treatment and consistently shows staying power in its enduring spicy intricacy. 2010 last tasted; no one grape variety obvious. "It's the blend, the fit of the diverse components, that provide that authority and reach," says Arnold.

Gamely, because he'd just stepped off a plane and was at an unfamiliar course, he once took up my challenge to play a round of golf for The Jem - and handed it over cheerfully when local knowledge – and luck of course – prevailed.

YOU MUST ALWAYS
CLOSE YOUR EYES

Giorgio Dalla Cia is a fellow Italian from the North. A fungiphile. For years we tramped the forests of Stellenbosch together, beginning 10 days after the first winter rain, rootling for boletus mushrooms. It was very catching, that gleam of a hunter's greed whenever he came upon the firm brown fungi peeping through the pine needles. "Got them!" he would shout, to summon his troops, strung out in the depths of those dripping forests. There were protocols. "Take care, cut them cleanly at the bottom of the stem," he would instruct, and he allowed only wicker baskets (no plastic bags), so we'd spread the spores for future growth.

Sometimes we kept the spoils greedily for ourselves. More often, there'd be a Porcini party. Many friends, much wine, usually Pinot Noir. Giorgio would bring his Italian coffee machine, ours being deemed sub-standard. Slicing the mushrooms one Sunday morning, before a sizzle in parsley, butter, olive oil, garlic, lemon, he put a plump specimen to his nose, and then to mine: "Beautiful, don't you think? Such a sexy scent. More pulling power than a locomotive."

It was these mushrooms which kept Giorgio and his winemaker wife Simonetta from returning home to Friuli as planned, after a short-term work assignment in the Cape. They stumbled upon them while out for a wintry walk. Incredulous, they filled the boot of their Beetle. They had never dreamed their favourite family activity in Italy, the mushroom-hunt, could happen here.

Giorgio is resignedly proud of his portliness. It speaks of fine food and a majestic indifference to exercise, unless in the gathering and making of food and wine. He once tried to induct me into his distinctive dieting methods. "In winter you open the windows, throw off the duvet, and let your body spend its energy fighting off the cold. You lose kilos." I've waited until now to tell him: "Scusa amico mio, doesn't work for me."

So, am I biased about his **Dalla Cia Teano 2011**? You bet.

In the best traditions of a wine, like a faithful hound resembling its master, this is a large-hearted and robust but also kindly and generous red. Inspired by the dramatically-priced Super Tuscans of Dalla Cia's homeland, this too is priced beyond the casual punter. The familiar, savoury, dried sage and rosemary notes of Sangiovese are there and provide a firm finish, but French varieties in the blend deliver flesh. There's emphatic, all-new oak barrelling.

"Close your eyes, you must always close your eyes when you smell and taste; do you get the marzipan and chocolate, the tobacco?" he instructs rather than enquires. And then more directions, towards all-important food partners: "Track down the finest T-bone, dress simply with olive oil and rosemary. Or Simonetta's tagliatelle with ossobucco sauce. Or Elena's Stinco, beef shin."

This is a big-occasion wine. The town of Teano is where Garibaldi and King Victor Emmanuel shook hands, uniting Italy.

THE TEMPERAMENT AND THE BUCKS

It's furious and cruel, the speed at which today's exciting modern labels and estates can turn into tomorrow's ho-hum. Not to be pitied or forgotten entirely perhaps, but too often we're wine label-drinkers, seduced by new designer-logos, quick to abandon loyalties and move on. Selling wine in today's congested terrain is brutal. One of the most successful bankers of his generation, GT Ferreira - FNB, Rand Merchant Bank — has the temperament and the bucks to enjoy such competition. His wine portfolio is not an executive toy; egonomics is not his game; he seems to like getting his hands dirty in the day-to-day routines at Tokara, his Helshoogte Pass vineyards, winery and gourmet restaurant. The Simonsberg towers to the north, Cape Town and the oceans shimmer below to the south west. He lives on the farm, delights in his olives and vineyards, and in the oil and wines they produce.

He decamped from Johannesburg with his wife Anne-Marie — the olive enthusiast - a couple of decades ago. During the 10-year start-up, budget-breaching, non-equity-returning phase of Tokara he had the no-nonsense Gyles Webb of Thelema as an immediate neighbour and the pair collaborated in laying the critical foundations of a vineyard and winery that are anything but ho-hum. It all now looks tastefully well settled, among gnarled olive trees. Webb lured the talented Stellenbosch and Californian-trained Miles Mossop, a 'critical foundation' choice. Tokara's top wines are world-class.

Tokara Director's Director's Reserve Red 2011 Ripe dark berry fruit quality, deeply complex. Cabernet Sauvignon may dominate but Petit Verdot — deep-dark colours — shows brilliantly, adds spine, excitement, with Cabernet Franc, Merlot and Malbec for balance and width. Full-house Bordeaux blend. As with all Tokara's top-line reds, unsparingly oak-aged. Wild yeast- fermented, partly whole-bunch pressed. Can be laid down 10-15 years.

THREE HALVES AND A RENEGADE

"I'm a quick study," says Ken Forrester, fixing you with a playfully – you hope - menacing grin. Long pause. "It only took me 16 years to realise this isn't a Sauvignon Blanc farm. I've ripped it out." His Stellenbosch farm features plenty of fine bush vines of other varieties.

Forrester is large and extrovert. He's wavy-white-haired, serious but playful, about wine, food, beef – his locally-reared, grass-fed Wagyu in particular - and horses: thoroughbreds, jumping, farm hacking. And world politics. Anything actually.

A hot Joburg restaurateur - first in Hillbrow, then Sandton - after a boyhood on the Zambian copper-belt, he's applied an inventive energy – and that quick-study mind - to winemaking. He's an out-there man, marketing a forté. Travelling the world. But also exploring remote corners of the Cape. He was among the first to venture into the 'wild west' – up the coast – to track down old vineyards of then unfashionable grapes like Grenache – long a special favourite of his - for the Forrester blends. In the swift turns of modern Cape wine farming, he's usually been in front. A visit invariably turns up a surprise. One year it was large and plump home-smoked hams sharing cool space with the wines in the barrel cellar.

On his front lawn under giant, shady oaks on a bright pre-lunch summer day at his Stellenbosch vineyards, a dozen or so wines are already opened, a daunting sight, as we turn up – to say a quick hello, grand-daughter in tow. Nope, says Forrester. We'll have "a few sips and a bite". A day turns upside-down.

His wines are works-in-progress around a few settled winners; they're promoted, and demoted among his ranges of 15 or so labels, from vintage to vintage. It's that febrile Forrester mind. You have to keep up. And think beyond his Mr Chenin persona. Give his reds, like these two, a chance.

Ken Forrester Three Halves 2009 on paper could sound clumsy. Half Mourvèdre - too much, 20% is normally plenty (I say, airily). Then half-and-half Shiraz and 30-year-old Grenache Noir. So, actually, 3 partners in roughly 50-25-25 proportions – at least this vintage, but we're certainly all in southern France – Forrester's comfort zone, matching the Cape's *vin de soleil* climate. Mourvèdre's usual dense, gruff, black olive thickness has almost evaporated, magically. Instead, there's a limpid, sleek generosity - also brassy quality, with plummy-savoury notes. It went up manfully against the dark and richly-meaty, salty Wagyu. Adaptable food wine.

Ken Forrester Renegade is not his top-ranked Cape-Rhône red. But this big-hearted friendly and juicy red does the business at a significant discount. About half Grenache, backed by Mourvèdre, Shiraz etc. Enough earthy-spicy oak. Not so much a sipping and thinking wine as a drinking, with a gulp or two, wine. Burger friend.

KNOBKERRIES OR GOOD SCIENCE

Chris Keet has been a Cabernet Franc freak for nearly 25 years. Okay, make that specialist now. The grape is moving out of the shadows. And so is he. It was his main variety at Cordoba, the Helderberg winery where he worked from the early 1990s. More recently, going solo, he's become a sought-after consultant, specifically among growers keen to improve their own Cab Franc. His services, unusually, encompass both viticulture and oenology.

He dismisses with cheerful clarity and admirable brevity much of the new age 'hands-free' wine-making that shuns the use of cultured yeast in fermentation in favour of wild yeast. "That's going back to the knobkerrie when we've got good science and better weapons to keep us out of trouble," he says. It's complex, but whether in its 'wild' or 'domesticated' form, Saccharomyces Cerevisiae yeast, he says, will eventually take over once sugar is converted into alcohol, from about 4%-5% alc. onwards, elbowing out other, feebler wild yeasts. So why wait and risk stuck or sluggish fermentation? Inoculate from the get-go.

Cab Franc is a hard sell in the market. Consumer recognition is scant. Appreciation low. It's a much tougher flog than Merlot. But neither is easy to grow or make as wine on its own – in South African conditions. The grapes don't produce the often stellar wines they do in Europe. Here, the wines are often distinctly 'leafy' or 'green' or 'herbaceous'. But among scores of growers who use it in their blends, you'll often hear them say Cabernet Franc is the most charming wine in the cellar – in years when it behaves.

Keet knows a few tricks about taming and harnessing it. All to do with opening up the vine's canopy. And it shows in his own exclusive (only 1500 cases a year) all-Stellenbosch-sourced Bordeaux blend. He has yet to launch a solo Cab Franc. Wait for it. Meantime, there is **Keet First Verse**, an exquisite 5-way blend: Cabernet Sauvignon, Cabernet Franc, Merlot - each between 22%-to 29%, with Petit Verdot and Malbec. Luscious fruit and fine tannins for long ageing. Classic minerally penetration. 2011 tasted. 2009 was a Platter Guide 5-star.

FRIENDS' BLENDS

A modern Cape wine success story. The internationally-decorated **MR de Compostella** is, most years, headlined by Cabernet Franc, the grape with a patchy history here, only recently showing promise as a single variety or blend leader. Launched with a 2004 by Mzokhona Mvemve and Bruwer Raats, M and R, it's been totting up outstanding 93-95/100 marks from the two most closely watched 'ratings agencies' in American wine, Robert Parker's *Wine Advocate* and *Wine Spectator*. How so?

Raats and Mvemve met when the latter (a Durban exile) did his Stellenbosch University Oenology practicals at Delaire, while Raats, also a Maties graduate, was winemaker there. They became friends and later business partners, deciding from the outset to concentrate their collaboration on just one wine. It would have to be brilliant – each vintage. It would feature five Bordeaux varieties: Cabernet Sauvignon, Cabernet Franc, Merlot, Petit Verdot and Malbec. It should meet the highest international standards.

To achieve this, neither M nor R being vineyard-owners, they would have to search out and nail down regular and reliable growers of the finest, ripest, most supple fruit. From diverse soils and micro-climates, but all from Stellenbosch. Though the composition of their blend varies by vintage: some years Merlot may produce lesser quality than Cabernet Sauvignon, for example; its proportion of the blend is cut back accordingly. Malbec and Petit Verdot are regularly the lesser partners, by volume.

Raats and Mvemve, each tasting blind, sample the separate wines after a year in barrel. There are a few weeks of back and forth, combining their preferences into an agreed blend, which is then matured in barrel for another year. Raats reports he has shown five vintages of the MR Compostella beside five vintages of Ch. Cheval Blanc (also Cabernet Franc-led) at blind tastings in New York, London, Cape Town and Johannesburg. "Combining the results at all tastings, the two wines came out about equal," he reports. The 2009 was a 'freakishly' great year: Cab Sauv and Cab Franc and Merlot were equal partners. A buy – wherever you can get it. Otherwise it's always been Cab Franc in the lead. The only blip has been the 2010 – not a bad Stellenbosch year, but it didn't meet the friends' exacting standards, wasn't bottled.

MR de Compostella A one-of-a-kind South African masterpiece. Typically shows a grand, many-layered, dark-fruit elegance, rich but also fine. Long, searching finish. 2013 tasted. Only 900 (x 6 bottle) cases tops each year, mostly exported.

AND

David & Nadia Sadie Elpidios 2012 Healthy complement of compatible Rhône grapes – mostly Syrah with Carignan, Cinsaut and Grenache. Only old wood. From at least six vineyards. The blends of soils – shale from Riebeek mountain, granite from Paardeberg, clay from western reaches of Swartland, reflect David Sadie's penchant for creative wine-making. (The name means to have hope, he says.)

De Trafford Elevation 393 is David Trafford's flagship, from his own vineyards. Super-dense, compact, substantive beauty – blend Merlot, Cabernet Sauvignon, Shiraz, near equal parts. Uncompromising, all new French oak. Huge. A sipping wine. 2010 tasted in 2015, still tense, a stayer. Released after long bottle maturation. 393 refers to altitude in metres above sea level.

Fairview Extrano Spanish inspiration, Cape interpretation. Tempranillo, Grenache, Carignan blend in 2011. No ponderous gravity here. Surprisingly light-textured and fresh, grippy, very savoury, penetrating, lingering. For spicy, robust dishes. Curries? Grapes widely sourced, some old vineyards.

Hartenberg The Mackenzie Polished, integrated Cabernet Sauvignon, Merlot, fruit framed by Petit Verdot; small yields, big flavours, firm backbone — and generous new oak finish adds to fine minerally qualities. 2011 recent standout. Ditto probably for 2015.

Jordan Cobblers Hill The estate's Cabernet Sauv-Franc and Merlot blend, selection of best barrels each vintage. Top-rate, intense, with charming quirky, faint liquorice-mint edging rich blackcurrant fruit. 2009 and 2010 fine years.

Abrie Beeslaar and Johann Krige of Kanonkop

Kanonkop Paul Sauer opens up more quickly, more prettily, than the estate's initially grumpier, tauter straight Cabernet Sauvignon. Deep-coloured, powerful and intense, suffused with black berry flavours, 2 years in oak gives fine lustre to the 2011. Usually 75% Cab Sauv to 15% each Cab Franc and Merlot.

The **2013 Klein Constantia Estate Red** gets respectable enough mentions, but I'm far, far more excited. The wine has some of the unmistakable attributes of quality Bordeaux — fine, rounded tannins that anchor, without elbowing out the pure juicy grape. Cabernet Sauvignon dominates (70%); there's no moderating Merlot or Cabernet Franc. But equal parts — about 15% each — of Malbec and Petit Verdot - buttressing rather than leavening grapes. And prudent oaking. Younger vintages show penetrating zing. These are keepers.

La Motte Pierneef Collection Shiraz-Viognier
Ambitious, grand red. Everything is grand at La Motte, a Rupert Family establishment purchased by the founder of the international business empire, the late Anton Rupert, for his daughter, the mezzo-soprano Hanneli, who is married to export wizard Hein Koegelenberg, formerly a winemaker. The plush tasting rooms (left), reached by a bridge over dribbling ponds, the unambiguously gourmet restaurant — al fresco under giant oaks, weather permitting - the hushed, minutely curated JH Pierneef Museum. There you can listen to a video of Anton Rupert, like so many magnates in their sage years, an enthusiastic intoner of philosophic aphorisms, worry about the general pickle mankind has got itself into and our power to destroy ourselves in a jiffy — like "scorpions in a box". This flagship red - a temporizing antidote to such woes - is a serious, sumptuous Shiraz-Viognier - 89%-11% - blend, ripe soft fruit, with open-armed generosity, enough spiciness for length.

Marvelous Blue A four-way Bordeaux grape variety blend without the usual alpha lead singer, Cabernet Sauvignon. I was tickled by the powdery-chalky, leafy — sometimes terms of opprobrium among sniffier tasters — aromas and tastes and softer structure of the 2012. Merlot — 59%, Cabernet Franc — 20%, Petit Verdot 14%, Malbec 7%. Slighter, less complex perhaps without the Sauvignon, but voices the less demanding charms of the others.

Marvelous Red The missing 'l' is because winemaker Adam Mason's computer was spellchecking in American. He gave up trying to correct it. No problems in other respects: an enjoyable, friendly wine, not hugely complex (the 2012), but its bright, direct Syrah spicy-pepperiness, and nicely rounded mouth feel is just the thing for merry, informal, round-the-fire occasions. Part of the Yardstick range, a joint venture between Mason of Mulderbosch, and chef Peter Tempelhoff.

When one says **Meerlust** most people think of the famous **Rubicon**. A great South African wine, steady, unmitigated class, this Cabernet Sauvignon, Cabernet Franc and Merlot blend. It's been part of the furniture for so long, in a showroom overflowing with new models, that we can forget how stylish it is. Its enduring allure? It doesn't shout. Winemaker Chris Williams believes it speaks in the Cab Franc's voice. It is plush, elegantly fleshy, quietly ripe, rich. There's some inky minerality, however (for the claret buffs) - and the kind of bite in the finish that leaves no teeth marks. For some, it is lost in the scrum. Count me in, though. The 2009 is particularly fine.

Meinert Synchronicity Always classy, Cabernet Sauvignon (mainly, with Merlot) blend. Rounded elegance – rather than turbo-powered thrust. Martin Meinert's philosophical, detached craftmanship shows in relaxed, fine oaking. An intellectual winemaker's interpretation of Cabernet from Devon Valley, Stellenbosch. Meinert consults for some grand names and was the start-up winemaker at prestigious Vergelegen.

Miles Mossop Max Tokara winemaker Mossop doing his own thing here, and aiming high: intense, powerful, spicy, sweet, and rich. Cabernet Sauvignon – about half, with equal parts Petit Verdot and Merlot; from Banghoek and Bellville vineyards. French oak treatment. 2012 tasted. Serious, will last good decade. Named after his son.

Nederburg Edelrood Find this Cabernet Sauvignon-Merlot blend on a list in a platteland hotel when you're on a road-trip and sigh with relief. Whatever you eat, you will drink well. And not expensively. Those who sniff because it is so widely available should rather be thankful. A notch up on its stablemate Baronne, but round a braai, in the bush, with supper rather than dinner, respect!

Paserene Marathon 2013 Trouble here – to contain my excitement. Petit Verdot (mostly) and Carmenère in striking partnership, a first in Cape; dark inky-tinted, super-fine tannins, spread of claret-like ripe fruits. Sensationally appetising – savoury, limpid elegant dryness washes palate. Grown-up food wine. Doesn't tip into sweet-spicy blandishment. Carmenère - a Bordeaux grape, is big in Chile, there from pre-phylloxera times. Winemaker Martin Smith has found a coastal vineyard, blended with Stellenbosch Petit Verdot. Crafted with light touch – no filtration, 30% new oak, beautifully tucked away, for 16 months. Smith, Stellenbosch University-educated, spent a decade in California at Louis Vuitton. Back home – he works at Vilafonté - he believes Cape wine is now "more exciting than California."

Rall Red The aim is "lighter and fleshy" says Donovan Rall of this elegant Syrah-dominated, Grenache-supported blend – and we should no longer be surprised at elegance from the Swartland! Loads of perfume (from the Syrah) and ripe, strawberry-dark plum juicy fruitiness. 'Soft hands' approach, no new oak – 22 months in used French barrels, all wild ferment, gentle hand pressing, no fining, filtration. The way Rall tells it, anyone could make this in their garage if they're happy to have purple-stained hands for a few months.

Rupert & Rothschild Baron Edmond The 2012 one of those polished reds fit for smart dining, where the oak and the 3-way grape composition – Merlot, Cabernets Sauv/ Franc - are knitted together completely. Alive and modern in its freshness. Fine tannins, blackcurrants, bit of leather, sturdy core, all in place for ageing - 10 years at least.

Savage Red 2013 Duncan Savage has built his reputation on scintillating white maritime-influenced wines at Cape Point Vineyards. Recently, he's emerged as one of the country's most eloquent young proponents of lighter, lower alcohol reds too. In this own-label he's navigated an admirable middle ground between too fresh-fruity and too limp-weighty. And kept alc. at 13%. (He will doubtless aim lower as vintages allow). Sourcing widely, he's assembled a mainly Syrah blend with Grenache, Cinsaut and Mourvèdre, managing to retain lively spiciness, and really fine tannins that don't dim a sweet-ripe finish. "I want people to be able to drink a glass or two and still go back to work," he says.

Savage Follow the Line Red A new-age, breakout wine, the 2014. Beguiling sweet perfume, savoury palate. Texture so silkily light – the translucence! - and juicy, dangerously moreish. If ever evidence were needed that Cinsaut (58%) and Grenache (21%,) two lower-rung grapes until recently, and no oak to speak of, can offer unpretentious and refined pleasure, this is it. (Shiraz 21% too). Delicious.

Sijnn Flagship Field Blend comes from a move you'd expect from David Trafford: go south, go maritime, go cooler. And plant warm-climate grape varieties. He's seen what's coming: warming in the decades ahead. In 2014, with like-minded partners, he put up a winery and is making wines at Malgas, at the Breede River mouth. Yield-crimping slate and stone in the vineyards determine a fresh, leaner style – for the table. This is a Cape original, a vineyard mix of four grape varieties – French and Portuguese; Syrah, Trincadeira, Touriga Nacional, Mourvèdre. Oak aged 18-22 months. 2010 tasted. Sinewy, grippy, earthy. Needs careful partnering – rich, fatty dishes perhaps? **Sijnn Low Profile** is also interesting, a lighter, fresher mix of all the above reds. Tasted the 2012. Would make a good-value house wine.

Steytler Pentagon Kaapzicht's outstanding serious red blend. Concentrated, blackcurrant fruit has absorbed long, partial new oak maturation. In 2012, anchored by 60% Cabernet Sauvignon with 15% each of Cabernet Franc and Merlot and 5% of Petit Verdot and Malbec: the complete 5-grape, 'pentagon' deal. "Americans love the name, some other visitors aren't so sure," says Danie Snr (right).

Swerwer Red 2014 "Why should I bring an oak tree [in barrel form] from Vosges in France and stick it into my wine grown here in the Swartland, South Africa?" asks Jasper Wickens. "That's not the impact I want." This is purist, new-wave talk. Only used old barrels – containers rather than oaking vessels - for his lusciously limpid 56% Cinsaut-31% Grenache-splash of Syrah blend. Fresh, sweet-smelling – the Cinsaut talking. Swartland grapes, fermented together. The Cinsaut is "*die boer se tros*, big berries for big, big taste," says Wickens. Keep an eye on this label: "We're experimenting all the time – and always drinking wines better than our own to learn."

The Blacksmith Vin Noir 2014 Tremayne Smith's day job (or masterclass?) is with the Mullineux Family. So perhaps unsurprisingly this light, delicious, inter-regional blend of 59% Paarl Cinsaut, 41% Swartland Carignan shows finesse and originality. Will delight fans of southern Europe's (and North Africa's) Carignan, and win over others. Smith worked in Roussillon for 2 years so has in-depth experience with this grape. Whole bunch-pressed, foot-stomped.

Webb Ellis 2010 Biggest statement-red from Neill Ellis Wines in 40 years. The founder, Neil Ellis, left it to his son, Warren Ellis, to finish crafting this Jonkershoek Cabernet (65%) and Darling Groenekloof Syrah (35%) family landmark wine, celebrating his mother, Stephanie Webb's partnership with his father. Powerful harmony. In the wine too. Superlatives apply. Syrah more on the nose, Cabernet mineral grip on palate, tons of spice from (mostly) new oak. Leave it till about 2017. And it'll go another 10 with ease, probably more. Only 780 bottles. R1000 a bottle in 2015. Solid liquid investment.

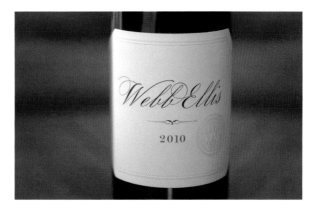

Riesling ranks beside, some believe above, Chardonnay in white wine's hall of fame. Devotees of each acknowledge the beauty of the other. The two greatest dry whites of the world. So why is Riesling so under-rated in South Africa? Perhaps there is a bit of a stigma, still, hanging around the name: until quite recently we were still labelling lesser Crouchen Blanc as Cape Riesling, an astonishing charade perpetuated by cynical commercial interests. Consumers remember how boring the old so-called "Rieslings" were… and were confused and un-tempted when the real thing arrived under the label initially insisted on by officialdom, "Weisser" or Rhine Riesling.

A thought strikes: that old Crouchen. Perhaps it, like other maligned and discarded varieties, could make a comeback in the new Cape Dry White Blend category…

Back to Riesling: the variety isn't difficult to grow here. It ripens – that's easy. But turning those grapes into a match for the stunning, tense, dry-fruity-racy flagships of the Rhine, Mosel, Nahe and Alsace has eluded Cape growers. You have to doff the hat to those who persevere. Is it our climate, our sunshine, cellar handling, or what… that exacerbates its terpene-petrol esters? Some people love them of course. So do I, but only if muted enough not to introduce off-key notes to a delicate shellfish dish.

We had a little Riesling vineyard once, at Delaire on the Helshoogte Pass in the 1980s. The grapes ripened into a translucent light green. I loved those vines, walked the rows most days, picking off a berry here and there. The first harvest and fermentation went swimmingly. I had two fabulous, eccentric and profound fellow Hungarian-born gurus, Julius Laszlo and Desiderius Pongrazc, guiding me. Great expectations. I learned a lot of Hungarian history. But consumers pronounced: the wine was too dry, not enough "flavour".

So, I can understand the Cape's default answer: sweeten up these wines a bit, or a lot, and mask the kerosene. It can work but usually at the expense of that essential knife-edge balance between ripe fruit and natural acid which is the grape's masterpiece. When those qualities are "finely counterpoised, they have the inevitability of great art", says the maestro of world wine-writing, Hugh Johnson.

The Cape has many eminently drinkable off-dry, sweet, and sensational dessert botrytis Rieslings. But like many, I have been waiting for a breakthrough, "great art" dry Riesling. I detect some excitement, some hope, but we're not there yet. We're at the end of the beginning.

RIESLING

BETWEEN THE EARS

He seemed a little suspicious, did Koen Roose-Vandenbroucke in his deerstalker cap when we pitched up at the end of the steep dirt road on Spioenkop hill in Elgin. The tiny pourings of his precious Riesling should be reserved for real customers, is perhaps what he was thinking. Winter was setting in and the bare, and even steeper hillsides (no tractors) and leafless vines made for stark vistas across these shivery highlands. His and his wife Hannelore's little white home beside a small, functional winery, all seemed inspiringly Spartan: a remote frontier couple standing apart from mad civilization. We'd been warned. Koen was… well, a little off-beat.

"I am a crazy Belgian," he announces, after first politely asking if we would like to converse in Afrikaans. He proceeds to show he's not - though he is talkative. He's studied his climates and soils – iron-rich laterite - done his research, long apprenticeships (including with Francois Naude in Stellenbosch) and set his precise goals after buying Spioenkop in 2004: world class quality on a tiny scale, completely individual, wines to reflect, in the purest, most uncompromising way possible, their aspect and origins. "A Petrus-pinnacle," he ventures, and he's not joking. The highest bar! The couple has made some oddly strict personal rules. They hardly ever drink their own wines. "You get familiar with them, you lose acute, objective assessment," says Lore. "Wine is all about between the ears," Koen adds. And there he's surely completely right. "But I also want to make sexy, sensual wines."

Vines here would struggle anyway. How he treats them, with unwavering neglect, toughens them even more. To survive, the roots need to grope deep and wide, siphoning up the minerals in that red iron ore. At the end of an expressive Koen lecture you're beginning to salivate – imagining all that earthy, spare, natural, flinty, lean linear minerality and purity. I interrupt to ask about 'linear minerality'. What is it? "Chalky, stony, salty, direct. But we're not there yet." We taste through a couple of Pinot Noirs and Pinotages. A fresh take. Spare, angular, different. And fresh. And then! Out comes the **Spioenkop Riesling 2013**. Whackingly arresting! Steely. Glorious clarity. Never tasted anything remotely like it in South Africa. Whisks me back to the Rhine. Not strictly comparable of course – it shouldn't, couldn't be - but some of that chilly, resolute quality. Way more austere than most Cape Rieslings, which often show distracting tropical fruit flavours, are too sweet or too oily. This wine will be too unyielding for many drinkers: its crispness and ultra-low pH (lean and spare on the palate) gives it an untamed coltish quality. But that's for me sometimes! With a few oysters… or some creamy dish.

As we leave I make a silent, private bow to these hills. They've generated something beautiful and unique. Later the emails flew. Koen Roose-Vandenbroucke made his sale.

FAMILY SOUL

"So why aren't you out there on a tractor?" I ask Paul Cluver. He's the soft-spoken, silver-haired neuro-surgeon who runs one of the finest large-scale farming operations in Africa. He was the first Elginite to get into wine 25 years ago – and then vinify on the property. First-class wines are – quantitatively, in the area the vines occupy, and financially – probably almost a sideline. From apples to conservation in its myriad ways (night-time photographing of leopards) to social empowerment projects, to working indigenous timber (the sales rooms are modern museums of his handiwork) to botanical-scale fruit and vegetable gardens stalked by fabulously orange-russet, red-and-black primordial chickens, there's almost nothing this polymath hasn't turned his mind and hands to. Driving a roaring front-end loader used to be his way of relaxing after returning home from the operating theatre in Cape Town.

He says: "Come round here, let me show you something." Off the gleaming tasting room – comforting smells of hand-worked wood and leather chairs – there's a tucked- away office with a few shelves outside the door, stacked with models of the huge yellow machines he once manoeuvred precariously round these slopes when he prepared vineyards. "They're hiding me away nowadays," he jokes. "I've only got the models." He's handed over to the next generation, a son, three daughters and son-in-law, Andries Burger, the winemaker, an Alsace obsessive determined, too, to master the difficult Burgundy conundrum in Africa, Pinot.

Two **Paul Cluver 'Close Encounter' Rieslings**, one dry, the other sweeter, are seamless, balanced and so, so easy; they're a joy to drink, partly because they're a very civilised, under 10% alcohol. The Riesling raciness is there. The old Cape problem of oily-petrol Riesling isn't. The sweeter (34 gms/l) is one of the classier 'any time' drinks around. The dry one is a great way to start a serious meal – and continue with it, especially if the food is fishy (in the right sense).

AND

Jordan The Real McCoy Riesling 2014 recently won a serious 5 Nations (Southern hemisphere) challenge in the category. We are tasting in the restaurant on the farm. Ducks quack on the dam below; chef George Jardine conjures up a complement in the gleaming, open kitchen, his every move and (quiet) instruction visible and audible. It arrives: a steaming parcel of herb-scented Saldanha Bay mussels. The salty ocean scents mingle deliciously with the Riesling's tangy, tropical-lemony flavours. A fine match. And something's on the horizon which could prove an even better partner: Kathy is Greek, so they've planted the Greek 'Riesling', Assyrtiko. A goose bumper in prospect?

Eendevanger Riesling 2013 A discovery wine. A tingling beauty. Lucinda Heyns, back home after a two-year stint in California, with profoundly widened wine horizons, found a tiny bush-vine Riesling vineyard in Darling – and bagged the grapes instantly. "I knew this was it!" This delicate little marvel bares its (characteristic Riesling) terpene teeth just enough. Personally foot-stomped. Only one barrel made. Destined for cult status.

Nitida Riesling 2014 The floral spiciness is well developed but not intrusive. What's so appealing is the balance: there are citrus blossom scents, and edginess and steeliness on the palate. The acidity is coated with imperceptible sweetness. Delightful.

Rosé is a visual wine. Puts us in a light-hearted mood, al fresco lunches, country picnics. It's about informality. Careless pouring, splashing, sloshing. No rules. And there are no rules, really, about its growing and making either: any grape variety, red or white (with a bit of red blended), dry or sweet, bubble, no bubble. Dedicated rosé growers frown on blending white and red grapes, but it happens. Blanc de Noir – blush – is a variation on the rosé idea. I am not sure that we have altogether cracked this style here, yet. But you might say the same about Provence. There is a lot of mediocre pink there… Here are my current local favourites. With a bit of poetic licence.

ROSÉ

Graham Beck Gorgeous First released 2015. Complete cracker – and priced for "the rest of us". Plus the alc. is only 11%. So, a carefree lunchtime glugger. All the sassy tastes of juicy, discreet Chardonnay blended with red-berry Pinot Noir. A permanent place in our fridge. A joy with light meals on a sunny day. Packaged to raise a smile.

De Toren La Jeunesse Délicate Yes, the consistently fine Stellenbosch Bordeaux-blend reds, Fusion V and De Toren Z produced here by Emil den Dulk and Albie Koch grab the headlines and international praise. Newcomer to the range Book XV11 is winning "Luxury Red" contests; it is made in tiny quantities, and is harvested and de-stemmed by workers wearing surgical gloves … But, a confession: our favourite in the range for its personality and deliciousness is this far less grand, lunch and summertime wine, served chilled. Not strictly speaking a pink, but not a fully paid-up red either. Four varieties, mainly Cabernet Sauvignon. Absolutely beautiful, fragrant and savoury at same time, just touch of oak to raise the profile. Superb with all sorts of food.

Eendevanger Pinot Gris Rosé 2013 Inspired by a skin-fermented white from Romania, a Pinot Gris, that Lucinda Heyns tasted – reluctantly, after much persuasion from wine friends, in Santa Barbara, California. Her début vintage here turned out – naturally - pinkish; SA authorities declined the varietal label. So she had to label it Rosé. It's a fresh, dry, savoury delight. Her label, The Duck Catcher, is meant to convey a straight-from-the-farm idea: a barefoot child in a meadow, chasing ducks. The wine has that same natural charm. Only one barrel. Watch this rising star, former viticulturalist at Mulderbosch.

Felicité Rosé – a Newton-Johnson Family and Stettyn collaboration: Worcester grapes. Unusual blend of Shiraz with about 20% Sauvignon Blanc for a crisp lift, with smattering Viognier. Dry, tasty, light.

FRAM Grenache Gris Thinus Krüger's deadpan humour has tasting audiences in stitches. Explaining how phenolic and sugar ripeness don't always coincide, he's says there's a third "blerry" problem: trying to dovetail with "logistical ripeness – when the blerry truck breaks down over the weekend and can't collect the grapes… So we winemakers make mistakes, but at least we're not your doctors, and you won't die. But you may wake up in the morning and wonder 'why the hell did I spend that kind of money on a bottle of wine.'" No such worries over this succulent Grenache from the Swartland. "Only problem I had was haggling with the grower over the price of his beautiful grapes. He wouldn't accept my offer. He insisted I pay him less. So I end up feeling guilty." Kruger did not seek out this Grenache, the farmer offered it. He could have said no thanks. "But I didn't want to stand on my stoep aged 80 and say, what if…" And so, a new wine was born in 2015.

Ken Forrester Grenache Rosé From single vineyard, dedicated to making this style of wine (for specific early harvesting). Launched with a 2015 – should become another household KF label; crisp, light and racy, whispers of raspberry. We tasted it with a prawn curry: what a match! Delightful on its own, too.

Klein Constantia Rosé From Constantia Cabernet Franc, with the grape's appetising savoury edges, presented here in dry, gently-crisp, stimulating style.

Sutherland Grenache Rosé From Thelema's Elgin vineyards. Thoroughly fresh, dry, clean, silkily light-textured (the grape speaking) and light-tinted to match.

Tokara Siberia Grenache Rosé 2014 Juicy, cheerful, cherry-like, dry on palate. Light – 12,5% alc. Though fresh, crisp, not too bracing. Good all-round food match. The name is that of a Tokara vineyard near Hermanus — colder, and supposedly "in exile" from Stellenbosch.

ROUSSANNE

Joostenberg Roussanne Full, round, nutty-sweet and slightly oaked, stands up for itself with Asian dishes, likes a bit of chilli. Excellent value. Mostly used in blends, this one of the few stand-alone examples of this white variety.

SAUVIGNON BLANC

The high-profile punch of these wines comes from high pyrazine levels in the grapes, determined by when they are picked. Pyrazines, detectable by us at 10-15 parts per trillion, decline sharply as grapes are given more hang-time on the vine, and ripen fully. Such ripe-picked sauvignons have more body and weight to cushion the variety's aggression. I prefer these less nettly, more relaxed, fuller and calmer sauvignons, often in blends. And I enjoy the variations in flavour which local sauvignons offer, reflecting their very different mountain and maritime terroirs. New Zealand and Sancerre, long the comfort zones of international sauvignon fanciers, have the Cape snapping at their heels.

UP THE MOUNTAIN
DOWN THE COAST
ACROSS THE OCEAN

Why, when you have one of the rarest, loftiest, most secluded vineyard sites in the world all to yourself, with *lebensraum* to expand, 1100m above sea level - would you want to go, first, to the opposite end of the South African winelands, and, then across to another continent, to Chile, to grow more of what you already have in quality and abundance, Sauvignon Blanc? There isn't exactly a shortage.

It's a question I will ask David Niewoudt if we survive, in our tiny hired car, the long, corrugated dirt, dizzy drops and hair-pin bends of the two mountain passes en route to his remote farm in the wilderness of the Cederberg, 200km west of Cape Town. The indigenous cedars, incidentally, are now almost extinct. Another question: what compelled his forefathers to trek here, and his grandfather eventually to plant vines, in ground so rugged they have been known to dynamite holes for the *stokkies*? Looking back explains the way forward. It's in the Niewoudt genes. He is curious and driven, like his ancestors. Perhaps even *bedonderd* as they say in Afrikaans, a bit crazy. If it takes a day to collect the post from here, why not an overnight trip to get to and from his coastal vineyards, and a cross-continental flight to South America?

The **Cederberg Private Cellar Sauvignon Blanc 2012** won UK magazine *Decanter*'s World's Best Sauvignon award in 2014. But I succumb to his Chilean beauty, the joint-venture **Longhavi Sauvignon 2013**, from the Atlantic coast region of San Antonio, west of Santiago. It is so exquisitely different, with a Sancerre-like acidity. I'm hooked.

Finer, more individual than anything I ever tasted in Chile – though some time ago – and I suspect will make waves there even now. There's a very European deep, damp earthy underground cellar vinosity. Plus on the bouquet, an intriguing topping of fruit – though none of the usual Cape Sauvignon descriptions, gooseberry, guava, capsicum, fit. This should dissipate after a year or two in bottle. It's the quality of the fresh acidity and (imagined?) ocean salinity that won me over. They love their sea urchins in Chile. This Nieuwoudt Longhavi Sauvignon is exactly right to wrestle down that seaweed-astringency – or any other set of untamed flavours on the plate. The striking individuality of this wine is also explained by daily ripening-period temperatures: significantly lower than at his recently acquired Ghost Corner vineyards at Elim, near Cape Agulhas, and a full 9 degrees a day cooler than in the Cederberg - a whole bunch of flavours not given away to the sun and heat.

There's a sub-plot here, a simmering low-intensity rivalry, genteelly waged - he's all old Cape family charm - from these spectacular uplands, famed for their rock art, rock formations and Cape mountain flora. The Nieuwoudt winemaking regime is "reductive" - he is obsessed about not letting his picked grapes near a breath of oxygen. This is in determined contrast to lately fashionable, sulphur-shy, minimalist handling of grapes – the "oxidative" approach.

"Once that berry is picked, until the wine is in the bottle, no air, repeat, no air," says Nieuwoudt with a shove-it-to-them grin. "My wines must be fresh, aromatic, clean, fruity, reliably stable. And yes, I use sulphur. Of course, well below legal limits."

There are three local Nieuwoudt Sauvignons, one regular smart one from the Cederberg Private Cellar range, and two from the coast under the **David Nieuwoudt Ghost Corner** label. Picked fruit is packed in dry ice for the overnight journey from Elim to Cederberg; kept at a cool 8 degrees. One is conventionally fermented but I prefer the **David Nieuwoudt Ghost Corner Wild Ferment 2014**. Fresh, complex, creamy – if that's the right word for any Sauvignon?

He modernised his cellar in 2013/14 to reinforce his ideas; a new German press blasts out oxygen-denying nitrogen, to keep the grape mash air-free. What he does at Cederberg, so he does in Chile. "My partners took some convincing, but I told them the dry ice part is only a few days – after a year's work." He'd just been to Chile when we met, and on his way back stopped over with his London importer. They went to dinner at a restaurant with a full list of "oxidative" boutique wines. The importer ordered two. "He – not me - sent them both back," reported Nieuwoudt.

David Niewoudt in his Cederberg vineyards (left)

THE NEW DEAL

Matt Day is a handy golfer. A good thing. He's obliged – by the wildly competitive modern wine game - to be an obsessive and finds golf unsettling enough to keep the mind in a wine-free zone for a few hours. Plus, it's good preparation for the highs and lows of growing and making. A harvest from heaven turns into hell in an instant, as happened when Table Mountain roared into flames in early 2015, threatening their vineyards. So Day is composed and wry about such laurels as his placement among the world's top 30 most brilliant young winemakers by *The Drinks Business*, 2014. But when his peers nod in approval, which they do, it counts.

In his mid-twenties when he took over this cellar in 2009, he has re-aligned this historic and modern but once coasting estate. It is now "authentically terroir, naturalist-orientated". The new guardians of minimalist purity can point no fingers here. No acid adjustments, no interventionist fining nor filtrations etc. One beautiful irony: Day has been given a gleaming battery of expensive new cellar toys - like a super-gentle bunch de-stemmer - with which to achieve this back-to-nature regime.

So what's the new deal at Klein Constantia ((KC), where wine was first bottled in 1824? Day is not shy of wide horizons.

"I want to make our **Sauvignon Blanc** the best in the world."

They offer several Sauvignons here, all serious. The **Metis** is a team effort with Loire producer Pascal Jolivet. There is the regular but always outstanding **Klein Constantia**. And one from a single vineyard - **Block 382** - the highest vines on this elevated estate. Of course he can't admit to favourites. But one senses that this is Day's first among equals. He took us up the frighteningly precipitous slopes to Block 382. Stepping out of the 4-wheel drive, all-terrain vehicle you promptly begin sliding down on the rolling gravel. He patrolled the rows, bending down to peer proprietorially into the leaves and bunches. I thought he was going to give the vines a Prince Charles pep talk. No vineyard-to-cellar miscommunication here. Longtime punters of previous KC Sauvignons may miss the louder thrust of the past – the shrill, exciting higher notes (from pyrazine) and added blasts from yeast fermentation. But these more modern, Matt Day KCs are beautifully balanced, just as delicious, held-back and decorous.

He rather scarily recommends eating crocodile with these. Less challengingly, pigeon. We suggest summery salads, anything with mayo, calamari.

AND

Buitenverwachting Hussey's Vlei Sauvignon Blanc The veteran winemaker here, Hermann Kirschbaum, has had three decades to master Constantia's signature grape. This label is his personally fashioned, magnificent, not-so-in-your-face Sauvignon, with true grapey freshness and balance, searching but unaggressively so. Brilliant with salads. A no-hesitation wine. Latest tasted: 2014. Can last a few years too.

Delaire Graff Coastal Cuvée Sauvignon Blanc The pride and joy Sauvignon of this winery; its own, combined with coastal Darling and Durbanville grapes. Neither raspy nor skinny; pure, beautiful, bright fruit – crisply tropical and ripe. Full-bodied. Has won the Sauvignon prize at the annual Mutual Trophy twice, only Sauvignon with that distinction. Superb match for chef Michael Deg's classic Delaire Caesar Salad.

Iona Sauvignon Blanc All the flinty fruity acidity you need - without the wallop of high-octane, unresolved nettles, grass, whatever. And also from Iona, **Sophie Te'blanche**, a cute everyday Sauvignon. There is no Sophie: the name is the farm workers' phonetic twist on Sauvignon Blanc.

La Motte Pierneef Sauvignon Blanc A grown-up Sauvignon, doesn't shout. Balanced, restrained, but enough fruity-dry presence – some flinty stone, muted gooseberry. 2014. Should grow in complexity for three or four years. A hit in our house.

Reyneke Reserve White My on-the-spot, at-the-farm notes on the 2014 read: "Incredible! Creamy, dense, fresh palate. A new take on Sauv Blanc! The usual assertive fruity attack subsumed. Appetising. Touch of spicy oak, whiff of flowers. Balanced, charming." Showers of show accolades, Platter guide 5 stars, and a confession from a sauvignon-bashing mate: he's invested in this wine.

Springfield Life from Stone Sauvignon Blanc A glance at the vineyard's stone-filled subsoil tells a story; the wine has the minerally, flinty thrust that cries out for a generous helping of something rich and assertive too – risotto, tomato-based pastas, pizzas, buttery-spicy prawns, maybe even a fish curry. Ages well – five years or so.

Steenberg Black Swan is the former, regularly fabulous, Sauvignon Reserve, from a 25-year-old vineyard yielding only 2,5 tons a hectare. It is complex, perfectly filled out with generous, crisp figgy flavours. A little help from a small blending dose of Semillon. No oak. The purity of the match irresistible.

Tokara Reserve Sauvignon Blanc 2014 From Tokara's cool-climate Elgin vineyards. Seriously full-on fresh Sauvignon - passion-fruit, apple-cider qualities. Flinty and lacy on palate. Should improve 3-4 years. Sauvignon category winner of 2015 contest among Australia, New Zealand, South Africa, Chile and Argentina.

Vergelegen Schaapenberg Sauvignon Blanc has been a personal Wow-wine for decades, with a few vintage wobbles – a Liverpool fan, I have learned one only intensifies the loyal support in lean years. The 2,4 ha. vineyard, on a wind-ravaged ridge staring at False Bay, is nearing the end of its useful life. It was planted in 1987. I will shed tears if/when they grub up these ragged vines. As they yield less, why not raise the price? The 2010 is a very Wow year, such pure, stunning European-like acidity. Winemaker Andre van Rensburg likes Thai dishes with his Sauvignons. Also "the best that the ocean can give you". And insists "not even Champagne comes close" to their affinity for wild oysters.

In his dainty **Villiera Bush Vine Sauvignon Blanc**, Jeff Grier's ability to put a consumer-friendly twist on wines jumps out of the glass. All he has done (all?) is to mute the powerful pyrazine flavours of the variety. By pushing his picking date to the limit. Riper, later-picked grapes provide more friendly fruit salad flavours than early picks, which attack your nose and tastebuds like a bunch of green nettles. These are from low-yield bush vines, unusual for Sauvignon Blanc. And no need to gulp down immediately: matures nicely for a few years.

I lost my heart and soul to John Seccombe's **Thorne and Daughters Tin Soldier Semillon 2013**. The palest, shimmering sunset orange. Clean, muted honey aromas; ample, silky, savoury, herby palate. Finish is all gentle generosity. Superb backing for all manner of light summer meals. From 33 year-old Semillon Blanc and Semillon Gris (or pink) vines in Franschhoek, sourced for him by viticulturalist Rosa Kruger.

It brings back memories of the tiny vineyard, one of the many Franschhoek La Provences, we bought (to escape journalist deadlines) in the late 1970s. It was planted mainly to these Semillons; close planted bush vines, 1x1m, and weeded by horse-drawn harrow! We called them "Groendruif", green grape, in those unfancy days. I was told that the random pink grapes, the Semillon Gris, were nuisance mutants, and was advised to cull them. I was too lazy, or disorganised … and then we sold, and most lately our little patch has been swallowed up and incorporated into showpiece Grande Provence. Which does not have a traditional Semillon of any shade on its list.

John Seccombe has turned some venerable old vine gems into gold.

SEMILLON

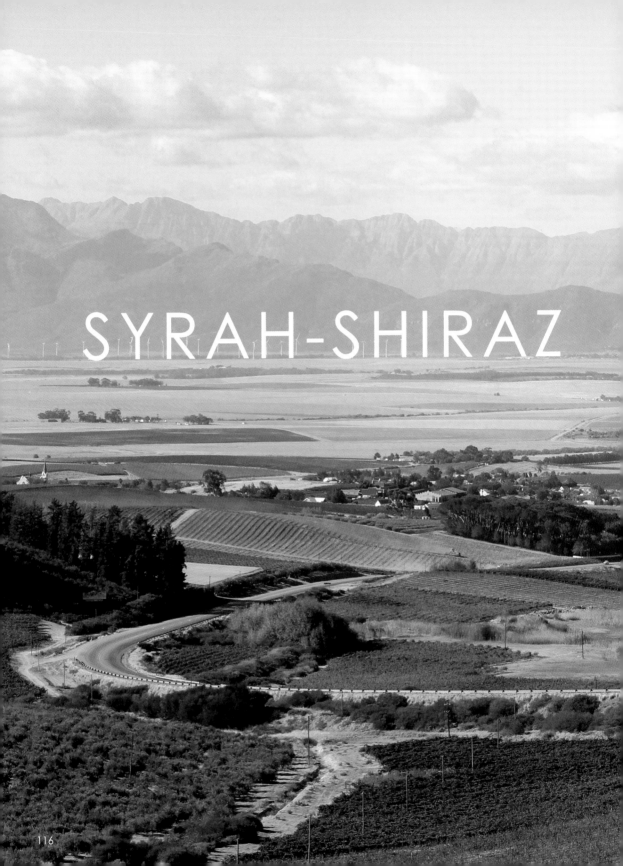

SYRAH-SHIRAZ

Shiraz or Syrah? Different names for the same grape. It did not originate in the Middle East, as was long believed; it is originally French. Now grown all over the world, it is used solo, in blends and even to make sweet bubblies. Red wine traditionalists sometimes appear unsettled by its versatility and less formal image. Ruminating on the reluctance of "entrenched claret and Burgundy drinkers to stray from the safe, marked paths" Remington Norman in his book *Rhône Renaissance* concluded such "inflexibility seemed to me narrow-minded and a mark of snobbery rather than a genuine love of fine wine".

That was in 1995. Today's wine drinkers know – or are they less snobbish? - there's simply too much adventure, and sheer quality, in Syrah not to range well beyond the confines of Burgundy or Bordeaux, Pinot Noir or Cabernet Sauvignon. South African producers have hedged their bets with numerous Cabernet-Shiraz blends. Since both varieties take well to oak, their individual grape qualities are synthesised, blurred – or, as winemakers would argue - integrated and harmonised during barrel maturation.

Despite smashingly good blended exceptions, I prefer Syrah alone in its striking glory – spicy, peppery, dark but not too stern; it has a less headmasterly quality anyway than Cabernet. Or when it's distinctly in the lead in a blend, supported by complementary (not competing) role players like Grenache, Cinsaut, Carignan - the first two very capable of fine wines in solo form.

Perhaps it's a questionable generalisation, but Northern Rhône styles, where Syrah often flies solo, are characterised by a peppery, tighter and more direct and dense, black olive character. That's riveting to me and found in the Cape more often in straight Syrah, in cooler climes. The spiciness – clove, coffee, liquorice – comes more from the oak.

We're producing South African wines, of course and comparisons can be invidious; but Southern Rhône wines tend to be broader and more diffuse versions than from the Northern Rhône, the Syrah subsumed, less defined, among a spread of grape varieties in the blend. The Swartland specialises in such wines, more regionally and terroir-driven, the Syrah a co-ordinator rather than a tall poppy. Though there are conspicuous exceptions, especially from the granite and schist mountainsides.

THE RUMBLING EARTHQUAKE

Two of the very finest Cape reds, Mullineux and Vilafonté, fetching stratospheric prices here and abroad, are made by American women. Not a great ego-booster for the men in South African wine. But they only have praise for Andrea Mullineux and Zelma Long (see Red Blends). The two of them are so indisputably at the top of their game, with precision winery techniques. And uncouth crowing would be beneath them. Which is all fabulous for the general image of Cape wine, still in need of more flag-bearing icons.

Andrea is the more recent arrival. They're both smart scientists, Andrea the product of the University of California, and its prestigious Davis oenology faculty. With her viticulturist husband Chris, she is at the epicentre – and a catalyst - of the rumbling earthquake in 21st Century South African wine, the Swartland Revolution. Travelled and trained all over the wine world, they met at Waterford in Stellenbosch, where Andrea was working a season. Chris came to buy old barrels, Andrea spotted him. And as she tells it, knew instantly (Chris was unaware) he was the man she was going to marry. They reconnected in France. Could have set up anywhere in the wine world. But chose sleepy, rural Riebeek Kasteel, with its three and a half restaurants, in the Swartland - for decades an underwhelming backwater of Cape wine.

What did this young couple know?

The Swartland, named after its original habitat, the grey-black Renosterbos or Rhino bush - *elytropappus rhinocerotis* - though warm, is not as hot as it's made out; its proximity and unsheltered openness to the Atlantic Ocean helps. From Kasteelberg you can see Darling on the coast. There are other cool, windy elevations. The soils of the Swartland and its various rugged ridges and protrusions, remnants of tectonic convulsions 540 million years ago, are well delineated. There's Kasteelberg , and then Paardeberg, the Porcelain ridge and lower foothills; in between, rolling flatlands of straw-gold wheatfields, with red and iron-heavy soils. The areas of shale-derived schist and decomposed granite are defined, so there's the opportunity to grow and make wines to reflect those soils with some clarity.

In general – granite-based soil, with its clay base under coarse sand and its slow-release moisture properties, makes for more even growth in the vineyard and more extrovertly-scented wines. Shale-schist is leaner, scratchier, less moisture-retentive and reflects this in firm, austere – but often beautifully so – food-specific wines. So the top Mullineux Syrah bottlings are labelled by their soils: Schist, Granite and, more recently, Iron. And there are labels that incorporate them all.

The couple also liked the dryland conditions, which don't compromise vintage distinctions. Nature and the year deliver their highs and lows unadorned: "truthful" wines, undoctored and uncommercial.

And the Swartland is a trove of scarce, old – some very venerable 70-year-old - vineyards of previously neglected varieties whose stock and value now have risen dramatically. The Mullineuxs are plumb in the middle of this revival – with dozens of sources of different grapes, rich ingredients for distinctive blends; whether of single varieties from multiple sources or multiple grape varieties from, say, predominantly single soil types. The scope is Burgundian in its labyrinthine complexity, Byzantine in its potential for scheming side-deals among growers, grower-producers and landless winemakers.

For all the straight-from-nature promo lines, the hand of man remains crucial in wine. And interventionist. Beginning, if we want to go basic, with the choice of the grape vine, *vitis vinifera*, an import – intrusive, alien, monocultural, ravaging the Renoster bos and banishing the poor old Rhino which roamed these parts. My notes on the rest of this stuff are extended minutiae, esoteric, eye-glazing stuff...

Let's cut to the wine. I had met the **Mullineux Syrah Schist 2011** before – at one of Andrea's polished tastings where her stories hang together compellingly, a difficult feat she achieves with charm. Next I drank it, under a billion stars in the bush in 2014, with the afore-mentioned Remington Norman, MW, Oxford don, author of beautiful books on the Rhône, Burgundy, and a philosophical one, *Sense and Sensibility* in which he writes: "Civilization is disappearing downhill faster than a greased pig." We agreed the Schist was superlative. It performed the near-impossible: obliterated the woes of a rough day on the golf course. A little youthful perhaps – but that's never bothered me. Minor niggles can serve merely to reinforce beauty. The **Mullineux Granite** of the same year – a fine vintage for keeping – seems to have won marginally more favour elsewhere. Robert Parker in the Wine Advocate, gave the Granite an 'extraordinary' 95/100, the Schist a merely 'outstanding' 94/100.

These and succeeding vintages are now international collectors' wines. No other Cape label has been showered with so many glittering prizes and accolades recently. Mullineux was the Platter Guide Winery of the Year in 2014; 5 stars twinkle throughout their range. In a wine scene so frenetic, new starbursts are inevitable. But I think they are ready for them. They recently teamed up with Cape wine's latest celebrity investor, the Indian magnate Analjit Singh, to secure a new base and vineyards on the farm Roundstone, high in the hills (and through a riverbed) outside Riebeek Kasteel. A warm and spiritual man, Singh says: "I just love the energy of Franschhoek". So that's where his base is, and a cellar, where **Mullineux and Leeu Family Wines** will be made (Leeu, the Afrikaans for lion; Singh, Hindu word for lion). The focus in Franschhoek will be different to that in the Swartland. The Mullineux team – commuting wine-makers now - will remain in charge of the wines and retain the regional and stylistic identities of the different labels.

THE BORN PIONEER

Callie Louw is the tall, square-jawed, silent type. He looks as if he's stepped out of one of those survival TV shows: dropped onto the top of a lonely hill and told to get on with it. Plant vines, make wine, bottle it, print the labels, run Ngunis, pigs and chickens; grow veges… he does it all here in the Swartland, on the small mountain of Porseleinberg and the slopes beneath.

Wind and schist and his own no-fripperies inclinations shape the character of **Porseleinberg Syrah.** It is a tannic-fresh, spare, no-compromise wine. Without (new) oak-leavening. No velvet cushions, no sweet-ripe induce-ments. For purists. The elegance is in its purposeful purity and functionality.

Louw is also a producer of custom-made wine labels. You order a case of Porseleinberg, you get to design your own label, and he does the rest, firing up the antique press which dominates the glass-fronted, wind-blasted tasting room between his home and the simple winery. His press is a French import, and also second-hand. One catch: you have to fetch the wine yourself from the mountain. "We're doing this for the people who believe in us," he says with the finality of a man with sure objectives. Only about 1600 bottles a year – 130 cases. That scarcity, that individuality: a snip at R500 a bottle, R6000 the case, in 2015.

He and his family live here, on the crest of the long schist ridge – the 'Porcelain' – which runs to your left on the road approaching Riebeek Mountain from the direction of Wellington. It's a trek getting there, opening-closing farm gates, around and over dam walls, up hillsides. And then on top, with a wrap-around vista toward the distant coast, across to Malmesbury, inland to Tulbagh, you're buffeted by whistling winds.

"Like this 90% of the time," Louw says. "Tough life for the vines. Good for them. Small berries." Except, where we're standing now they are not Syrah vines but Grenache. "The Syrah were no good, all died. The Grenache survive on half the water and can take the wind better." The Syrah vineyards lie in the more sheltered valley below.

This is all organic wine farming. Louw, trained in the States, is a founding member of the Swartland Revolution, helped draw up its producer guidelines. "We stomp the grapes ourselves, we're up to our armpits." Then over to natural-yeast ferments in cement tanks – and the usual 'Revolution' things: no additives, no filtration etc.

With one curious, significant exception – which Louw brought from his experiences in California. He doses grapes with sulphur, in significant quantity – nearly 100 parts per million - when they're harvested. "No trace of sulphur is left after the wine's safely fermented," he says. You don't hear that often from winemakers, never from the new, no-additives promoters. So I'm curious about sugar-to-alcohol conversion ratios, with, supposedly more fragile, wild yeast working under those sulphurs. And that's when I'm told: "Too many questions!"

So, to the wines: Louw has opened several, of various vintages. The experts tell us not to expect too much Syrah perfume from schist soils; those wonderful aromas are more evident from vineyards in granite soils. That seems to be borne out here. These are dark, tough food wines. Not bulky or heavy. Should age elegantly. The 2012 long sold out. The 2013, just bottled when we visited - 50% matured in concrete, 50% in used barrels – has powerful depth on the palate and should evolve impressively over a decade. The 2014 was still finding itself.

Porseleinberg is much more than 130 cases a year. It's the brainchild of innovator Marc Kent, über-winemaker at Boekenhoutskloof, Franschhoek, and its chairman, Tim Rands. They've been on a buying spree of brands and lands during difficult economic times and are in the forefront of the sustainability movement, especially in the Swartland. Porseleinberg's eventual 85ha of grapes will be handled by Kent for various labels. He's given Callie Louw, a born pioneer, a long leash.

THE DAREDEVIL
AND THE STEADY HAND

"Bring that chair a little closer, I want to look into your eyes." And so, of course, Carl Schultz, who wanted the job, moved the chair nearer to Ken Mackenzie in a big, green rocking chair, the man so tall they nicknamed him Stork when he joined the RAF as a Spitfire fighter pilot in World War Two. The Stork trained an unrelenting gaze on the young interviewee, interrupting occasionally to probe – with an intimidatingly deep-gravel tobacco voice - fidgeting with his pipe to keep it alive with endless matches. This was their first, and a one-on-one-meeting, and it went on for three hours. That was in 1993. Carl Schultz is still at Hartenberg; Ken Mackenzie is no longer with us, and his two daughters, Fiona and Tanya, now preside.

"He wanted to be quite convinced I wasn't going to flit," said Schultz. "I learned how strongly he valued loyalty and trust and that they would be reciprocated if given unstintingly."

Mackenzie told Schultz: "Okay, so let's make the best wine in the world." Gilbey's (from whom he bought the farm in 1987) had told him it was the best estate in Stellenbosch. As carefully as he could, Carl said he'd try, but it wasn't simple nor quick. Mackenzie, who knew little about wine, was all enterprise and free-spirit and gusto; old-timers still remember him flying his plane above Durban's main street, executing some daredevil (and forbidden) rolls en route. From nothing virtually, he grew a diverse international conglomerate which thrives under his daughter Tanya today. First love – beef cattle. He was a philanthropist. The Drakensberg Boys' Choir one of his many beneficiaries, and his old school, Michaelhouse, another (he was a scholarship boy).

Hartenberg had always made decent Shiraz. Now Schultz has built on this variety to take the estate to a pre-eminent position in Cape wine at a time when the competition has never been hotter. While retaining its unpretentiousness and visitor-friendliness. The long list of wines – to suit all pockets – is dominated by Shiraz labels. Their annual Shiraz and Charcuterie event, in collaboration with Joostenberg, is a highlight of the Stellenbosch foodie-wine calendar. Their Cabernets are outstanding, topped by The Mackenzie. In some years, I prefer it to the Gravel Hill. Hartenberg is among the few Cape wineries to hold back their top reds for several years to mature in ideal conditions at their cellars at no premium charge. But It is not a red-only estate. I have a soft spot, too, for The Eleanor – see in the Chardonnay chapter.

Hartenberg Gravel Hill Shiraz Consistently one of the grandest of South Africa's Shirazes since its first vintage in 1995. The estate's icon, signature red from a gravelly, of course, gentle, eastern-facing slope on the estate. Effectively the first single vineyard wine and marketed as such, the brainchild of then marketing supremo James Browne. Schultz – who calls this "undoubtedly the finest wine I have had the privilege of crafting…" - has been disciplined about striking a balance between intense, strong, dark - typically Stellenbosch Shiraz - fruit and the outcomes of long oak ageing, formerly up to 22 months in 100% new barrels; now since 2009, cut back to 60%-70% and harvested a little earlier, also reining in alcohols for a juicer, less compressed style. The array of spices - clove, cinnamon and others – suffused in the ripe juices still showing. Suitable for the finest dining occasion but also a treat with the obvious: roast lamb and rosemary. Stablemate The Stork is a past winner of Syrah du Monde, the Best Syrah in the World competition.

Hartenberg Doorkeeper Shiraz A go-to, dependable, friendly-priced Shiraz; less complicated than estate's high-flyers but with reassuring hints of liquorice perfume and sweet, ripe fruit.

THE VINE WHISPERER'S LAIR

Now we're in the vine whisperer's lair – on a Stellenbosch hilltop, cooled by onshore swooshes from False Bay, curdled with the nearby whiffs of Johan Reyneke's lactating Nguni cattle – and two dear old Jerseys, Daisy and Kleintjie, their dainty little horns curled harmlessly inwards after eons of straightjacketing, genetic-modifying domesticity. The Ngunis have widely spaced, viciously sharp horns that say: don't mess. There are birds and bees and hives and wild shrubs with busy crawlies in a pulsating oasis, a self-contained biosphere above and below ground, nourished by cowpats. And vineyard soil so friable you stick a hand into it without much resistance. It's home to a febrile growth of weeds where vines are condemned to compete in undemocratic Darwinian battles. That limits the crop of grapes almost to leftovers from the tussle - 4-6 tons/ha of smaller berries, richly-flavoured. Singular footprints in a bottle.

Reyneke is a Stellenbosch philosophy graduate who decided his place was in the vineyards. He learned from the ground up, working as a labourer beside his staff to return over-worked, over-fertilised, over-sprayed vines and soil to a more natural state. He was a fully paid-up Rasta then, by his own account, with extravagant dreads doubtless rich in a biosphere of their own. That's gone. The dreamy intensity hasn't. Today he and his very like-minded – scientifically fully degreed - winemaking partner, Rudiger Gretschel, are among the most highly-rated, peer-respected duos in the Cape. At one of the rare registered biodynamic vineyards.

Gretschel is the chief winemaker of large commercial outfit Vinimark, which has an interest in Reyneke. He isn't sold on 'natural' winemaking in its entirety; he cherry-picks from the roster of dos and don'ts, subscribing to wild yeast and some whole-cluster ferments, but avoiding – "I hate it" - the slightest bit of carbonique maceration. "We foot-stamp thoroughly." There's a feathery hand with sulphur. And intuitive berry tasting - dispensing with saccharometers - to set harvesting dates. "Not before the white pepper flavours appear in the skins of the Syrah do we harvest." One variety that has him stumped, cowpats notwithstanding – at least for now: Merlot. For the rest, soon, one suspects, only special pleading will secure bottles of these authentic, site-driven wines.

Reyneke Reserve Red is a Syrah of singular character and a contender for the Cape's A team. Is it a compliment or an affront to call a South African Syrah French-like, or specifically in this case, Northern Rhône-like? Cape winemakers are often fastidious, even touchy on this point, insisting they are not trying to emulate wine from another country. However, they are usually using French grapes! Some genetics will out. If the finest French Syrah is about focused, penetrating, minerality and spice, then this 2012 could be a ringer, at least when I tasted it. It's stunning, poised. It makes many Cape Syrahs look floppy. The ferment, and smart, light oaking, have cleaned out the cowpats – without the help of filtration, a biodynamic no-no.

Rudiger Gretschel (left) and Johan Reyneke

LIFE ISN'T BAD

Jean Vincent Ridon buys grapes all over the winelands, many of which he and winemaker Laurence Buthelezi (far from his ancestral home in Zululand) vinify for their Signal Hill 'Single Barrel' range. Original curiosities and blends – a Pineau Chenin Blanc-Colombard; Mourvèdre (just 250 bottles from a garden overlooking the chic beach of Camps Bay); Malbec; Crème de Tête Muscat d'Alexandre NLH; Grenache Blanc and Noir, Mathilde Aszü 6 Puttonyos; a Petit Verdot – he was the first in the Cape to bottle this individually; ditto the first to make an Eiswein - in a refrigerated container in the Cape Town Docklands. "But only the second to bottle a Straw dessert wine, missed a trick there."

He professes to "know about wines to drink, rather than talk about too much". But his fund of stories is inexhaustible. He's been a sommelier, wine-broker and wine bar owner in France, launched the Classic Wine trophy in South Africa, coaches the national Wine Tasting team. As he opens a Cabernet Franc he's been hiding – never yet seen on his ever-changing 20-label list, he pauses to make a point: "In wine, there's no one truth, do you agree?'

Walk through his Cape Town inner-city winery to the adjoining al-fresco courtyard of restaurant Bizerca and in a corner you may notice a lone vine. Not a décor item. It's the real, ancient thing: 240 years old Chenin (Jean-Vincent has had it DNA-analysed in France, to find it's a 'Gros Chenin' a kind of precursor to our present-day Chenin). He's made 20 bottles from that.

Just as adventurously, he's planted a few hundred ungrafted Syrah vines on an unirrigated, terraced plot in suburban Oranjezicht. Looking to do a Clos Montmartre in Cape Town, he went onto wine-loving broadcaster John Maytham's Cape Talk radio show and brazenly solicited a vacant lot anywhere in the city where he could do his thing. Someone rang in, and offered the bottom of their family's garden. The vines, in the modern way, are not overly weeded so they contend with competing elements, including occasional campers in tents. "Oh, the birds steal more than they do". The result is an authentic terroir wine, **Signal Hill Clos d'Orange Syrah**, with the rarest of addresses, without much evidence of interference from the hand of Jean-Vincent. There are wide-angle views of Cape Town harbour. Jean-Vincent stands there among the (almost) bush vines (a single, low trellis wire) and breathes in heavily. "Life isn't bad."'

He had piled us all into his suspiciously fragile, ancient Citroen, to inspect these vines, weaving through the traffic, waving regally to the crowds, hooting for fun, exhaust – what was left of it - backfiring with the gear shifts, taking selfies. Capetonians love him. He owns the place. Worth a detour when you're in town. But make an appointment. Jean-Vincent is in perpetual motion. And don't bother to bid for the car. "Too precious, never for sale." He hires it out to film-producers and ad-makers.

UNADORNED

Alex Dale's Winery of Good Hope crew smiles with amusement at the loud tom-toms beating from the Swartland proclaiming their Revolution. "What revolution? A revolution over there, but already institutionalised here in Stellenbosch. They're catching up," laughs Dale. "The buzz is good for the industry."

Unlike some, Dale is tickled by, supportive of, these bursts of experiment, and eccentricity among the 'upstarts' of Swartland and Walker Bay. "Wine stretches from commodity all the way to art; some of what's happening now is funky, even faulty, cloudy, forced, and that's when they get flak. I admire the way the experimenters ride the censure. But many of the wines are also honest; I love watching the evolution toward art; there's serious, committed talent there," he says.

They've been at it quietly, deepening 'authenticity' aspects for years at The Winery of Good Hope: natural yeast ferments (for 10 years or more for reds); minimal to zero fining and filtration; whole bunch fermentation, within reason; grapes from dozens of different soils and climates, with an emphasis on mature vineyards; low or near-sulphur-free. And, most important, harvesting dates and wine-making methods that emphasise lower alcohols. They are looking for palate substance with a balanced, lasting tannin and acid structure. And an honest reflection of grape variety and soil and climatic origins.

So here, proving their points, is the **Winery of Good Hope Nudity**, a 2014 Syrah – grapes sourced from under the noses of the Swartland Revolutionistas at Voor Paardeberg. A zero-sulphur, low alcohol – only 12% - dry red, decidedly for the table, with a robust dish – ox-cheek, ox-tail? Purity of bright fruit provides both contrast and freshness. Not thick, unctuous weight. So, Nudity.

AND

Boekenhoutskloof Syrah Winemaker Marc Kent planted his flag more than 25 years ago with this Rhône variety. No signs of letting go. The fruit is bought in, typically from Wellington, but Kent's vineyard sources, Boekenhoutskloof-owned or managed, are now so vast and varied, he can cherry-pick for this flagship label. And for relative vintage consistency. It's a sumptuous, plummy-spicy beauty with fine-grained tannins.

Craven Syrah Faure 2014 Exceptionally fresh, sappy take on Syrah, from Jeanine Craven's family vineyards at Faure, Stellenbosch, overlooking False Bay. Exceptionally light too – 11.4% alcohol. "A smashable wine," says Mick Craven. Natural – unadjusted – acids. New age minimalism. Remarkable.

De Trafford Syrah 393 In stand-back winemaking house-style: the craftsmanship lies in fine-tuning the non-interventions! Evidently a vineyard-driven wine, from ripe grapes, red and black berry flavours and peppery notes dominate the oak barrel seasoning, bracing, spicy-sweet. The flavours balloon nicely on the palate. 2012 most recent. Ample structure to last another decade.

Jordan The Prospector Syrah Generous, comforting, wide-bodied, some dark chocolate notes with spices, plush texture. "Synergy between sun and soil," says winemaker Gary Jordan. Dependable vintage to vintage. A beautiful accompaniment to quail and game.

Keermont Steepside Single Vineyard Syrah Intense, energetic fruit purity. Juicy-sweet quality on palate and lasting finale in 2012. Unfined, unfiltered, minimal use of – old – oak. **Keermont Topside Single Vineyard Syrah 2012** is luscious, with a fleshy texture; peppery power too. A blend of the two 2012 Syrahs, with a touch of Mourvèdre – therefore no longer a 'single vineyard' label – was rated 95 points by *Decanter*.

Kleine Zalze Family Reserve Shiraz Outstanding Stellenbosch example, spicily oaked, manages from vintage to vintage to be grippy and mouth-fillingly generous at same time.

Richard Kershaw Elgin Syrah From selected parcels in cooler Elgin, based on two Syrah clones. Clonal selection a Kershaw speciality, still a new labelling concept in the Cape. One of his descriptions for the 2012 is "iodine". Whether or not you agree, this is a distinctive, dense and focused Syrah taking its place among the best of the Cape. Probably comparable to the tighter, dark, spicy style of northern Rhône. Peppery too. Oaked. Light-touch vinification.

Stark-Condé Three Pines Syrah Spicy, sensual and serious. Edgy blackberry and olive notes. Terse, fine-grained tannins. From one block on this singular, individual farm, in one of the wettest, coolest valleys around Stellenbosch. Oaked. Capable of long – 10 years, plus – ageing. Recent 2013 superlative; two previous most desirable too.

Terra Cura Kasteelberg 2014 "I believe in single sites," declares Ryan Mostert. And this deep-soil Swartland Syrah comes from "our incredibly rugged, old earth" showing unusually earthy, herbal, fresh notes. No wood.

Tokara Director's Reserve Collection Syrah 2011 Stellenbosch single vineyard. A dense and tight, deep Syrah, direct and powerful. Smallest crop recorded, tiny berries. Also wild yeast ferment, partly whole-bunch pressed; oak-finished.

Vondeling Erica Shiraz 2009 Named after Erica Hippurus, a wild red flower unique to the Paardeberg Mountain: there is a botanist at this environmentally conscious project. The Shiraz is "touched up" with a few other Rhône varieties. Brimming with peppery, dark-fruited spiciness with dark olive notes. Savoury weight and fine on palate, sound tannins. Long finish. Minimalist wine-making by Matthew Copeland.

Waterford Kevin Arnold Shiraz You'd expect the only wine in the range carrying his name would warrant a cellar master's special fine-tuning. It shows. A Shiraz you open with confidence, variations in tone, no shocks from vintage to vintage. Friendly, broad flavours. A little pepper lifts a savoury black olive quality some years. Restrained oak.

Wine Cellar Syrah 2014 has light, limpid texture of a fine French Rhône, with similar inviting complex, low key ripe grapey-plum perfumes, fresh and savoury mouth-feel, airily nimble finish. Been nowhere near new oak. The 12,5% alc. spot-on. Beautiful. Made by Wine Cellar cellarmaster Ryan Mostert, observing the rules of few rules - as few interventions as possible - trying to deliver the vineyard in a bottle.

Intellego Kolbroek Shiraz Jurgen Gouws (above), a free-agent winemaker formerly at Lammershoek, is enjoying producing wines in uncommercial quantities, free of commercial constraints – only 1400 bottles in 2013 - in the style he personally likes. Might be unyielding for some, the "freshness" perhaps a bit too elegantly austere. I liked it a lot. Not for casual imbibing, but good company for a bubbling winter casserole. Light in colour, and splendidly low alcohol (12,5%). "The last thing I want is overstatement," says quietly-spoken Gouws. But this wine is a statement.

TEMPRANILLO

Rioja fans might like to try **Nederburg Ingenuity 2012 Tempranillo** – to compare and contrast with the Spanish grape, in a Cape setting. Some echoes of spicy vanilla sweetness from part American oak ageing; but there's a punchier (than Rioja) quality here too. An earthy food wine, firm to the finish. Romanian-born winemaker Rasvan Macici, an inspired hire more than a decade ago for this South African wine institution, has recently moved on and up to head the entire Distell winemaking operation. A massive job.

TINTA BAROCCA

Tinta Barocca often features in Portugal's heady after-dinner (and sometimes aperitif) Ports. Only relatively recently have the Portuguese been luring new buyers by turning these ancient varieties into interesting dry red table wines.

Sadie Family Old Vine Series Treinspoor Tinta Barocca A few sips of 2014 changes any notions of Tinta as a roughish, raffish grape fit only for Port. This dry red from Swartland Revolutionary Eben Sadie glides over the tongue with a range of savoury, dried-herb-strewn wafts and tastes, and underlying friendly sweetness, friendly tannins.

SO CHIC

If Marelize Jansen van Rensburg – a leading young light of the minimalist winemaking movement - can rescue an ancient, ruinously unviable vineyard at Bot River for a few more years, she'll turn her **Momento Tinta Barocca** into a celebrated label. The decrepit 40-year-old vines she harvests – at a laughable yield of 1,5 tons per hectare - have long outlived their ordinary commercial life. You get the picture from the gnarled root illustrated on the label by her artist husband Hennie Nieman. At Marelize's boutique price, she may just be able to pay the grower enough to keep him from yanking out the vines and replanting afresh with more productive varieties. Meantime she is establishing a reputation as an original and determined winemaker, hand-crafting wines also from Grenache, Chenin Blanc and Verdelho. The grapes come from vineyards and microclimates she knows well even though they are not her own. She went to school in Elgin and worked for some years in the Beaumont cellar at Bot River. This 2013 is uncommonly elegant, with a sweet-berry perfume and lightness on the palate, and a sufficiently firm core. Without the slightest throat-catching bitterness. Delicious. Uncowed by robust cuisine. A feat for so chic a wine.

VIOGNIER

This aromatic white grape variety was once confined mostly to Condrieu and Côte Rotie in the Rhône where it produces fabulously spicy, expensive wines. It's also used in small quantities to ginger up Syrah. The grape has now spread across the world – losing much of its exclusivity value, and, some say, its expressive French intensity. The most frequent description used in South Africa is peachy – but it has rather more than that, a spicy piquancy, litchis too, some muscat hints. It's also used to add complexity to some of the Cape's outstanding Rhône style red blends.

Pronounce it, more or less, Vee-on-yee-ay…

AHEAD OF EVERY SWERVE

Charles Back is the unquestioned individual dynamo of Cape Wine. Somehow, he sails way above the scene of a hundred bickering, over-lapping committees, and an industry tangled in regulation, with a long history of quasi-government, monopoly controls – only recently loosened. Why? Because he knows how to sell wine in a world awash in it. And because he's a lightning-quick initiator of new ideas in a cut-throat business, getting tighter every year.

He's hands-on, knows every trick in the cellar, sound on basic chemistry, and out in the vineyard he twirls the secateurs like a magician. At a push, like me, he could still milk a goat – for Fairview's cheeses. (I learned in the Italian Alps, aged five.) Back considers every customer, from a giant UK supermarket chain to a hesitant, walk-in buyer of one bottle of rosé, as the boss. He's always been purposefully non-corporate. The brand himself is shaking your hand, looking you in the eye, remembering your name. And there's irreverence written all over him.

For the past 30 years he's been well ahead of every swerve in Cape wine's many lurches. After South Africa's re-entry to world markets in 1994, he leapt on planes and worked European – mainly British at first - wine outlets from the bottom up, first mixing with the people who unpacked boxes and chose the eye-level shelves, then picking the brains of the wine advisors selling to the public, finally getting to the upstairs suits who place orders. "I've tasted what sells downstairs," he'd say. "If you give me your official specs, I'll do my best to match them, and I'll see you back here in a few weeks. Or, would you like to come out to see my vineyards, help me adjust to European tastes?" The trail to Fairview became well-worn; the wines juicier, friendlier and the labels as catchy and cheeky as Back himself.

Stiff delegations of grey crocodile-shoed gents from other outfits would arrive in London, present wines and announce: "These are the products of our long and glorious tradition." Chauvinism unbowed. Cape wine got off to a dreadful start.

Goats have always loomed large at Fairview – actually, a very mixed farm; his father Cyril was easily distracted, very resourceful, attracted to the unusual, his always too-long trousers trailing in the dust; Fairview was pigs, chickens, sheep, pheasants, ducks, goats and cheese; goats' cheese at first, then every kind of cheese.

When Charles Back started a line of easy-drinking wines with flippant goat labels – Goats du Roam, a fun word-play on Côtes du Rhône, for example - the French became testy. There were threatening calls. Far too good an opportunity for Back. He gathered workers, went into union-harangue mode. The French are undermining us, he told them, threatening our livelihoods. Shameful first world colonialism-imperialism all over again. T-shirts and slogans were produced. Struggle songs practised. Buses hired. Media alerted. Banners printed: 'Frogs, can't you stand the temperature? Aren't you rich enough? Don't starve the poor.' The chanting convoy thundered from Paarl into Cape Town, picketed the French Embassy. Crowds cheered. Riot police stood by. News-cameras whirred. Worldwide publicity. Priceless Fairview exposure.

"We became friends later, with the ambassador," says Back. "We had a good laugh and they left us alone. The ambassador told me: 'We won't give you that chance again.'"

A few critics might say Back's wines have never quite achieved the ultimate levels of quality and consistency. Frankly – though this isn't him speaking - I think it would simply be a huge yawn for him to try to make the finest, most elegant, stratospherically-priced southern hemisphere Côte Rôtie, year after year - and keep trying for 99 points. The futility of that would strike him as banal. Why submit to that capricious casino? Much more to his liking are research, experiment and innovation. He's in touch with his customers; they like the excitement, the constantly evolving styles, labels and ideas that stream out of Fairview.

He turned 60 in 2015. Has begun thinking of legacy. He's always been mindful of social responsibilities – his grandparents fled Lithuania with nothing, early in the 20th century, just over 100 years ago - but he's churning a few projects that would articulate a typically original and unstuffy approach to those goals. I am sworn to secrecy.

One of the (many) gifts he brought to Cape wine was, still is, **Fairview Viognier**. He pioneered this spicy French grape in South Africa, in a vineyard immediately below his home, back in the 1990s. It was overtly peachy, noticeably scented but less savoury than its Rhône namesake, and reflected Fairview's warmer climate. These latest vintages – 2014 tasted - come from cooler Darling, altogether more refined, with a salty minerality at the core. Gorgeous.

Prospecting for oil, consulting for international conglomerates – Vietnam, Syria, Indonesia, China, Dubai – may not be the usual launching pad to wine–growing in the KwaZulu Natal Midlands. But it was a perfectly logical idea and destination for Ian Smorthwaite. Wine and oil are very geological. He met Jane, a London Festival Ballet dancer, in Singapore. When they found Abingdon farm they decided: "This is our last stop, our Utopia." She's furiously busy running their eat-drink-and-let's-get-married-here destination, the Café at Abingdon. Ian is the vini-viticulture boffin: his wine quality, and the unique locality, now project enough appeal to leave him short of stock! Except at the Abingdon Café of course, where he happily discusses the wines with guests. Abingdon's altitude – 1150 m above sea level – negates some of the disadvantages of KZN's latitude, and its summer rains. (Rain in summer is not unknown to Bordeaux and Burgundy, either.) He's shown Chardonnay can be a winner here. He's nailed an attractive bubbly. He has his sights set on Nebbiolo. Laurie, their very highly qualified daughter, runs KZN's most serious wine education courses here, too.

Abingdon Estate Viognier 2013 is a triumph of appetising refinement – and no allowances made for its un-Mediterranean location. So appetising the vervet monkeys do their best to share the harvest. Has true – in fact quite vigorous - Viognier spice and aromas, carried by a fresh, ample and sappy palate. Peach, apricot and litchi wafts.

Eagles' Nest Viognier is an expressive, but not over-expressive example of this grape, perhaps because it's stylishly oaked. The floral spiciness and fruit in step alongside barely noticeable barrel notes. A beaut. Anytime drinking. 2013 tasted.

Chris Williams' **The Foundry Viognier 2013** reflects his personality, which is held-back, amused restraint. This is what you'll find in this elegant and quite soft dry white. Grapes are from Stellenbosch, fermented in barrels previously used for Chardonnay. An original approach which produces an original wine. So, while you do get floral and peachy Viognier wafts, they are subdued, allowing other intricate grapey nuances to insinuate themselves, and vary as you get deeper into the bottle. Williams' day job is at Meerlust; proprietor Hannes Myburgh encourages him to indulge himself with some tinkering on the side, provided the varieties and labels don't compete with Meerlust's.

WHITE BLENDS

Grenache Blanc, Clairette Blanche, and Palomino: lowly varieties? No longer. With old workhorse Chenin Blanc they feature in the modern Cape Dry White blends which are being hailed as a "discovery" for – and by - the wider wine world. A new South African wine of distinction. The girl next door has become a beauty right under our noses. These old vines have become valuable assets. All sorts of new and traditional winemaking techniques are being applied. And soils are being left alone to express themselves in the grapes.

Other felicitous dynamics have imposed themselves: the prohibitive cost of imported French oak has deterred the temptation to use this ubiquitous 'seasoning', so terroir uniqueness has been preserved, wine styles not blurred. The self-confidence among the crop of young winemakers has been palpable. And planting of numerous other warm-climate grape varieties has begun. Already Viognier, Roussanne, Marsanne, are enlivening blends.

The Swartland, and regions further west and north are headlining this news, but fine dry white blends are showing their paces in several other regions. Semillon has long featured in classy wines with Sauvignon Blanc, from Stellenbosch, Constantia and from around Cape Agulhas. Growers there are also intent on re-asserting themselves. The Great White Wine race is on…

THERE'LL NEVER BE ENOUGH

"They are adjusted for the unforeseen and accustomed to the unexpected": writer Karen Blixen's observation on the gifted and complicated Kikuyu people of Kenya where I grew up. It's a gear I try to engage when I'm about to meet Eben Sadie. The Eben whose horizon is now "rough, tough Africa" and "wine linked to our continent".

You need to expect big new bends among the verbal flourishes in his ever-evolving philosophies. He's a wisecracking, free-spirited surfer ablaze with new obsessions - and a guru of the current makeovers in Cape wine. He may be, like many others, about back to real basics and to nature, but he has twists all of his own. Some say he's the modern movement's patron saint. Friends call him "baby Jesus". Even detractors ambivalent or dismissive of his theories and wines love him. In the past 15 years he's both shaken and stirred. And been shaken himself.

"I'm thinking now wine must not even touch stainless steel tanks," he says as he wrestles with a large key and flings open the door to his tiny, white, chapel-like barrel cellar at Aprilskloof in the Swartland. Those oaky, dank, cobwebby, spilled-wine smells always stir the juices and we're looking at 20 super-thinly staved, custom-made French casks. Their contents are travelling 1st class. For centuries, this is how the greatest wines have been matured. We're juiced up, ready.

But Sadie announces he's now off wood. "Why do we rely so much on oak? I want to phase it out from my wines." Out with all that evocative folklore, really? This is some ratcheting up of the tenets that have earned him and his exclusive, expensive wines, fans all over the world – by keeping things sustainable, ethical, pure, authentic, simple, wine true to its origins - and beautiful. The beauty is in the absence of adornment. No acid, or other adjustments, no additives, subtractions, like filtering. Oak has been absolved, by ritual and tradition, and its own 'naturalness', of the 'additive' charge. But Sadie is right: a wine poured into a new oak barrel absorbs a deluge of powerful, non-grapey aromas and tastes – vanilla, caramel, spice, clove, smoke, char, toast and scores more. The most expensive wines in the world are all tarted up with oak. Until now, including his own.

The lonely little chapel on a slope I first saw many years ago was rented space then. Now he's bought part of the property and it's an outhouse guarding a growing cluster of buildings with, as you'd expect from this archetypical rugged individual, no concession to landscaping, artifice or symmetry. The winery is filled with imported egg-shaped cement tanks, re-modelled successors to the classical amphorae that preceded the wooden barrel as a wine container, based on the much-trumpeted 'golden ratio' – and here we're tipping into the philosophical end of things and the biodynamics of wine farming – and life.

Back to gadgets – or the lack of them in this cellar. He's always detested machinery. Crushing, mashing grapes, de-stalking grinders, violent pumping: not for Sadie Family Wines. The minutely porous cement gives wine life, inert stainless steel can't. "In a steel tank it's buggered, life snuffed out, wine in a coffin." So long, steel and oak, in Sadiedom. But in a while. It'll be a phased outing.

Another denunciation this morning: Sauvignon Blanc. "It should be banned from the face of the earth. So coarse and loud." He thrashes his fists up and down as if he'd like to beat it to death. "We have hundreds and hundreds of grape varieties and what have we done? The wine world is dominated by just five of them. How dumb is that? We should plant what belongs, not what sells."

Above all, he worships venerable, aged vines. And he's a strugglenik: vines must suffer, must have to crawl deep down into soil to suck up those precious elements that form a wine's taste and character and confirm its origins. No pampering irrigation or fertilizer or weeding. They must win out against the competing undergrowth, so their berries are small, thick-skinned, flavour-packed. They must overcome nature to authenticate their naturalness. Otherwise they're like fat, wobbly battery chickens or crowded feedlot cattle stuffed with antibiotics. How strange, he seems to say, that you'd want to manipulate, soften, acidify grapes and deny or blur their pedigrees.

A wine that smacks of the commercial, of assembly-line ordinariness, of meaningless blending, of man's unnecessary interference, of anything that renders wine a mere product rather than an 'expression' of its birthplace, its soils and vines, is common. Not for him. He's targeting drinkers and collectors who understand art. Not the all-I-want-is-what-I-like hordes. He makes only 50000 bottles a year, or 137 bottles a day, for thousands of Sadie Family followers and restaurateurs here and in the 30 countries he exports to. There'll never be enough.

Stephen Fry said it nearly perfectly in his *Chronicles*: "As in food, so in the wider culture, anything …. savoury, sharp, complex, ambiguous or difficult is ignored in favour of the colourful, the sweet, the hollow and the simple."

A few messianic types among Sadie's flock there may be; you sometimes pick up a certain sanctimony, and mutterings about "dinosaurs of the industry", wedded to commercial wines. From the other side, there are acerbic rejoinders about young know-it-alls; and "dodgy wines by dodgy winemakers". But despite his occasional hyperbole, Sadie himself does not come over as particularly puritanical, and certainly not arrogant or derogatory about those who disagree with him.

The crucial evidence of course lies in the wines: marvellous – in my view. Nothing funky, dodgy or rustically cockeyed about them. Actually, pretty much like him – complex, original, individual and expressive, though that's only partially true. His colourful, attractively reckless chatter sometimes might suggest he's a bit breezy in the winery. But he's a very careful and dogged winemaker. Those who value balance, especially tannin balance, and structure, will not find his wines wanting. They are not easy, simple, fruity, forward, over-smooth or floppy. His frantic tasting of European wines is all about improving his own performance. "Sometimes those tannins of theirs are so beautiful, they cut you at the knees with envy," he says.

Sadie Family Palladius This Cape White is already etched into South African lore as a pioneer of the new national way with Chenin Blanc-led blends – in this instance, with Roussanne and seven or so other white varieties, allowed to integrate over a leisurely couple of years in cement tanks, the 'golden ratio' egg-shape ones. Sadie has the latest versions, said to improve both fermentation and ageing, the oxygen held and exchanged in the tank walls micro-oxygenating the wine, and the shape beneficial in other complex – even mystical, some say - ways. They're increasingly in vogue worldwide. In any event, the wine is light and expressive at the same time, a rounded generosity. Old, dryland bush-vine grapes make up a large proportion of the wine, contributing to its hallmark absence of fussy fruitiness – a grown up, earthy-savoury maturity with mid-palate intensity and width; 2012 last tasted. Restrained, integrated, a beauty from a modern Cape winemaking star. Sold out the minute it's made.

The blends in the **Sadie Family Old Vine Series** are rare and difficult to find, too. And very good. If you come across any of the following, you will be fortunate: **Kokerboom** – Semillon blanc and gris; '**T Voetpad** – Chenin, Semillon, Palomino; **Skerpioen** - Chenin and Palomino.

OVER-PERFORMANCE

"The Viking I presume?" A 2m – 6 ft 7 inch - blond with a bottle under each arm is striding up the street in Riebeek Kasteel, the epicentre of the Swartland Revolution, and he laughs: "That's me." Donovan Rall (left, opposite) would be noticed anywhere. As are his wines. At home, in 2015, these were R200 a bottle. Steep, some locals thought. Not influential UK wine writer Jancis Robinson. "Under-priced," she told her Financial Times and website readers. Exactly the reaction Rall intended: "My aim is to have my wines over-perform at the price."

We repair to the hotel veranda, people-gaze a bit, but this is a very sleepy place, and he opens the bottles, pours, shoves them back into the coolers, and we chat. The "Revolution" – laissez faire, oxidative winemaking, sustainable and organic vineyard management – gets more pushback these days and I ask why.

Long pause. "Let's turn that around. Why," wonders the man they inevitably call the gentle giant, "when you can make great wine pretty naturally, farm naturally without pesticide and the rest, would you not want to farm and make wine that way?"

Rall lives and consults in Stellenbosch – he graduated from the university there with an Oenology and Viticultural degree and then, as you now do, worked all over the world including France and New Zealand, to widen horizons and experience. After-hours and between his day jobs he makes just a few of his own wines, grapes sourced mainly in the Swartland where he rents cellar space. They're very smart, very 'in'.

Rall White has the experts in a flutter of approval; has been showered with 5 stars. Mainly Chenin Blanc. "Chenin translates soil so well," he says. Teamed with Verdelho, Chardonnay and bit of Viognier. Fermented very unhurriedly – 3 to 9 months – in old oak, on its fermentation lees, stirred occasionally. With a stirring result: balanced, pure, fresh and lingering - with a gorgeous limey, mineral core. Very individual. Tasted the 2013. Loved it.

SHATTERINGLY GOOD

Wendy and Hylton Appelbaum of DeMorgenzon would lace anything – wine included, obviously – with their anything-is-possible sense of adventure. Hylton sets up speakers to entertain and ripen the vines and wines, literally, loudly. Baroque Bach, he explains with a straight face, enjoying your incredulity, does make a difference. In the Cape's blustery winds, can they hear anything? "Of course." I wonder whether some Touareg Kora strings might work too. "That'd be African, Bach was not of our continent - where's your sense of place"?

Colourful diversions abound here: floral archways edge the close-planted vine rows; there's a vast sacred lotus pond (Hylton's special interest); the loos are papered with sheet music; the extravagantly curated tasting rooms echo, yes, to Bach. But the wines rise above the sound and special effects. They are brilliant. It is the Appelbaums' calm, organised, confident young winemaker, Carl van der Merwe (above, right), who seems to supply the safe, steadying pair of hands here. A killer combination. As is their **DeMorgenzon Maestro White**, a shatteringly good blend.

I have a – doubtless misplaced – aversion to messing with decent Chardonnay and relegating it to second, or third fiddle in some mix. But this is grown-up, broad, mouth-filling, silky, with a muted spiciness and lemon-tang finish. Van der Merwe has combined barrel-fermented Chenin, Chardonnay, Roussanne and Viognier, all made separately before blending. The 2012 was the Platter Guide's White Wine of the Year in 2014. That's not me, but a team of serious judges tasting blind, for pay. Is it a lesson? Don't get hung up on single varieties? Think about hybrid – mongrel? – vigour.

Van der Merwe blends fussily – even without music (if Hylton's not around). He tries to mute Viognier's peachy bounce where others might try to enhance it. He uses Roussanne for texture, Chenin for acidity. He intends to include Grenache Blanc in future – the in-grape now, even in its red form. Does he need to gild this lily? Let's see.

OH BUT WE HAD FUN!

Abrie Bruwer is a Cape wine iconoclast, with a permanent, naughty gleam in his eye. An Afrikaner who, unusually, abhors both rugby and hunting. Scores of idiosyncratic adaptations - he's an inveterate machine modifier, lately with grape harvesters – have not survived long at Springfield. Before they are adjusted, re-made. But one experiment hasn't been repeated: ocean-ageing his wines.

The family seaside home was designated for the idea. Large iron cages, with racks, were specially made to contain a few hundred bottles. Bruwer and family, including his sister, Jeanette, the Springfield partner and marketer (once a practising dentist), hauled them aboard their boat and sailed out to sea to lower the cages into the waters – not too deep, sandy beds. "Where's a pen?" he shouted, as the boat drifted. He needed to record co-ordinates. By the time he'd scratched the details on the side of the vessels with a fishing lure, he was no longer over the maturation spot. It took 15 years of intermittent diving around the shifting sand banks to locate the barnacled stash. Result: no discernible difference when tasted with the vintages stored quietly – unrolled by the tides - at Springfield's winery.

"Oh, but we had fun!" says Abrie. Jeanette's memories are not quite as rosy. She recalls bubble-wrapping a few bottles for a London wine show. When she unwrapped them "the whole hall smelled like a fishmonger's," she said. "I had to grab them and flee outside onto the pavement, Knightsbridge, or somewhere. We hadn't scraped off all the stuff clinging to the bottles. Putrefaction deluxe!"

Bruwer has often been ahead of the game in wine-growing and making; among the first to get into wild yeast fermentation. He's adapted trellising widths, heights and directions for his machine harvesters – though, naturally, he first modified the machines themselves, at the factory in France!

"Twenty years or so ago, these were rough machines, berries and leaves were mangled, often together. The latest versions are beauties," he says with pride. He's not defensive: "Hand-crafted wines, from hand-picked grapes, blah blah," he says. "This technology is a life-saver. We harvest swiftly in the cool, dead of night; the berries are clean, they're dosed, automatically in tiny spurts, with anti-oxidant sulphur, and long before dawn they're in the cellar perfectly cold and safe to start their journey into wine. We lose no freshness or fruitiness."

Robertson's lime-rich soils accentuate acid liveliness in wines and in Springfield's case, especially in the Sauvignons, they've sometimes been over-crisp for some palates. They're designed around Bruwer's own keen appetite. I asked him about the brisk acidities. "We've pulled back a bit in the latest vintages," he says, by shifting harvesting dates. The lime soil means these wines never have to be adjusted upwards for higher acids. Natural wines?

Bruwer insisted we arrive for lunch. Robertson folk are famously hospitable. It means tasting 'over the mountain' as they say, is always a slow affair. He had flown in a couple of hours earlier from Stellenbosch in his Mooney. "Just nicked my wing on the way out – some guy parked badly." No hair turned. "Squid's on the menu," he says. "I eat fish five days a week, would be seven if my wife (an English GP in Robertson) didn't insist on meat sometimes!"

His wines are labelled to describe how they're made – Wild Yeast – Work of Time – Méthode Ancienne – Whole Berry – Life from Stone (from formidably rocky, boulder-strewn soil). The reds include a wild ferment, 35 year-old single vineyard Cabernet Sauvignon – the Ancienne - which encompasses all of the above. Now comes an exception. **Springfield Miss Lucy 2014** features Sauvignon but with Semillon and Pinot Gris to widen and calm the blend. Delicious, unpretentious. An all-day friend, not clawing for constant attention. Miss Lucy is a name for the Red Stumpnose, native to the South African coast – and now endangered. Predictably, brilliant with seafood.

THE MIXOLOGIST

Adi Badenhorst's 60-plus-year-old Chenin Blanc and Grenache vines – their fruit quality is at the core of his success – are part of the nature-in-naked-glory idea, unirrigated, untrellised, weeded only notionally, unpampered, brusquely pruned. Treated, he says, "as organically as possible". Is there a gap for some doubt in the "as possible"? Possibly. "Well, we have to remain practical; we're in the wine business." A few spot - rather than blanket - sprayings against some disease; but non-systemic dustings of sulphur to ward off leaf-shrivelling fungal mildew attacks don't count – this is sulphur free of a 'pesticide' charge, as 'clean' and everyday as soap in the bathroom, he says.

The vineyards' main duty is to supply small crops - 4-5 tons/ha - of small bunches and smaller berries, the smaller the more naturally and powerfully flavoured the better. The vines in their orange-red autumnal colours are also useful visuals surrounding the collection of unassuming old Cape Dutch buildings strung out in a line overlooking the wide Swartland landscape.

He steers us away from the winery through a huge kitchen where chefs are prepping food for a wedding to the strains of a saxophonist practising her musical gift for the bride and groom. Cornelia Badenhorst is a famous master-minder of rustic-chic parties. By the time her husband has herded us into his office-den, pulled out bottles of "my new, drier, tonic water", changed the music, he's well into a tangential disquisition on the horrors of "overly-sweet" commercial tonics that "pulverise" decent gin. "And I love my gin," he says. Almost as much, apparently, as his new Caperitif – a Vermouth-style assemblage recreating a local product once one of the staples of international cocktail bars, known as the "ghost" ingredient. "I'm actually a mixologist," he says, but won't reveal more about what's in the retro-labelled bottle, except buchu from the Cape mountains. And there's mint among the herbs in his tonic. Both beverages are commercially available. Expect more.

His private quarters have the crowded, curated look of a museum – a considered jumble of posters, glass cases containing stuffed animals and fish - and now he's pouring thimbles of a dry Muscat de Frontignan distillation - from a Calvados bottle. Very arresting. "Perfect with Eggs Benedict at breakfast," he says. His riotous and serious, in parts, food-and-wine events are always overbooked. He chooses chefs who chime with his organic sympathies. It's raucous-thoughtful.

"I don't want to be defined just by my wines," he says – superfluously. "I don't want to fall into that trap, it's only part of what we do." Is this the start of a little detour into mysticism and biodynamics? Ecological harmony and our duty to the wider social environment, beyond personal financial ambition? If so, it's unnecessary. We don't need convincing. We are stumbling away happily, out of time. And forgotten – or been deviated from – wine tasting! "Happens quite a lot," he admits when I call later to plug the gaps in my notes. And probably just as well; I taste samples later, alone, quietly.

To this brief – and inadequate – sketch of so colourful and thoughtful a man, I can add something I learned decades ago, when on a committee to give higher education bursaries to 'previously disadvantaged' students. Badenhorst was at the time growing vegetables and trying to flog them to Cape Town chefs. He sneakily snuck in an application. But he is from an old Cape wine family. Of course we had to bin it on racial empowerment grounds. However, I got to see his grades. This is one sharp cookie – all that risk-taking is finely and scientifically judged. That may take the edge off the no-interference-from-man line a bit. But not the thrust of the Swartland movement as a whole.

In profile, Badenhorst – big-beard, jutting jaw – is a ringer for another revolutionary, Karl Marx. But our man's gaps between revolutionary theory and practice are more palatable.

AA Badenhorst Family Wines White Blend Free-style wine-making at its most interesting. 2013 dry, with Chenin at the core, the largest ingredient. With some 10 other white or whiteish varieties, like Grenache Gris, Verdelho, Palomino, and other usual suspects - Marsanne, Roussanne, Viognier. As if Badenhorst is reluctant to leave anything out, even Chardonnay gets a look in, and Semillon. Oak doesn't. Large – 1200 and 3000 litre – old oak vats. Theme is old, bush vine fruit, from the home Kalmoesfontein vineyards, plus bits and pieces from Paardeberg Mountain and wider Swartland. An instinctive, cheffy, bit of this, bit of that, season to taste, recipe. Relaxed, non-reductive (see My Take notes) wine-making, no filtration, no fining, no cultivated yeasts, sulphur at minimums. This guy could become an habitué of any Rhône village. So what about the wine? Quite advanced straw hues, quiet, grown-up nose, not wanting to draw much attention. The palate builds slowly, then fills your mouth. I'm getting bit of peach, almonds, heather, minerals. Badenhorst says: "Stone fruits… and slight phenolic edges supporting the fruit." Whatever. A Swartland charmer? Absolutely. How long will it last? Not sure. But the way it's made, don't see any quick collapse.

AND

John Seccombe goes along with the broad artisanal winemaking principles of minimalist intervention by man. But he is also a reassuring antidote for the growing body of cynical punters unamused by what they call "all this evangelical bullshit, earth-mother authenticity, I'm-only-a-midwife, not-a-winemaker". He says: "We mustn't box ourselves into a corner. I intend to remain flexible, undogmatic. However, I do want to surprise and please my clients; I want them to say, 'Oh, this is a wine from left field but I like it'." And they have, and do.

This relatively new kid on the vineyard block, with his new family label – Thorne and Daughters – is an experienced hand. After making a huge career leap from computers to wine, he studied in the UK, and worked stages all over the world – Barossa, the Languedoc, California, England, Alsace - where he still does each harvest, during the Cape's winter downtime. (Which means he's a Riesling specialist. I wish he'd put that to use locally.) Back home he picked up more skills in the wineries of Thelema and Iona, until he and photographer wife Tasha were ready to fly solo. Their maiden 2013 yielded a minuscule 4500 bottles. And a shower of encore-requesting bouquets. It looks as though he's here to stay. Happy to let his French rust and decline repeated job offers from Alsace.

Thorne and Daughters Rocking Horse Cape White 2013 This honeysuckle-scented 4-way blend of Roussanne, Chardonnay, Chenin Blanc and Semillon, is made for seafood and roast chicken. Lovely. Much appreciated, too, by John Seccombe's advisor and business partner: father-in-law Richard Poynton. A ruddy-faced, Hemingway-bearded, charmingly rowdy culinary legend, who led a revolt against the food while a pupil at posh Michaelhouse, Richard is chef, host and owner of Cleopatra Mountain Farmhouse hotel, in the Drakensberg. His trademark "first butter your oven" style established Cleo as a gourmand-gourmet destination decades ago; he has a cellar to match. The family wines are clearly conceived with the simultaneous pleasures of eating and drinking in mind.

David Aristargos Complex dry white blend from David and Nadia Sadie; composition varying each vintage. Latest 2013 and onwards with Viognier and Roussanne ascendant. Satisfying, savoury aromatics plus peachy, white-fruit scents, snatches of aniseed dancing in the background. Should become even more complex in the bottle.

David and Nadia Sadie's cellar at Paardebosch (above)

B Vintners was launched in 2015 to "celebrate Africa – the vine, our heritage, our terroirs and our future," says Gavin Bruwer, of this partnership-range with his cousin Bruwer Raats. "To tell a story about our land, open horizons." Their **Haarlem to Hope** is an unusually complex, savoury Stellenbosch blend: mostly Chenin – flinty fruit, with pear and melon notes; plus 9% Semillon for texture, and a bit of spicy Muscat d'Alexandrie, "it flutters in and out," says Bruwer. Haarlem was the port from which early Dutch navigators sailed to the Cape of Good Hope; the three grape varieties are "African", or at least, more African than others. The first two were among the foundation stock brought by the Dutch, the last is regarded as indigenous to Africa – grown in early Egyptian vineyards near Alexandria.

Chamonix White Semillon-Sauvignon Blanc benefits from former winemaker Gottfried Mocke's off-duty interest in food, cooking and re-inventing traditional dishes with his wife Anna Marie. "Green Sauvignon with any 'green' food – vegetables etc - tastes horribly metallic," he says. So he toned down Sauvignon with peachy-straw Semillon and came up with this clever, generous, not too steely, Bordeaux-style white blend. Delicious.

David Niewoudt Ghost Corner The Bowline Sauvignon with barrel-fermented Semillon, serious all-round food wine.

Fable Mountain Jackal Bird Tulbagh's deep shale soils, in the Witzenberg foothills, were the reason for American Charles Banks to include this property in his selection of international (Australia, Chile, Argentina, California,) terroir-specific vineyards. Run by organic-conscious viti-viniculturalists Rebecca Tanner and Paul Nicholls, whose wines are finding global favour. A good representative of the fashionable 'New Age' South African dry white blends: Chenin Blanc base with Grenache Blanc, Chardonnay, Roussanne, Viognier. Generous, wide mouthfeel, solid core. Stand-back wine-making techniques: wild ferment, no fining, no filtration etc.

Fairview Nurok White Blend About 25% each Chenin, Viognier, Grenache Blanc and Roussanne. You may pick up traits of one or two of the grape varieties; I don't bother. It's a complete, wholesome and complex, invigorating, totally versatile drink, for fine dining and al fresco sipping. Suggestion: read the back label, one of the few worth the effort; it tells a stirring story of bravery and loyalty among Di (née Nurok) Back's ancestors in Arctic adversity. 2013 tasted.

The Grande Provence White 2013 Significant plaudits for Karl Lambour's blend of "noble varieties", says the label, perhaps a bit ambitiously upgrading Chenin Blanc and Viognier. But the result is serious, weighty; opens with faint signature Viognier floral notes; mouth-filling, rounded, Chenin on palate – more satisfying substance than flighty fruitiness.

Mullineux White These Swartland white blends last brilliantly – surprisingly to those who've, evidently, been under-rating Clairette Blanche's (and its alcohol-moderating?) role in a blend. A 2011 tasted in 2015 was fresh as a daisy, not a hint of ageing. Chenin provides the core – about 65%, with Clairette at about 25% and rest Viognier. Quiet nose, but there's integrated harmony with a savoury, nutty-almondy aspect; eminently suitable at table. Alc. at 13% also a bonus.

Nitida Coronata Integration 2013 is simply superb. And individual – in the benign and optimistic sense. One can buy the hyperbole for once; the barrel-fermented Semillon does smooth and fill out, where the tank fermented Sauvignon Blanc, the other blend partner, so often shrill, is in its corner whistling quietly. There's flinty grip, there's palate generosity. There's fruit, there's savoury width. Certainly meets owner-winemaker Bernhard Veller's memo to himself: "Make wines that our customers enjoy drinking as much as we do." And, too, "rely on distinctive Durbanville fruit for impact" (not wood). We ordered a case immediately.

Savage White A Cape White Blend in full cry, another coup from Duncan Savage. The 2014 from Sauvignon Blanc (73%) and Semillon (27%). Superior minerally substance combines with fleshy, complex but muted capsicum and green melon notes. Beautifully deep, flowing food wine. Tune to change in coming vintages. In 2015 this White will feature 5 varieties. And in 2016, possibly up to 10. Exciting stuff. Keep a look-out.

Simonsig Red Ox is Frans Malan all over: "He couldn't resist planting 'new' vine varieties; he tried 25 of them, including – then – obscure vines like Verdelho," says Johan Malan fondly, recalling his late father. This is a brilliantly playful, original dry mix of barrel-fermented Roussanne touched up with about 14% Chenin Blanc in 2013. Substantial but graceful; savoury-fruity flavours vying interestingly.

Sijnn Dry White A big-hearted dry white, with the generous quality and complexity that's generating respect internationally for this category of Chenin-based South African blend. Attractive savoury-spicy fruitiness on palate; wide spread of flavours, starting with a honey-blossom bouquet. Slick, glossy texture. Wild ferment in big used oak, no filtration. Predominantly Chenin - about 75% - with Viognier and Roussanne from relatively coolish Malgas coastal area. 2012 and 2013. From painstaking, up with it winemaker David Trafford of Stellenbosch.

Solms-Delta Amalie A clever dry white blend, 2013 generous, palate-drenching Grenache Blanc-led with Roussanne, Viognier in attendance – hints of the Mediterranean - then back home to be filled out with Chenin. From a Franschhoek property with organic sustainability high on its agenda. And equally sound worker participation programmes.

I often prefer Sauvignon in a blend, as in the **Steenberg Magna Carta**. A grand name for King John's much-ignored undertaking at Runnymede in 1215. Steenberg MD and former cellarmaster John Loubser explains – or doesn't: "It established the precedent that the law is above Kings." Well, yes. And it's great to drink, too.

Sumaridge Maritimus 2012 Sounds good on paper – Sauvignon Blanc 49%; Chardonnay 25%, Semillon 21%. Even better tasted. No grape dominates: even Semillon's lanolin, and Sauvignon's flinty thrust are tamed; it's lightly oaked, is integrated with pleasingly faint peachy-lime wafts in the finish. A wine superior to the sum of its parts. Made by Gavin Patterson, whom we first met in Zimbabwe, trying to make wine under the baleful eyes of farm-invading "war-vets".

Thelema's immaculate vineyard management extends to their Elgin farm, the cool, distinctive climate and its soils broadening Gyles Webb's wine options. All grapes are cold-trucked down the mountain to be vinified at Thelema in Stellenbosch. The **Sutherland Viognier-Roussanne** is among the very best of our Mediterranean-variety whites; peaches-and-pears Viognier marries with Roussanne's smooth amplitude for a deep, elegant mouthful. Good for glugging on its own. But also a food partner, especially white-meat dishes.

Vergelegen GVB White 2010 A grand, wide-bodied, full and complex combination of oaked, barrel-fermented Semillon and Sauvignon, varying proportions, but usually more Semillon, 50-40%, than the Bordeaux norm. "Softer on the teeth," maintains winemaker André van Rensburg.

THE NEW WAVE

Something beautiful and strange has been happening in South African wine. And it may, just may, rejuvenate the industry. Local per capita consumption has never been lower. We're export-dependent, in a flooded world market. One of our problems is that wine isn't more like beer. It is simply not as easy to drink. Alcohol levels in Cape wines have been soaring. It hits me every time we return from Europe and endure the shocks of re-entry: the sheer brawn – 14,5% alc. and 15% alc. - of so many local wines, leavened, but not sufficiently, by their softer prices.

These are not easy drinking. And it is a defeatist cliché to put it all down to our climate.

A new generation (not age-specific) of adventurous winemakers is now on the case, targeting significantly lower – in the 11%-12,5% range - alcohol wines. Lightness, freshness, tastiness – easy drinkability - are their goals. They're making real breakthroughs. Not all the experiments have come off; they're taking flak for some unconventional bottlings. But relief is in sight. The grand heavies will always be around. But the choices are widening. The new, more manageable wines will gather up converts - and retrieve others who've drifted away from the grape.

Critics of these alternative wines and their makers should trust the markets and consumers: they'll make the call on ultimate viability. Cape wine has nothing to lose – probably a lot to gain – from all the fevered experimentation. It's a healthy change, pushing boundaries. The past was constricted by excessive conformity.

Among those allowing their wines to emerge naturally from the vineyard instead of being nipped and tucked and botoxed in the cellar, are, in particular, two groups of young winemakers whose name-tags are misleadingly belligerent. A bunch of nice guys and girls making nice wines: what's to get revved up about? But label them young guns, or even vintage muskets, as the older-generation modernists are dubbed; or flaming revolutionaries: now you're talking. It's a wine war! Much sexier. And not just good marketing: behind it all is a package of solid expertise, real flair, and a commitment to make wines that shout: South Africa, and not France or the Rhine. It's an exciting time to be a winemaker here. It's an even more exciting time to be a wine drinker. Here a brief resumé of the two most visible groups re-energising Cape wine.

Elsewhere in this book, many more examples of how other winemakers, some activists of decades ago, are now clearly upping their games.

THE SWARTLAND REVOLUTION

The idealistic (and realistic too) enthusiasm and the chemistry among five young, like-minded individuals based in the Swartland, determined to create an authentic wine identity for their region, has been a brilliant marketing – and wine quality-enhancing – success. For all of South African wine. The five: Andrea and Chris Mullineux of Mullineux, Eben Sadie of Sadie Family, Callie Louw of Porseleinberg, Adi Badenhorst of AA Badenhorst Family are a team of 'all the talents' – including the gift of the gab. And backed by solid oenology and viticulture degrees and extensive international experience. They drew up winegrowing and winemaking codes to emphasise the authentic, the natural and the organic – in vineyard and vinification, where minimalism was a priority. If followed, wines can carry the Swartland Independent Certification sticker on bottles. Soon, nearly 30 growers and winemakers signed up to this voluntary code. Many included free-spirited winemakers, without properties, buying in grapes, renting cellar space. They haven't boxed themselves into a corner though; in weaker years – 2014 was one when low acids needed adjusting upwards - a grower/maker can opt out temporarily from certification, without expulsion. And qualify in following years.

The "Revolution" is celebrated, renewed, at an annual – few-holds-barred – festival in Riebeek Kasteel drawing hundreds from all over South Africa. Celebrated speakers come: Lebanese Chateau Musar's acclaimed Serge Hochar was the 2014 guest of honour shortly before he died. "Some people think we're just a bunch of pot-smoking hippies…" smiles the leader of the Swartlanders, Eben Sadie. "It's true we don't ban surfers!"

Fusillades from envious competing regions have followed: "Scavengers without commitment nor capital," said some. "Men at arms without farms."

So-so, perhaps too adventurous, speculative wines seeped out of the Swartland sometimes (even embarrassing Revolution founders – none of whom is exactly landless) but there are also stunners made by youngsters with only a surf board to their name. "Why should the size of our wallets be the metric of worth?" they complained.

It's a lovely war. And it's provided at least three invaluable benefits: because they're situated among old and untrellised vineyards, many of the newly fashionable Chenins and Cape White blends have distinctive qualities – and Swartland origin labels on them, winning international kudos, batting for South Africa; many of the old vineyards, destined for grubbing up, have been saved. And, third, the Swartland success has revved up every other Cape wine region.

Envy and excitement have spread and the schisms have wreaked renewal everywhere. Four men and a woman, sharing beliefs and a coherent plan, have had fun – and spread it.

(from left) Jeanine Craven, Lucinda Heyns, Gavin Bruwer, Ryan Mostert, Tremayne Smith, Jasper Wickens and Mick Craven: Young Guns class of 2015.

THE YOUNG GUNS

This is a group invented and championed by the crisp, cutting-edge young Cape Town (but online everywhere) wine merchant Roland Peens of Wine Cellar. Importer of French, Italian and Spanish wines but also energetic promoter of local wines that "push the boundaries". Since 2011 Peens has chosen a handful of Young Guns a year and organised the liveliest tastings of innovative wines at road shows around the country. The mantra is "Tossing out the Textbooks" on wine.

The 2015 show included 14 wines from 8 of these New Frontiersmen and women. Some from the Swartland, others from Stellenbosch, whose youngsters are not to be outdone. Many of the most original and engaging – and internationally-acclaimed - wines in this book come from past or present Young Guns. There's loud music, anything from Led Zeppelin to Johannes Kerkorrel (chosen by each winemaker in turn); there's no formal, dreary tasting routine, but irreverent chatter; the dress code is totally casual - shorts, flipflops, skateboard caps, tattoos. The Guns pour for each other, support each other, it's all dynamic accord; they're committed to innovation, to organic farming, to minimal, uninhibited, "oxidative" winemaking; to letting the land and their sites speak; to disdain for new oak.

It's revivalist – but they politely do not smear the old guard. Their expertise and knowledge is usually astounding, their attitudes freed-up. Every one of those 14 wines had something significantly different to say; one or two strayed up the alcohol levels but each had evident points of departure. I invested in 10 of them. They feature in this book under their respective varieties or blends. The (mostly) young audience loved them, too.

THE ADVOCATES

Here are two strong and visionary individuals who both came to wine from the law and drove astonishing changes, in Rosa Kruger's case helping to save precious old vineyards and opening new taste horizons for South Africans and the world; in Robert Parker's, challenging conventions, shaping palates, rocking markets. In very different ways, both have influenced the course of South African wine.

THE VINE ADVOCATE

If you go to find these vineyards, perhaps you'll also find a basketful of fresh pomegranates, the perfume of ripe quince, or mullet on a fishing line, a drop of fiery witblitz at Dwarskersbos, the scents of buchu under your heel, dried rooibos, the subtle odour of a vineyard in flower, strands of barbed wire from the Boer War – to keep the Tommies off the farm... Rosa Kruger, from her website listing 3538 hectares of old vineyards, seven planted before 1905. **iamold.co.za**

Viticulturalist Rosa Kruger is the warrior queen of South Africa's modern wine makeover – riding to the rescue of a priceless, fading heritage in ancient vines; championing humble, long-ignored grape varieties like Grenache and Cinsaut; fighting her corners all over the winelands, from the most remote, marginalised vines up the West Coast to forgotten pockets in fashionable Franschhoek.

Her fieldwork has nourished the growth of a new, national wine genre, the South African Dry White blend – centred largely around old vineyards, Chenin Blanc in particular. The genre, and its growing recognition globally, have done much to boost local confidence. After 20 years of forever "coming in from the cold" of apartheid isolation and sanctions, still dependent on exports and patronising views of overseas "experts" as a New World wine country overshadowed and out-priced by New Zealand and Australia, Cape wine needs this morale-boosting jolt.

Rosa Kruger is unafraid of confrontation. Perhaps, I wonder, even relishes it. She gave up a newspaper (*Die Beeld*) job in Johannesburg because she loathed the claustrophobic politics – though she is clearly very political, as you'd expect from a great, great granddaughter of President Paul Kruger. She then qualified as a lawyer but finally, in her 40s, found her metier in the winelands and in exploring the soul of the vine. She is self-taught; two Stellenbosch University academics, Prof Eben Archer, a viticulturalist, and Dawid Saymaan, South Africa's leading soil scientist, became her guru-mentors, and she read widely, internationally. Then she invaded a world of male viticulturalists. 'You've no idea how difficult it's been," she says.

An early benefactor was Johann Rupert of Rupert Wines – and Richemont, the Swiss-based international luxury goods company with brands like Cartier, Piaget, Van Cleef & Arpels, James Purdey, Dunhill. He provided financial backing and inspiration for her vineyard researches and restoration initiatives and was an early beneficiary, gaining access to distinctive and rare fruit for his portfolios of wines. She then

moved from Stellenbosch to live among the Swartland Revolution growers at Riebeek Kasteel, where she works with Eben Sadie, Adi Badenhorst, Mullineux and Leeu Family Wines and many others further afield, including in Franschhoek and Stellenbosch. It won't be this restless, enquiring woman's last move.

But an enduring legacy will be her still-unfinished work on codifying the Cape's oldest viticultural treasures, beginning with a register of the location, age, variety and vineyard size of blocks 35 years old and older. It's on the web and shows South Africa has a respectably large acreage of aged vineyards. Most of their production has gone into bulk wine, and will continue to do so. Many gems have been found, more remain to be discovered.

Her role is tricky: she's become, effectively, a vineyard winebroker. A confidante to land owners and competing winemakers and virtual arbiter of many of their relationships. This is uncharted terrain for a vineyardist in South Africa. Who does she choose to alert first to some new hidden jewel? Often she parcels things out among several winemakers she believes would best 'match' the grapes. These are minefields. Futuristic wines formed in my head – and on my palate - when she outlined the prospects of securing unique vineyard X of old variety Y and steering the grapes to winemaker Z.

And what about plan B? As the Cape – on a drier, hotter climatic trajectory for a decade now - becomes even hotter and drier, what then? "We have to go further up into cooler mountains," she says. The wider industry doesn't seem to have much of a plan B yet. They'll be looking to the Krugers and other viticulturalists for a lead. She's been arranging the import and plantings of scores of grape varieties and specific clones never tried here before. They might provide some heat-resistant clues.

She delights in demolishing clichés. "They're always going on about how tiny yields make quality. Every vineyard, and its location, is different. Sometimes an old vineyard can provide quite handsome yields without compromising quality. These one-liners, one-size-fits-everything statements are nonsense. You have to know the grape variety and the vineyard. Above all, respect it. Don't bully it. We can safely prune for higher yields sometimes," she says.

"Long hang-time is another thing," she adds, referring to the idea that an extended period of grape bunches hanging on the vine improves flavour and quality in wine. "It's bullshit, that's often the way to take the heart out of a wine." She believes vines are individuals, responding differently to their handling; and that they have to be herded, sometimes with careful neglect, toward quality. There are 9-hour days in the burning sun or the driving winds of winter, when, at the end of the rows, a fire of vine-cuttings warms workers huddled for a quick coffee break. In my day, this was when I'd sneak a dop straight from a bottle, a good way to taste.

These are Rosa Kruger's best times. "I just love being out there. Okay, it's back-breaking but it's so stimulating. I want to listen to nature, learn; and listen to the vineyards too. They tell you a lot about themselves." And, she also enjoys mixing it with, training workers; salty humour never gets better. I am paraphrasing, but if the grandees of the shiny, air-conned boardrooms could hear the raunchy commentaries - amusement and contempt in about equal measure – of the people they employ, they might think harder about many things. Rosa Kruger is universally admired for her fieldwork, even among detractors who've been subjected to her asperity. Her vineyards are models of creative distinction.

She has been quoted as saying: "I don't like to speak about wines, only about vines… I love viticulture." I asked her about this: how can she go about her business shaping the character of vineyards – and therefore wines - and not be intensely, minutely interested in the outcome?

She explained what she does when winemakers ask her about new – actually old – vineyards, and whether she can locate a likely source of grapes. "I'll go and taste the guy's wines," she said. "Then I know what he's about, where to look. I'll know where to find a vineyard for him." This wasn't a complete answer. But one came soon enough when we got onto funkier wines. "You know, people are paying good money for a bottle. They don't want cloudy wine. That's silly. Producers have to be realistic."

So, she can and does wax on wine. There's a Rupert & Rothschild Baron Edmond Merlot-Cabernet Sauvignon/Franc blend she says I should try, with a whistle of admiration. "That is good." A fine tasting note. And a Kendall-Jackson-Anthony Beck collaboration, a new American-South African project, one wine from three vineyards which she supervises. Loads of character here, coming together in a wine named Capensis (see under Chardonnay).

THE WINE ADVOCATE

Baltimore lawyer Robert Parker launched *The Wine Advocate* in 1978, and swiftly became the world's most powerful wine critic. He doesn't mince words. He's swayed tastes and styles, ("Parkerised wines") cowing wine growers – including the mighty Bordelais – wherever American markets are their targets.

He popularised and refined his own 100-points ranking system, sniffed at by the French and British, though many of them now use it too. Any wine taking itself seriously, scoring in the eighties from Parker, was more or less toast. The 90s were safe, but it was the high 90s which sold wines. Retailers and restaurants used Parker points as the ultimate ratings agency.

Parker's palate favoured rich, ripe, deep, dark and dense reds. And the equivalent in whites. High alcohols were fine. I'm simplifying here, because he appreciates finesse too, especially in Champagne. But in general, his high-point wines were the antithesis of restrained, quiet elegance – a supposedly European preference, with fine cuisine. To Parker, and many others too, 'elegance' was a euphemism for mean, thin wines. To the European palate Parker's "fruit bombs" were simple, colonial, New World ruffians. To his European – Old World - critics, reducing quality, tradition, historic fame and acclaim, and anything as complex as personal taste, to a number was outright crassness.

Parker always gave as good as he got. And he was untainted by commercial advertising and promotional, consulting or trade hook-ups. He declined freebies, which he said clouded the writing of a number of British wine critics. He shook the French wine establishment to its foundations. But the French eventually began bottling less austere, richer riper, Parkerised wines.

The pendulum has since swung back, with a much greater diversity of styles – patterns discernible in South Africa too, which is why I'm recording this. Parker has sailed on, disputes notwithstanding.

The Burgundians eventually sued him – a wrangle settled out of court. Then French President Jacques Chirac awarded him France's prestigious Lègion d'Honneur, a 'defensive move' wrote *The New Yorker's* Adam Gopnik, in September 2004. Parker apparently shed a tear at the grand Paris occasion– and has since apologised to the Burgundians. But he remains unbowed, at the head of an enlarged team at *The Wine Advocate*, which he has sold to Singaporean investors. Nor has his growing infirmity – he walks with two canes, has chronic back problems and is large – dimmed his fighting spirit.

In the *New York Times* in 2015 he castigated the "Natural" wine people as "the Jihadist movements of non-sulphured wines, green, under-ripe, low alcohol insipid stuff promoted by the anti-pleasure police and neo-anti-alcohol proponents, another extreme and useless movement few care about". You have to admire this gumption. But where to cast our vote? Dense and deep, or taut and delicate, or green, neo-anti-alcohol?

It's not a cop-out to keep an open mind, to believe too much of the same is as boring in wine as in anything else. A favourite *vin ordinaire* house wine needs a rest after a few days on the trot. I like restraint in wine, especially next to any delicately-flavoured dish, but an emphatic Parker wine can be dramatic and fun occasionally. We need to interrupt the oats with bacon and eggs.

Parker has played a pivotal role in shaking up the world of wine. We now have healthier, broader choices everywhere.

MY TAKE ON...

ALCOHOL

If I were president for a day, the alcohol % on labels would state the figure within a decimal or two, more boldly, on the front of the label. At present there's a whole 1 degree leeway. A 14.5% wine is probably nearer 15.5% - too much. With rare exceptions – when you savour a couple of glasses over an hour or two – is a wine worth that alcoholic punch? You can't drive home. Science and viticulture are catching up with modern trends to lighter wines – at the quality-and health-conscious level. But surveys show 1 in 10 people still believe higher alcohol equates to better quality! In wine contests and shows, headier alcohol wines generally have more impact, collect more gongs. Only the most disciplined judges, tasting slowly, methodically backwards and forwards in a line-up of wines, can search out balance and elegant moderation in a thicket of alcohol-powered bruisers. (Of course, I would first fix the economy, balance the budget, strengthen the judiciary, jack up education, disarm the populace, jail the corrupt, revive the medical services, narrow the trade gap, obliterate racism and unemployment…)

BLIND TASTINGS vs SIGHTED

Endless hullabaloos. Commercial contests should be blind, where judges and tasters can't see, hear, read the label. The outcomes of those contests are not infallible and they are, like all wine drinking, utterly context-dependent and a fleeting snapshot. But they're at least demonstrably fairer, or should be: a level playing field in a competition. Critics of all kinds, however - of music, food, art, theatre, restaurants, beauty pageants, motor cars - review performances based on what they observe, hear and taste after gleaning, sighting, as much information as they think they need. And they're not necessarily ranking things; they're often simply cruising a gallery or exhibition admiring different artists or performers, who may all be geniuses! In matters of taste, there's a deficit of objective truth. It's emphatically subjective. How do you measure 'best' in food and drink, when each of us has thousands of differently calibrated taste buds and memories? Like this book, it's only an opinion. An invitation to dialogue. It's the big, should-be, well-understood caveat; constantly worth re-stating.

BUSH VINES, OLD VINES, DRYLAND VINEYARDS

All very in. A few generalisations: bush vines are free-standing - no trellising - lower to the ground, less gravity for the sap to defy. These tousled vines come into 'balance' easily - specially with age – and balance, as in leaf-to-bunch ratios, also favours fruit quality; crop yields are usually lower than in trellised vines. Older vines mean deeper, searching roots, equal more flavour, say the ampelographers. And lower yields of smaller berries - so again, finer wine quality potentially. These newly fashionable bush vines are invariably of an age. Veneration for the elderly. Now, a number of growers are replanting vineyards without trellising - as bush vines. Dryland means unirrigated. Wines reflect the vintage more clearly. Usually means smaller yields, struggling vines, ergo more characterful wines. And costlier.

CORKS AND SCREWCAPS

For everyday drinking, the screwcap is a sensible, safe option, with several advantages: easy to open; the bottle doesn't need to be stored on its side to keep the cork moist (otherwise it dries out, allows air into the wine and certain spoilage); the wine can't be "corked" – damaged by the chemical compound trichloranisole (TCA) sometimes present in cork bark, which gives off a musty wet paper/dishcloth smell that the human olfactory system can pick up in a few parts per trillion; and screwcaps don't crumble. The latest ones look much smarter, overcoming the "cheapness" charge. But they render a wine inert, completely sealed. Corks, by admitting minute amounts of air, allow a wine to "develop" over longer periods and so winemakers of age-worthy bottles, and many of their buyers, will continue to prefer corks. And of course they like corks for the aesthetics – and a bit of ceremony.

DECANTING

Breathing – decanting and hyper-decanting. How to "ready" a wine. The old, big question. Bill Gates's friend, physicist Nathan Myhrvold – for many years Microsoft's head of technology and research – prides himself on myth-busting. According to *The Economist*, Myhrvold whizzed 1982 Chateaux Margaux (not a cheap experiment) in a kitchen blender, and served glasses, whizzed and unwhizzed, blind, in "triangle tests", to British Masters of Wine. "They couldn't give the same verdict on two glasses treated identically," reported Myrhvold. This doesn't prove hyper-decanting, as it's called, does the trick. But I've tried the Myhrvold *méthode frappé* on 75 doctors at a conference at Spier. A young Cabernet. Blind of course. Overwhelming preference: 85% - in favour of the whizzed wine. Conventional oxygenating - decanting - certainly airs and softens. There are good gadgets that 'cascade' wine, increasing air exposure as wines are poured, from bottle to decanter. I often pour twice. And drink within a couple of hours. Simply removing the cork doesn't do it. The molecular activity in the neck of the bottle is next to zero.

FOOD AND WINE

White meat with white wines, red meat with reds? Usually a sensible idea, but strict food and wine pairing conventions are generally out now. Modern is free-style. So relax. But Pinot Noir, so fussy as a grape, is a slut as a wine: goes with anything. Ditto any time, anywhere MCC - including with curries, the prickles helping. Curries, in our experience, don't need sweetness. High profile aromatics, as in Sauvignon Blanc, or dry Riesling, work. So on, ad nauseam. It often does help to chill the wine – white, of course, but also red, though less so.

GLASSWARE – STEMWARE

No need to go ultra-fancy or expensive. But a few basics help a lot. Generously-sized, thin, clear, clean, plain. The bowl much wider than the rim; aromas should be funnelled to your lips and nose. The stem, also thin and long. The rim, clean-cut edges, not flanged, and again, thin. Good for red and white – and now Champagne and MCC too. Give the glasses a few long swooshes through the air to blow out stale whiffs collected in the bowl during storage.

HAND-CRAFTED/PICKED/SORTED

As opposed to machine-harvested – allegedly qualitatively inferior. Big debates about this. But there's technology and machinery all the way down the line in growing and making wine. (See Abrie Bruwer, page 140.) The 'sorting table' where damaged, under- or over-ripe bunches or berries are removed, is one of the biggest boons to quality wine-making in the past couple of decades. Cape wine was in the forefront of that worldwide development.

LEES, BATTONAGE, BARRELS

And new and old wood, barrel fermentation, maturation. Lees are the gunge, the sediment of the dead or dying yeast, settled at the bottom of tanks and barrels during and after fermentation. Beautiful creamy stuff – and creamily coloured in whites, thick velvety purple in reds. The 'mother of the wine'. Before they draw off the wine from this sediment, winemakers can stir the lees back into the wine, to enrich flavour, before it settles again. Battonage in French. Can be repeated – many times. With stainless steel instruments – or by rolling barrels, in which case the bung can be left in, limiting oxygen intake. Fermentation in barrels is said to enhance quality, especially in Chardonnays. Barrels are small vessels, so oak-to-wine exposure is high – more oakiness. In used barrels – say after 2-3 'fills' – oak uptake in wine diminishes. Fermentation and/or maturation in oak barrels then provides progressively less oaky character to the wine; ultimately such barrels are mere storage vessels. New barrels are blunt instruments in a sense: the intensity of scores of powerful oak compounds penetrates wine in potent ways. It can so easily be overdone. In much serious-quality wine, only a proportion of new barrels is used; or wine made in new barrels is blended, moderated, with unwooded wine.

MALOLACTIC FERMENTATION

Especially important in Chardonnays and most reds. Wines are broadened and softened by malo, often dramatically and pleasingly. It's the softening (malic acid to lactic acid) transformation by bacteria, usually after, but can be simultaneous with, alcoholic fermentation. Winemakers have options: prevent it, allow it completely, or just partially (sulphur and/or temperature deployed in first and third options). They can also choose whether to wait for it to occur spontaneously, or induce it with introduced bacteria. Next time a winemaker talks about hands-off minimalism, ask about his or her malo protocols.

NATURAL WINE

Grown in organic vineyards and vinified strictly with no extraneous artificial additions, subtractions, modifications. Many wines come out unconventionally: in colour, in spritz form, cloudy, with tastes unfamiliar to most wine drinkers, sometimes described as Sherry-like. But hundreds of Natural wines have been made in Europe, France and Italy particularly (where such traditions go back centuries), and are gaining devoted followers – often at dedicated Natural Wine bars. These wines are frequently low in alcohol with trenchantly (natural?) savoury flavours. Only a handful of practitioners dabbling in South Africa. A commitment ties the winemaker's hands severely. Still commercially risky. Many organic and bio-dynamically-inclined farms are edging closer to these ideas.

ORGANIC, BIODYNAMIC

Organic farming seeks to exclude artificial fertilisers and pesticides, and to produce grapes - and so wines - that are more eco-sustainable and free of artificial additives. Sulphur additions seem to get a free pass – sulfites exist in nature anyway. Biodynamic farming takes things a few steps further, incorporating a range of holistic farming practices that recognise lunar and other natural rhythms. Subscribers are usually admirers, if not strict adherents, of Rudolph Steiner's 19th and early 20th century agricultural philosophies seeking complete ecological harmony – drawing on much mysticism. Even evoking Native American Chief Seathl's haunting warning that… "all things are connected" and "man will die from a great loneliness of the spirit" if we disturb nature fatally. Delivered in 1855 – the year the French proclaimed the Bordeaux Chateaux Classifications - still in use.

OXIDATIVE,
REDUCTIVE (OR REDUCED)WINES

Controversial topics. These are kinds of complementary opposites, in wine-making - and the outcomes, the styles of their respective wines.

Reductive wine-making seeks to preserve the fruitiness of harvested grapes from oxidation by air (which can lead to oxidised wines, the dangerous slope to vinegar) with various vinification techniques, including additions of sulphur at one or more stages of the process. Sulphur is usually adjusted just before bottling. Sulphur is not the only preservative. Nitrogen and carbon dioxide – a bi-product of fermentation - protect against air. But the carbon dioxide blows off after fermentation. Reduced wines can be closed and hard, initially, especially if heavily sulphured, and will suffer from 'bottle shock' which can take a few months to dissipate. Thereafter the fruit should begin to show, though wine can remain in a 'reduced' state for much longer.

Oxidative winemakers – which does not mean the wines are oxidised - take a completely different route, eschewing sulphur, relaxed about air contact, before, during and after fermentation, while the grape skins – skin contact – remain with the juice or wine. The berries and skins float to the top, absorbing oxygen, protecting the wine, forming what the French call a 'veil' over it. This can go on for months – in some cases even years. The long soak. The wine becoming richer, the skins and pulp leaching their flavours into the must before the 'juice' is separated. There are risks. High temperatures can prompt and accelerate spoilage if the grapes, or the condition of the new wine, aren't near perfect, uninfected by bacteria. Then you're on the way to volatile acidity and vinegar looms again. Grape quality should be obvious from the start; winemakers can abort the oxidative route with sulphur, if in doubt. The oxidative wine, denuded of primary and evanescent fruitiness, aims at more complexity, stability. So, dumber on the nose, supposedly – and in fact often markedly so - more interesting on the palate. Uninitiated tasters can be disappointed initially by the lack of forward aromas. Palates habituated to conventional wines often discard oxidative ones as faulty. Oxidative punters relish the more savoury, umami saltiness underneath – on the palate.

POURING

Never pour a bottle with your knuckles anywhere but facing upwards. Just one of those things. In Stellenbosch, if you don't, you might be asked to start again, with a fresh bottle. Or so I used to be told.

SINGLE VINEYARD WINE

From an officially designated and monitored vineyard. No grapes from elsewhere in the wine. Not necessarily superior to a blended wine – where the winemaker's craftsmanship can often effect improvements. For collectors and purists, however, a single vineyard wine is a tidier proposition, potentially mirroring vintage variations with clarity. Chris Mullineux of Mullineux Family believes wine should be about building coherent stylistic consistency – subject of course to what nature imposes from season to season.

SOMMELIERS, ICE IN WINE AND...

Somms could and should be the new wine arbiters. They have to be social-media savvy – have to be right up to date. Many are now better trained and more knowledgeable than the better wine stores. The diner's comfort should be the somm's first priority. A somm shouldn't be entirely tip-dependent. Nor, obviously, open to 'incentives' from producers' agents keen to punt their wines on the list. If a Somm points you, non-condescendingly, in new wine directions – compatible with the dishes you're ordering – you've scored. But the first somm duty is to make you feel comfortable. Even if you choose the cheapest wine on the list. After all, it's on the list. Even if you ask for ice to put in your wine. Even water. It's not legal for winemakers to nudge their wine alcohols down with water. But drinkers can – and it's often a good idea. (The last few sentences are in because my editor drinks, balances she says, high-alcohol whites with ice and water.)

STRUCTURE – TANNIN AND ACID

Three frequently used words. If we reduce wine to its most basic - acid, alcohol, tannin and fruit (which evolves into a zillion flavours) - then tannin and acid, with their own flavours too, form the backbone that provides structure. Alcohol is part of that too, of course; without alcohol there's no wine. Acid and tannin provide the scaffolding or, more poncily, the architecture. Sales and promotional 'literature' sometimes use 'structure' euphemistically for overly, or unripe tannic, "green" wine; wines that will 'come round with time'. Careful. Longevity is impossible without structure, that's true. But body and flavour are needed to fill out the skeleton. And ripe flavours and tannins should be evident from the start in fine wine.

SULPHUR

Not always the culprit. South African wines are low in sulphur, well under worldwide legal limits. Under 150 parts per million in dry wines; normally even below that. Most well-made wines would be around 50 p.p.m. total sulphur, and 20-30 free (active). There's more sulphur in an egg, or a paracetamol (for fixing a hangover.) Mixing - or too many - drinks are far more likely to cause headaches.

TERROIR

French word embracing climate, soil and aspect (affecting heat, sun etc.,) of a vineyard, thus defining its wines, which should express their origins, or terroir, with a Sense of Place. Wine promoters frequently invoke this nebulous notion in support of their labels. It becomes apparent more easily to long-time collectors of wines with reasonably consistent and identifiable characteristics attributable specifically to terroir. I often think the personalities of the grower and winemaker belong in there too.

TOASTS

Look them in the eye when you clink glasses and toast someone… they won't believe a word you say otherwise. And, so it is said in the winelands, you are doomed to very bad luck in your love-life if you don't.

WHOLE BUNCH PRESSING, FERMENTING

Two different things: pressing whole bunches is a gentler process, therefore supposedly resulting in finer, less 'extracted', therefore less coarse wine (depending on the bar pressure of the press machine). Much modern wine making tries to avoid 'bruising' grapes. This avoids de-stalking, pulling berries from stalks by machine, a rougher process. Fermenting whole bunches leaves stalks as well as berry skins together longer, usually resulting in sappier tastes, the tannins and other compounds in the stalks contributing freshness to wine.

WILD, NATURAL OR INOCULATED YEAST FERMENTATION

The atmosphere is alive with wild - or ambient - yeast; vineyard populations and their characteristics are said to differ markedly; a large body of oenologists believes wild yeasts stamp their imprimatur on the wine during fermentation. Wild yeast ferment is in. It's part of the authenticity – wines with a 'sense of place' - badge. Others pooh-pooh these ideas, saying yeasts – both domestic and wild – are resident in wineries and all self-activate in the vicinity of sugar, and multiply rapidly anyway – several generations in the course of a wine's fermentation - and have little material effect on a wine's outcome. Some say the 'domestic' yeast present in cellars takes over regardless. Grape juice which isn't inoculated with cultivated/commercial yeast, begins fermentation sluggishly, sometimes 'sticking.' Stuck fermentations, and then having to fire up the juice to complete fermentation, are winemaking nightmares. Many winemakers, especially fermenting white wines, resort to no-nonsense, bulldozing commercial yeast - *saccharomyces cerevisiae* - from the outset; which, to cloud things further, are said to have mutated anyway and now exist in both wild, free, ambient and domesticated form. A few winemakers believe it's the wild, allegedly slower-acting yeast, that finishes off a fermentation, in the presence of higher alcohols. Conventional wisdom in the past has said they're asleep at a much earlier stage. Help!

WINE "RATINGS AGENCIES" AND WINE SHOWS

Internationally, Robert Parker's *The Wine Advocate*, and the *Wine Spectator* have serious buyer followings, their scores from 93+ points commanding respect. Also highly regarded, *Decanter* magazine, in Britain (though with more readers outside); now using the 100 points system. Domestically, the Platter Guide's top five-star rating and the Old Mutual Trophy winners, and Gold medallists, are gold-standard stuff in Cape wine, all decided at blind tastings. (Four-and-a-half star wines and below in Platter are not assessed blind). The Platter Guide throws a wide net, finalists drawn from the thousands of wines tasted. The Mutual Trophy winners are chosen from voluntary, subscribing entrants, a narrower field. It's a tough judging panel, including international palates invited by chairman Michael Fridjhon. A Silver at the Trophy Show would be the equivalent of the Platter 4-star and even higher often.

The Platter Guide has been edited by Philip van Zyl since 1997 when we sold the book to our printers, Creda Press. We founded it in 1979. I still sometimes attend the annual five-star taste-offs, but do not contribute to the guide otherwise. Marketers using the guide's ratings as tools should not be attributing them to John Platter but to Platter's, the brand-name of the guide. Currently it is owned by Diners Club and Jean-Pierre Rossouw has been publisher from the 2015 Ed. Van Zyl has been an outstanding editor. His wife Cathy, associate editor and taster, is a Master of Wine, Britain's highest qualification in the wine writing, judging and trade business. Angela Lloyd, still a member of the team was our first contributing taster years ago. She's brilliant, dispassionate and enthusiastic.

Christian Eedes' (*Winemag*) and Roland Peens' (*Wine Cellar*) reviews have become increasingly influential. And there are dozens of wine blogs and websites to keep modern drinkers bang up to date.

WINE WORDS,TASTING NOTES

Earnest, hilarious babel and I hesitate to leave my devoutly agnostic perch and add to it. I'm not remotely funny nor expert enough to offer something new or worthwhile. However, however, a personal, current – always evolving – take: a breathless avalanche of literal flavour and aroma words doesn't do it.

I'm flummoxed not enlightened by the jumble of often conflicting, always overlapping adjectives and comparisons. Iodine, medicinal, greengage, lavender biscotti, lifted florals, honey suckle and bath salts (yes, together), AA Kenya coffee (what happened to BB Columbian Highlands?) and violets. This last now banned from my lexicon. I used to deploy it, more as a feeling, an imagined state of regal beauty and colour (we drink with our eyes), but, on closer inquiry, at my editor's insistence, it turns out to be not only unfamiliar to most South Africans, but hardly a scent at all. Scientists say that only a small percentage of humankind is equipped to pick up this elusive smell! One MW (Master of Wine) we know says he has spent years smelling the violets and has never found one with a scent.

I didn't recognise one of my favourite wines in this book, in the following description. "Pale, lucid yellow, nose packed with straw, lemon grass, baked yellow capsicum and rich lemon curd… complex herbal dimensions, a pithy minerality of crushed gravel underpins notes of dried herbs, tarragon, dried bay leaves and buttered white toast." Enough already? No, it also has "full, bold fleshy entry with mouth-coating dry extract, concentration of lemon verbena, white citrus, passion fruit soufflé and peach stone fruit." There's more: "gravitas and weight of fruit, classical styling with immediate accessibility and allure…revealing trademarks of lemon and pineapple pastille fruits, textural richness, vibrant acidity, seamless integration and above all, balance."

Whew! Shome mishtake, shurely? With winemakers busy tossing out the textbooks, is it time for tasters to reconsider their ancient craft, rein in their tastebuds and nostrils, and offer more approachable wine descriptions? Many wine drinkers are intimidated when they find nothing more, but also nothing less, than a wine they like in a glass, but feel they are obliged to search out strings of comparisons. Especially when such conversations are "live". Time to consult Stephen Potter in *Wineupmanship*? He recommends long pauses, finally dipping your nose into the far side of the glass and after another breather pronouncing: "Too many tramlines, I fear."

My take on the wine above is much more prosaic. Though maybe still not down-to-earth enough for the Cape's new breed of winemaker, like Thinus Kruger of FRAM. He concluded his remarks at a recent tasting - many stories, no notes from orchard, garden, kitchen, farm, or deli counter: "It's just a wine; you just drink it; and enjoy it." And his colleague Ryan Mostert, of Terra Cura and Wine Cellar added: "What matters is the way wine moves you."

One useful word buried back there is minerality. It's now discouraged apparently – by the literalist camp, who, doubtless accurately, say it has nothing to do with actual minerals in the soil nor the wine. My minerally wine is about savoury, salty (some use saline) freshness, tension and grip that's tasty and energetic with a plate of anything almost, and applies to both red and white. Without it, there's often unbalanced floppiness and conversely, a wine too tart is unbalanced-astringent.

My tasting routine is to jot down a few self-evident words, some fruit flavours – ripe plum, tart pineapple; textures and mouth-feel words – silky or sandpapery; spices, spiciness (important) – clove, black pepper etc., especially in oaked wine; and whatever else may climb out of the glass. Some modern wines have only the faintest of scents; no need to stress and strain to find something, anything. Because while colour and aromatics provide important clues, and the finish, or aftertaste, signal quality impressions (the "before" and "after" of a wine), the palate, or as some call it, the mid-palate is the crux of the matter. I base my take overwhelmingly on this.

Delicious charm and balance – what it's all about really - are soon evident. And useful to all of us who prefer the fox's way: to be vaguely right rather than precisely wrong – though we should remember too that we cannot be precisely wrong about personal taste. One worry: sometimes it's only after a few more sips, or gulps, that a bitterness is revealed, masked initially by other elements. All wines change in an opened bottle, in the glass, with time and temperature shifts – and dozens of other variables, including the company and the weather!

Most tasting words and terms should be obvious: fleshy, toasty, dense, grippy etc.
But a word like typicity can be tricky. And probably increasingly meaningless. It refers to the qualities and character of a wine when it is "true to type" reflecting its grape variety or varieties, or is true to, or at least recognisably reminiscent of, a regional style. In the recent explosion of wines from more regions, made from newly introduced or revived grape varieties, in modern ways and styles, the focus has shifted more to terroirs than grape varietals (another word for varieties!) Typicity is losing its significance. To fault a wine because it does not taste or smell as the textbooks or tasting manuals say it should - or once did - is becoming out-of-the-window stuff. To many, especially keen young wine tasters, it's important now to "taste the site." So are we drifting toward soil typicity? In any case, varietal typicity always suffered from a weakness: the stage at which grapes are harvested determines wine character; early-picked Sauvignon Blanc (capsicum notes) for example is quite different to late-picked (gooseberry and tropical fruit.)

Another term you may hear is linearity. "You will find this in a wine that is focused, straight, running along tramlines," explains (or doesn't) one winemaker. Is it the opposite of breadth? Lean and sleek - or one-dimensional? Best avoided.

A bit of anthropomorphism – burly, loud, shy, aggressive – is fine, I feel, but frowned upon as frilly nonsense by literalists. The old "sensualist" school of wine annotating tolerates it, as it does even looser flourishes of metaphor. Wine lingo may be a standard object of satire but we're speaking of rituals developed over 6000 years of recorded wine drinking (over vast territories where wine is now banned from its birthplaces) to elevate wine from what otherwise might be alcoholic ordinariness. Should we be so impatient with these amusing literary flourishes?

An old favourite note from Hugh Johnson speaks of a wine "…wonderfully potent with promise but scarcely mature enough to do itself justice…less a statement than a suggestion, its structure that of lace, delicately woven with a sweet touch of sharpness in persuasive harmony, adding another element of seduction, a limpid texture that made me think of cream poured over gravel, smokey, autumnal, earthy roast coffeeish."

Some literary, rather than literal, licence there. More evocative than a percentage.

WINE
COUNTRY
FOOD

A warning before you dip into this section: please do not expect a normal, standardised cookbook style here. We have passed on the following recipes as they were given to us. Minimum interference for more authentic flavour rules in both cellar and kitchen… So, tossed together, you will find professional chefs and keen winemaking amateurs, precision and free-styling, measured instructions and bluntly unminced orders (take a bow, Abrie Bruwer). But all in the end saying the same thing: wine and food are made for each other.

DRESSING AN OYSTER

This dressing was shown to the Newton Johnson wine family by Tommy Poulsen, a Danish friend who worked at Copenhagen's famous Noma restaurant for four years. "It has a better taste than high acid lemon juice or traditional Tabasco," says Dave Johnson, and we agree. He always puts out an array of their whites, Chardonnays and Sauvignons, for guests to choose their own drinking partners.

Chop a small red onion very finely. Mix a 50/50 solution of water with a really good vinegar (wine, rice or cider). Add salt to taste. Steep the onion in the solution. Spoon a little onto each oyster.

SAUVIGNON MUSSELS

Instructions from wine action-man Dave Johnson, diver, fisherman, seashore forager, a magician with all things marine. Cook in Sauvignon Blanc, serve with ciabatta and more Sauvignon.

Collect 30 good-sized mussels, or whatever your licence allows. Scrub to remove barnacles, seaweed etc. Immerse them in a bucket (of seawater if possible) to purge the sand. Now you can start cooking. Put mussels in a pot with 125ml Sauvignon Blanc. Close lid. Heat rapidly. When mussels have opened (about 5-7 mins), remove from heat. Take mussels out of liquid, remove half the shell and beards if still attached. Check for grit and rinse if necessary. Put liquid through a fine sieve.

Now finely chop
4 large spring onions
2 celery stalks
2 cloves garlic

Fry in pan with knob of butter

Add
250 ml cream
Mussel liquid to taste

Reduce sauce (about 5 mins). Add mussels and chopped parsley. Season.

AN IRRESISTIBLE CURED FISH STARTER

This little yellowtail dish, conceived by George Jardine of Jordan restaurant (a South African Top Tenner), is so completely delicious you want to lick the plate. Especially every drop of the bright green nasturtium leaf pesto: an inspiration (picked from Kathy Jordan's garden). George cures the fish with salt and sugar; then adds the sort of finishing touches we expect from such a super-chef: aioli, and an artichoke and Parmesan dressing. His seasonal, local and often foraged dishes are exceptional; he does things with East Coast hake, for example, that make you wonder why anyone would rather fly in foreign fish. Add the beautiful breads from their Bakery, and the food-friendly wines; tick all the boxes. The Jordans recommended their Inspector Peringuey Chenin with this dish: a terrific match. Serves 4.

10g coarse salt
10g brown sugar
250g yellowtail fillet
100g nasturtium leaves
1 clove garlic

100ml olive oil
Salt, pepper
100g Jerusalem artichoke
50g Parmesan

Yellowtail
Combine salt and sugar, sprinkle over yellowtail. Leave to cure for 20 mins. Wash off salt and sugar. Slice yellowtail (6-7 slices per portion).

Pesto
Wash nasturtium leaves. Place in blender with garlic and olive oil. Blend until smooth. Season with salt and pepper.

Dressing
Wash and dice artichokes, roast gently in a pan until soft. Place in a bowl. Grate over Parmesan, moisten with a little olive oil, season.

Aioli
Make a mayonnaise, using olive oil, adding garlic.

Plating
Use our picture as a guide. A few dots of aioli here and there add richness.

TUNA TARTARE

A favourite starter at bistro-in-the-winelands Joostenberg, where Christophe de Hosse deftly manages to shrink the air-miles between the Cape and France with dishes that star proudly-local ingredients but speak with his own French accent. Which herbs? He uses any or all of the following: dill, chives, basil, chervil, flat-leaf or regular parsley. Accompany with toasted sourdough bread. And butter, he recommends. And one of his brother-in-law Tyrell Myburgh's interesting organic whites. The Joostenberg Fairhead would be good. Or the Kaalgat Steen. Serves 4.
Attention! Can stay in the fridge for an hour or so, but no longer: it does not really keep well.

450g fresh, raw tuna
2 shallots, peeled, finely diced
½ cup fresh herbs, finely diced
Juice of 2-3 lemons

Salt, pepper to taste
1-2 Tbsp extra virgin olive oil
Baby tomatoes, sprigs of herbs to garnish

Chop tuna finely with a very sharp knife, being careful not to crush or bruise the fish. Place in a bowl, toss lightly but thoroughly with all the herbs and shallots. Again, be careful not to bruise the herbs or fish. Season with olive oil, lemon juice, salt and pepper to taste. Serve with baby tomatoes, sprigs of fresh herbs.

SEARED SESAME TUNA WITH PEANUT BUTTER DRESSING

From Matt Gordon of French Connection Bistro in Franschhoek, consultant at Laborie's Harvest. Trust him on this: he has always been noted for his sauces, butters (his Café de Paris is legendary) and dressings. Classic French, modern Asian, the lot. A Riesling works well with this dish. And a good pink, like the frisky Graham Beck Gorgeous.

40g grated fresh ginger
¼ cup sesame seeds
1 Tbsp cracked black pepper

500g fresh yellow fin tuna
Good salt
3 Tbsp cooking oil, for searing

Peanut dressing
1 cup peanut butter
1/3 cup lime juice
¼ cup water
1/2 cup oil
2 Tbsp sesame oil
1/3 cup soy sauce
2 red spring onions
½ tsp finely grated fresh ginger
Freshly ground black pepper

Salad
1 medium-size, ripe avocado, peeled, pitted, sliced
½ cup mixed micro-greens
½ red onion thinly sliced
1 medium tomato, peeled, seeded, diced
100g fresh green asparagus tips, blanched
100g baby carrots, peeled, blanched,sliced
Assorted bean sprouts
3 red spring onions, sliced
100g baby leaves
Vinaigrette
Pea shoots for garnish

Mix together ginger, sesame seeds, and black pepper. Season tuna with salt. Roll in ginger mixture, pressing lightly so it sticks. Place in a pan over high heat. Add oil, sear 30 secs on every side. Remove from pan.

For the dressing: start with the peanut butter in a bowl, slowly add liquid ingredients, gradually thinning it, but not allowing it to split. If too thick, add a little more water. Add spring onions, ginger, and pepper to taste.

In a bowl combine avocado, greens, onion, tomato, asparagus and carrots. Toss with a little vinaigrette. Slice tuna. Place some dressed salad on 4 plates or 1 big platter. Top with tuna, surround with dressing, garnish with pea shoots.

WHY NOT START WITH PANNA COTTA?

Chef Lucas Carstens made a savoury panna cotta for the opening course of a recent dinner to mark the launch of Simonsig's The Garland Cabernet Sauvignon in the estate's classy Cuvée restaurant. It accompanied an array of baby pickled beets – red, pink, white and yellow. Which looked ravishing, tasted delicious. But the panna cotta stole the show. You could team it with just about anything – variegated tomatoes and basil, fresh fig - and it would delight and impress. Simonsig's bubblies move easily from aperitif to starter-partner.

500ml cream
3g salt
200g chevin goat's cheese
1½ Tbsp gelatine powder or 3½ gelatine leaves

Bring cream and salt to a boil, remove from heat, add cheese and sponged gelatine. Blend with stick blender. Pour into bowl, set in fridge overnight. When ready to use, whip the mixture with an electric whisk, till stiff and fluffy. Scoop into quenelles and plate with your chosen salad ingredients. Top with rocket or micro-herbs.

NOT THE USUAL SEAFOOD SALAD

We asked Matt Gordon, of French Connection Bistro in Franschhoek and Harvest at Laborie in Paarl, for a "not too cheffy" seafood recipe. We can make such cheeky demands because we have known him since he was 10 years old, and already putting us grown-ups to shame with his skills in the kitchen. This is his exciting, pretty, and undaunting suggestion: the chorizo brings an extra dimension. He serves warm. Matching wines from the valley might include Chamonix Chardonnay, or Grande Provence White. Or Colmant bubbles.

1 large chorizo, sliced thinly	**Dressing**
300g small calamari tubes, cleaned	100ml mayonnaise
8 tiger prawns, shelled, de-veined,split	50ml plain yoghurt
100g mixed baby leaves	Juice of 2 lemons
1 roasted red pepper, peeled, seeded, sliced	100g fresh coriander, finely chopped
120g peppadews, sliced	25ml olive oil
100g wild rocket	**Mix these dressing ingredients together.**
Salt and pepper	

Pan-fry chorizo until crisp. Reserve in cooking pan with oil. Season calamari and prawns, grill in a skillet. Now add chorizo and its flavoured oil to the seafood mix. Toss leaves, pepper, peppadews and rocket in the dressing, arrange on a platter or individual plates. Surround the border of the plate with dressing. Arrange prawns, calamari and chorizo on the plate. Drizzle over some remaining chorizo oil from the pan for colour and flavour.

BOERE SALAD

A dish we sampled at Bertus Basson's latest restaurant venture at Spice Route, where Charles Back has transformed an old Cape Dutch house, outbuildings and farmyard into a brilliant food and wine destination. Bertus, TV's popular Braaimaster judge, is updating traditional dishes and re-inventing Cape classics here. The shady oak terrace, the vineyard and mountain views are made for al fresco lunching. Inside, it's all rustic-chic, the country cousin of his more urbane (though still rural) Overture kitchen, a South African Top tenner. If you do not have a biltong-maker, or dehydrator, or are too frightened to hang your meat out on a sunny washing line (as John Platter did when growing up in Kenya), beg or buy the very best, and most home-made-tasting biltong you can find. As long as you nail "the essence" of the recipe, says co-chef and business partner here, Allistaire Lawrence, you will be fine. Team with a Spice Route wine. Serves 2.

Biltong
1kg top side, cut into strips
50g coarse salt
 20g brown sugar
5g black pepper corns
30g coriander seed
3g cloves
100ml Worcestershire sauce
100ml soya sauce

Vinaigrette
20g whole grain mustard
50ml lemon juice
120ml olive oil
30g mayonnaise

Salad
80g baby gem lettuce
20g witloof (or endive)
Salt and pepper to taste
15g white anchovy
25g home-cured (or best) biltong
5g powdered biltong (grated from the above)
15g toasted sunflower seeds
15g toasted pumpkin seeds
15g grated grana padano (Parmesan)
10ml whole grain mustard vinaigrette
4 slices very thin toasted ciabatta

Start with the Biltong, if you are curing your own
Roughly blitz spices in a food processor until well mixed together. Rub spice mix over meat, massaging it well into the grain. Place meat in a container, cover with sauces. Allow to marinate for 36 hrs. Remove meat and pat dry with paper towel. Hang in a biltong maker for 5 days or so. (The longer you leave it, the dryer the meat; depends what you prefer.) When needed, grate 5g of biltong.

The Toast
A tip from chef Allistaire: freeze loaf of bread overnight. Easier next day to slice perfectly thinly. Lay on a flat sprayed tray, drizzle with olive oil, toast until crisp and golden.

The Vinaigrette Dressing
Place mustard, lemon juice and oil in a bowl, and whisk to emulsify. Then add mayonnaise. Mix. Refrigerate.

Assembling the Salad
Place leaves in a mixing bowl, gently sprinkle with salt and pepper, then toss. Layer salad in a bowl, alternating with leaves, then other ingredients (except toast). Once complete, drizzle with the salad dressing, garnish with toasts.

EGGS ON TOAST IN PINOTAGE SAUCE

A Cape version of the French dish Oeufs en Meurette. Made by chef Frank Menezes, of the Red Leaf restaurant at Beyerskloof, featuring cellarmaster Beyers Truter's signature grape. A treat of a brunch, lunch or supper dish. You can prepare its different components separately, ahead of time, and simply warm, before assembling for the table; you could also fry the bread, instead of toasting. Serves 4, with a bottle of Diesel Pinotage. (See picture opposite.)

1 onion, chopped	**Garnish**
1 carrot	300g shallots
1 celery stick	30g butter, pinch of sugar
1 garlic clove	170g portobellini mushrooms
750ml Pinotage	170g streaky bacon
500ml beef stock	8 pieces toasted/fried baguette,
Bouquet garni	Garlic and parsley
8 eggs	**Beurre Manie**
2½ml black pepper	30g butter
Salt and pepper to taste	22g cake flour

• Sweat onion, carrot, celery, garlic in pot for 2 minutes. Deglaze pot with Pinotage, add beef stock and bouquet garni. Reduce by a third. Strain sauce. Poach eggs in this sauce. Season with black pepper. Keep warm.
• Place shallots in a little water with salt and poach until tender, strain. Add this poaching liquid to the Pinotage sauce. Place shallots back in pot with butter and sugar, cook until caramelised.
• Sauté mushrooms in butter, season to taste. Meantime grill bacon in oven for 6-10 mins until crispy. Rub bread with garlic, scatter with parsley.
• Place sauce in a pot back on stove. Mash together remaining butter and flour until they form a thick paste. Stir this gradually into the sauce in the pot, cook gently until sauce thickens, becomes glossy. Season.
• If eggs have cooled, warm in hot water. Place each egg on a round of toast/fried bread. Spoon sauce over eggs. Scatter with bacon, mushrooms, and caramelised shallots.

EGGS BADENHORST

Adi Badenhorst is not really joking when he labels himself a "gourmand". He's the one winemaker for whom all the hot Cape Town chefs and butchers will pack their knives and decamp to the Swartland to cook and commune, collaborate and celebrate, and, resoundingly, bring wine and food back to their roots on the farm. The Convivium hosted by the Badenhorsts at their farm Kalmoesfontein in February 2015 was perhaps the foodie event of the Cape year. In a previous life, Adi used to grow speciality veges for such chefs. This riff on Eggs Benedict is a family favourite, done best, he says, by his mother Judy.

"I like this with tomatoes and red onions - fried or shoved in the oven for 10 mins. Then with lots of fresh herbs - thyme, parsley, chives, wild rocket, watercress etc. To give it a Swartland twist, a few waterblommetjies on the side. In season, some veldkool (a sort of wild asparagus spear). So...

• In a pan fry up/sweat off red onions in olive oil. After a few minutes add a tsp or two of balsamic vinegar. Add tomatoes - any kind, any style, whole, chopped, halved, whatever you prefer. I pop this in the oven while I do the other stuff. Steam waterblommetjies or veldkool. Drain, season with salt and pepper.
• Poach eggs - easy enough if they are fresh koekoek eggs.
• Quickly make a Hollandaise type of sauce – an old moer-toe blender is essential. I usually add chopped chives, and try to make it quite tart with lemon juice.

We do not shy away from meat for breakfast, lunch or dinner! So the eggs are served with wors, bacon, skilpadjies or chops."

CHEESE TART

Olive Hamilton Russell is a brilliant cook and effortlessly (it seems) stylish host. Her book, Entertaining at Hamilton Russell Vineyards, features a year's series of seasonal dishes and menus, and highlights her special interest in local and indigenous ingredients. She would use cheese from nearby farms like Kleinrivier for this simply delicious tart, which she sometimes makes as individual tartlets, as we did for our picture opposite. HRV Chardonnay is the partner to choose. Serves 6–8.

Pastry
200g cake flour
Pinch of paprika, salt and pepper
75g butter
75g mature Cheddar cheese, grated
2-3 Tbsp cold water

Filling
3 eggs, separated
250ml cream
2 tsp Dijon mustard
Salt and pepper
150g Gruyere cheese, grated
75g feta cheese, crumbled (don't use Danish feta, too salty)
125g Camembert cheese, rind removed
¼ cup pine nuts (optional)

Pastry
Preheat oven to 180c. Sift flour, add paprika, salt and pepper. Rub butter into flour until mixture resembles fine breadcrumbs. Use a food processor if available. Add Cheddar cheese. Bind into a dough using just enough water. Wrap and chill for 30mins.

Coat a 28cm loose-bottom tart tin with non-stick spray. Roll out the pastry, line the tin. Using a fork, prick small holes in the base of the pastry, cover with plastic wrap and chill for another 20 mins (to prevent pastry from shrinking when baked). Line pastry case with baking paper ensuring to cover all the edges, fill with baking beans. Bake for 20 mins, remove paper, bake another 5 mins. Remove from oven, cool slightly.

Do not turn off oven.

Filling
Whisk egg yolks, cream and mustard, season with salt and pepper. Dice cheeses. Stir into the cream mixture. Whisk the egg whites to stiff points, fold into cheese mixture. (I stir in a quarter of the egg whites, and then very gently fold in the rest.) Spoon into slightly cooled pastry case. Sprinkle pine nuts over evenly. Bake 35-40 mins until golden and set. Leave to cool for about 10 mins before slicing and serving. Garnish as you please.

WHAT TO DRINK WITH CRAYFISH

"A good fresh cray has a nutty nuance to the flesh and this is matched by an elegant Chardonnay," says Dave Johnson, whose own Newton Johnson Family Vineyards conveniently offer a whole dance-card of suitable partners.

A UNIQUE WAY TO FRY A FILLET OF FISH

Springfield Estate's flying fishing foodie Abrie Bruwer (left, slicing his own home-made bread) confesses: "I stole this with my eyes from a Portuguese guy in Angola. The trick is to judge the amount of salt needed."

1 fat fish fillet
Clove garlic
Coarse salt

Vinegar
Breadcrumbs
Olive oil for frying

Cut the fish fillet in leaves (this is the first trick) ± 5mm thick, starting from the tail, much like you would cut a whole smoked salmon, just a bit thicker.

Using a small pestle and mortar, crush garlic with enough coarse salt for the fish. Add 2 Tbsp vinegar, mix into a briny paste. Wet your fingertips and pat this paste onto the leaves on one side. Place the next leaf onto that seasoned side, and repeat (as there will not be enough brine to coat both sides). Let it stand 15–20mins.

Coat fish in half breadcrumbs (bakery ones are fine) and half flour. Fry in shallow olive oil in a very hot pan

WHAT TO DO WHEN KINGKLIP LOSES ITS COAT

Another trick and treat from Abrie Bruwer, whose fish-cooking methods have been perfected over a lifetime of tight lines. When they aren't biting, he recommends Kingklip: "Always available, has a long life in the freezer, actually better frozen than fresh… Because it has a tendency to shed its batter when fried, I implemented this recipe…"

Salt the Kingklip pieces (once cut into the sizes you require). Coat with half-half breadcrumb-flour mix. Fry in olive oil with bay leaves (5-10) and 2-3 small cloves of garlic whole with the skin on. When the fish is fried on both sides, take it out. Squash the garlic in the pan, add the juice of 3 lemons and half a glass white wine. Sauvignon is good. Let it bubble away and pour over the fish pieces once reduced.

This method gets hold of all your stuck batter. The richness of the oil does the oil-free Kingklip a lot of good. And you will be a lot poorer if you leave the bay leaves in the kitchen. Serve them on top of the fish.

DUIDELIKSTE VISKOEKIES

Or in English: Better than Good Fishcakes. "I normally do this with big fish that is too grainy to eat any other way. Fry in the best olive oil, is my advice. If you are turning a beautiful old fish into a humble fishcake, the only honour you can bestow on him is to fry him in olive oil…And there is only one thing better than a fishcake…it's a day old fishcake!" This is Abrie Bruwer, oracle on all things fishy, again. And Springfield has recently made Miss Lucy, a delicious white blend specifically to drink with fish. Game, set, match.

Steam a fish in wine, bay leaves and black pepper corns. Flake fish. Chop onions to half of the fish's bulk, add breadcrumbs for the other half (now you have doubled your basic mix). Now mix together the following:

2 handfuls chopped parsley
½ cup bread flour
Salt, pepper (more than usual)
3-4 chopped chillies

Can of soda water
½ cup lemon juice
2 eggs
2 Tbsp baking powder

Combine this with the fish, breadcrumb and onions mixture. Form fishcakes. Fry in olive oil.

PLANK-BRAAIED TROUT

"One of our favourite braai-tricks," says John Seccombe of Thorne and Daughters Wines about this "more of a method than a recipe". He was shown how by a Canadian friend. There they use salmon. "We have used it very successfully for local salmon trout. We serve it with bread and dressed leaves. And perhaps a horseradish cream," he says. Even better when teamed with T and D's own Semillon or Cape white blend.

The first thing you need is oak or cedar planks that will fit on the grill of a Weber braai. They should be soaked in water overnight, preferably weighted down to keep them submerged. Note: the wood must be completely untreated. Specialist shops sell smoking planks, but Seccombe has used old barrel heads, cut down for the purpose. Photographer Clinton Friedman went foraging at the Neil Ellis Winery in Stellenbosch and found some discarded oak staves. He flew them home to KZN and followed John's instructions: a triumph!

Lay whole trout or fillets skin-side down on the wet planks, dress, baste with:

¼ cup olive oil
2 garlic cloves, crushed
1 tsp mustard seeds
½ chopped chilli

For the braai, wait until the coals are well settled and grey. Place wood on the grill and cover with the lid of the Weber - vents closed on top. Leave for 10 mins. The steam from the planks will cook the fish through gently and if the heat is just right, the planks will begin to char on the edges, infusing the fish with a wonderful hot smokiness.

FISH ON THE FIRE

Here's how Dave Johnson barbecues/braais his gamefish and yellowtail. Both of which like Pinot Noir, he reveals. And Chardonnay. Fortunately the Newton Johnsons grow and make both splendidly.

I like to use a good-sized fillet which I always debone. Take a hinged braai grid (or in Afrikaans, more descriptively, a *toeklaprooster*), and line one side with heavy foil brushed with melted butter. Place the fillet skin side down on the foil. Brush the flesh side with lots of butter. Close the grid and put flesh side down over hot coals. You want the butter to melt on to the coals and cause a short period of flame to caramelize the remaining butter on the fish. This should take a few minutes.

Turn the grid over and put over a cooler part of the coals. The fish is now cooking through the foil with the flesh side up. Baste with melted butter mixed with the juice of a lemon or lime. Sprinkle with chopped fresh herbs.

When fish is cooked through (should take about 15 mins depending upon size) remove from grid. The skin of the fish should remain neatly on the foil.

PRAWN AND CHILLI LINGUINE

Being a restaurateur long before he became a winemaker, and a great home cook too, Ken Forrester knows better than most which wines go with what dishes. But he would not be Ken if he played it safe. So: what to team with the Forrester Meinert Chenin, the FMC, the top overall scorer in Wine Cellar's 2015 tastings of "luxury" (expensive) whites? An end-of-meal dessert, seeing the wine is categorised in most books as Off-dry to Semi-sweet? Certainly not. Ken suggests a far more adventurous match: the key here is the chilli, which is beautifully tamed by this wine. The dish made for us by Tasha Wray, of the Forrester-Meinert "canteen", 96 Winery Road restaurant, an enduring winelands favourite.

Linguine for 4
2 medium onions, chopped
2 cloves garlic, crushed
Olive oil for frying
400g headless peeled prawns

½ glass Chenin Blanc
1 can peeled, chopped tomatoes
1 tsp brown sugar
Dried or fresh chilli, chopped, to taste

Boil a pot of water, add the linguine. While it is cooking, fry onions and garlic in olive oil until soft but not brown. Set aside. Put the prawns into the same pan with a little more oil on high and singe the outside for 1 min. Turn and repeat. Add wine. Stir, reduce by half. Add tomatoes and brown sugar. Add chilli to taste. Add cooked onions and garlic. Simmer.

Drain linguine, reserving a little of the water to add to the prawns if necessary. Whole process should take between 6-8 mins. Spiral linguine into a warmed bowl, add prawns and sauce.

OLIVE SALAD DRESSING

An Abrie Bruwer (of Springfield Estate) inspiration and innovation. His doctor wife, Michelle, refers to their home kitchen as "Abrie's food factory". He even cans his own yellowtail. This inventive vinaigrette gets the stiffest iceberg lettuce leaves dancing. And is brilliant over sliced, hard boiled eggs. Choose a good oil. "The shitter the oil, the worse the vinaigrette," warns Abrie.

750ml olive oil
½ bottle vinegar
½ bottle lemon juice
2 Tbsp Dijon mustard
2 Tbsp honey
2 Tbsp salt
2 Tbsp black pepper
2 Tbsp chopped anchovies
½ bottle of peppadews, with sauce, chopped
2 cloves garlic, crushed
2 cups black olive (stones removed, all of them) minced to a paste

Whisk the lot with a stick blender. Bottle.

FRESH HERB SAUCE FOR ROASTED BEEF FILLET

"When we entertain guests for lunch on a summer day, we like to serve a simple cold fillet, with a fresh herb sauce to complement the herbaceous notes in our Cabernets. The flavours are clean and rich, the dish not too overpowering," says Marie Condé. She runs the charming Postcard Café overlooking the dam and overlooked by mountains (a picture-postcard setting) on the Stark Condé family farm in the Jonkershoek Valley, Stellenbosch; her husband José makes the wines. "I prefer to cook the beef in the oven, especially when it's too hot to braai, and anyway I like to have lunch prepared well ahead of time. I serve this with colourful salads and crusty bread."

1 cup chopped Italian parsley
½ cup thinly sliced spring onions or chives
½ cup chopped basil or mint
4 Tbsp capers (rinsed, chopped)
½ cup chopped red onion or shallot
Zest of 1 lemon
1½ cups extra virgin olive oil
Salt, pepper
4 Tbsp lemon juice

In a bowl, mix all ingredients except lemon juice. Season with salt and pepper. Add lemon juice just before serving.

PINOT NOIR SAUCE
FOR PAN-FRIED DUCK BREAST

Dave Johnson has always loved Pinot Noir. His Cape Master of Wine thesis was on Pinot, many years before he and his family grew and made it at Newton Johnson Vineyards. And he loves to cook with it. More Pinot Noir (NJ Mrs M, perhaps) is obligatory to drink with the dish, which nowadays he slimmingly serves with cauliflower mash and a salad.

150ml Pinot Noir
35 ml balsamic vinegar
10 ml brown sugar
Few sprigs thyme, rosemary
700ml beef stock
Salt, pepper
Knob of butter

Gently heat Pinot and balsamic in a saucepan until reduced by half. Add sugar and herbs. Simmer gently until thickened. Season with salt, black pepper. Whisk in a knob of cold butter just before serving.

SORT OF
QUICK SPANISH CHICKEN AND CHICKPEAS

Here is an off-duty dish from Cape Town culinary star Peter Tempelhoff, boss-chef of five multi-starred restaurants. He won a string of eating-out awards when cheffing in London and remains at the top of his game. This dish is quick, easy, "we eat it all the time," he says. How comforting to hear that grand and glossy chefs are just like the rest of us and do not go near foams and drizzles and dishes made with tweezers when relaxing at home. Pete likes to use long thin pimento peppers, if possible. It is exactly the sort of quick, casual, flavourful, no-fuss food made for his and Adam Mason's range of Marvelously easy, everyday drinking wines. And vice-versa.

4 free range skinless chicken breasts, cut into large dice
Sea salt
10ml smoked paprika
120ml olive oil
2 medium onions, sliced
2 red peppers, diced
150g best quality thin chorizo, skinned, sliced

3 cloves garlic, finely chopped
50g tomato paste
2 440g tins of peeled, chopped Italian tomatoes
15g sugar
1 tin cooked chickpeas
1 handful parsley, roughly chopped
1 handful soup celery leaves, roughly chopped

Massage chicken in a large bowl with sea salt and smoked paprika, allow to rest for an hour.

Place a large heavy pot on stove on high heat until it begins to smoke, add half olive oil to pot, then colour chicken, for 3-5 mins. Remove chicken, turn down heat to medium, add remaining oil, lightly colour onions (4-5 mins) then peppers; simmer for another 2-3 mins. Add chorizo, continue to cook on medium for about a minute. Add garlic, cook for 42 seconds, no longer. Then add tomato paste. Simmer for another 2-3 mins until paste becomes a delicious rust colour. Add chopped tomatoes, sugar. Simmer another 15 mins (ish), until it thickens slightly. Season.

Return chicken to pot, add chickpeas, simmer for 8-10 mins. Add a garnish of parsley and soup celery leaves if you like. Serve at once with steamed rice, crusty bread or even a wrap.

193

MARINATED OVEN-ROAST LAMB
WITH AUBERGINE MASH

Globe-trotting Hartenberg wine ambassador James Browne is an accomplished and adventurous cook, and the dishes he likes to make could originate anywhere in the wine world, as well as places like Ecuador, Madagascar, Gabon, Papua New Guinea etc, all visited in pursuit of another interest – birds. Here, to accompany any of the brilliant Hartenberg Shirazes, he has stayed more or less at home, with Karoo lamb. The cheesy aubergine bed on which the lamb rests is an unusual accompaniment.

1,8kg leg of lamb

Marinade
200g plain yoghurt
4 Tbsp olive oil
2 Tbsp tomato puree
1tsp caster sugar
4 tsp red wine
4 garlic cloves, crushed
3 bay leaves, crumbled
1 tsp caster sugar
1tsp salt
½ tsp black pepper
1 tsp cayenne pepper

Mash
675g aubergines
Olive oil
40g butter
40g plain flour
275ml full-fat milk
25g Parmesan, grated
55g feta cheese, crumbled
Salt and pepper

To serve
Pomegranate seeds, watercress or fresh coriander

Score skin and fat of lamb. Make incisions all over with a small sharp knife. Mix marinade ingredients together, pour over lamb, rub into incisions. Marinate for 24 hrs if you can, and for at least an hour if you can't. Then drain lamb from marinade but don't wipe clean. Roast for 75 mins at 190c (for pink lamb) or 15 mins per 500g. Remove from oven, cover with foil, leave for 15 mins.

To prepare aubergines, drizzle them with a little olive oil, roast for 30 mins in an oven preheated to 180c. Remove, cool. Slit aubergines, scoop out pulp, press through sieve with a spoon to get rid of some of the juices. Purée pulp. Make a white sauce: melt butter, add flour. Stir over low heat until it forms a pale golden roux. Take off heat, add milk, slowly at first, making sure liquid is well amalgamated before adding the next bit. Put back on heat, bring to boil, stirring all the time, until sauce is thick. Simmer about 5 mins. Add aubergine purée and cheeses to this sauce. Stir, season with salt and pepper.

Carve lamb, serving the slices on a bed of aubergine purée scattered with some pomegranate seeds or chopped fresh coriander or watercress.

GAME BOBOTIE

First Catch Your Eland is the title of a 1977 Laurens van der Post book on African food: a collection of memories and descriptions, not recipes. So, there's a gap here, which the Niewoudts of Cederberg Private Cellar obligingly fill. This is their favourite version of a traditional Cape recipe, which begins: "First catch your kudu". You can substitute other game or minced meat. It was cooked for us by bobotie queen Mrs Jennifer Bock (aka Koekie), whose instructions were translated from the Afrikaans, and augmented here and there, by Cederberg's living replica of a bearded Boer War general, marketing man Pieter du Toit. He says: "This meal will serve 3 South Africans, or 4 to 6 people. Best with yellow rice and raisins, a few thinly sliced bananas and lots of Mrs Balls if your own home-made peach chutney has run out." Cederberg's singular Bukketraube is a fine companion. But so would be just about any of their wines.

1 kudu
1 butcher

30ml olive oil
1 medium onion, finely chopped
1Tbsp curry powder
2ml salt
20ml turmeric (borrie)
20ml vinegar/white wine
1 kg kudu mince
Cederberg Bukettraube
50 ml apricot jam
1 tomato, finely chopped
250ml fresh breadcrumbs
160ml peach chutney, preferably homemade
10ml milk
2 eggs

Make an appointment with a game farmer and fetch/kill/shoot/collect a kudu.Take the kudu to the local butcher – in this case at Prince Alfred Hamlet, near Ceres, and ask him to slaughter the kudu. Make sure some quality mince is included among the cuts. Share the meat with the butcher in exchange for his work.

When you get home, heat oil, fry onion until soft. Add curry powder, salt, turmeric, and vinegar (or wine). Keep stirring. Heat oven to 180°C. Grease one large casserole dish - or several small dishes for individual helpings. Now add kudu mince and decent dash of Cederberg Bukettraube (it does not work with others) and keep on stirring (and sipping) until you are happy and the liquid has disappeared. Use a two-pronged fork to separate the mince. Now add the apricot jam and tomato. Keep on stirring. Add bread crumbs and chutney, mix well.

In the meantime beat milk and eggs in a separate bowl. Add half to the kudu mince mixture. Spoon mixture into the dish/es. Only now pour the rest of the egg and milk mixture onto meat mixture. Bake until set, 30 to 45 mins.

A FABULOUS CURRY

Warwick winemaker Nic van Aarde's adventurous CV includes consulting for Zampa Winery in Nashik ("the Napa of India"). This wine growing area is about 180 km outside Mumbai. "But takes 4 hours by car in hectic traffic," recalls Nic. "While there I used to frequent the only wine bar in town, called The Cellar Door, and became good friends with the 30-year-old owner, Sachin Darade, who was doing his bit to get the wine scene going in India. I always ordered this dish with a glass of red wine - local Cabernet or Cabernet Shiraz. It was goat on the bone. Sachin let me spend some time in the kitchen watching the Maharashtrian chef cook. The fried onion base is the secret to the rich taste of this curry." Now, Nic matches this dish with Warwick's signature Cabernet Franc. Very good indeed.

150ml vegetable oil
1 cinnamon stick
12 peppercorns
6 cloves
8 cardamom pods
1 tsp caraway seeds
3 green chillies
2 bay leaves
4 onions, sliced
10 cloves fresh garlic, chopped
6 teaspoons fresh ginger, chopped
5 tsp coriander powder

2 tsp cumin powder
½ tsp turmeric powder
2 tsp red chilli powder
1 tsp green cardamom powder
Salt and pepper
300ml full fat yogurt
20g coriander leaves
1kg lamb knuckles
450g can of diced tomatoes
2 cubes beef stock
1 tsp garam masala for garnish
3 Tbsp chopped coriander leaves for garnish

Add some oil to a pan and fry cinnamon stick, peppercorns, cloves, cardamom pods, caraway seeds, bay leaves and green chillies for 2 mins to release flavours. Keep stirring, add 2 sliced onions, ginger, garlic and fry. Add powdered spices and a splash of water to prevent them from burning. Keep stirring, while frying for another 2 mins. Season.

Empty mix into a blender, with yoghurt and coriander leaves, whizz. Pour over the lamb knuckles and leave to marinate.

Heat some of the oil in a heavy pot. Add remaining 2 sliced onions, fry gently until golden. Stir to prevent burning. Cool down, then put in blender to make a paste.

Add some more oil to a pot. Add diced tomatoes. Fry about 2 mins, add onion paste, fry another 2 mins. Add meat and marinade to this tomato-onion mixture. Dissolve stock cubes in a cup of water, add to pot. Cover with a lid or foil. Place in a preheated 180c oven for 2 hrs.

To serve, sprinkle with garam masala, and some chopped coriander leaves. Accompany with rice, roti or naan.

SWARTLAND SHORT-RIB

This recipe comes from Peter Ceaser of the excellent Mama Cucina trattoria in Riebeek Kasteel. We went with viticulturalist Chris and winemaker Andrea Mullineux, locals who often eat here; they recommended this Special on the menu, we were bowled over. A knockout. And perfectly accompanied by the Mullineux' new-generation Swartland reds. You can replace the Darling Brew with your favourite local craft beer. Serve with wild mushroom risotto or potato-pea mash, says Peter. Feeds 6-8.

3kg beef short-rib
Sea salt
Coarse black pepper
2 tsp caraway seeds
1 bunch fresh rosemary
2 Tbsp creamy Dijon mustard
1 bottle Darling Brew Black Mist beer (550ml)
1 bottle good quality tomato sauce (750ml)
3 Tbsp maple or golden syrup
5 Tbsp good quality soya sauce
5 to 10 bay leaves

Cut short rib into preferred sizes. Sprinkle with salt and pepper, place in a roasting tray in a very hot oven to grill and get rid of the excess fat. (Or cut it off.) Once browned, put into a clean roasting dish.

Combine rest of ingredients in a saucepan on low heat. Pour over the meat. Cover with foil or a lid, cook in 150c oven for about 90 mins or until soft and sticky.

"Food and wine matching should not be about what to drink with truffles. Rather what to drink with KFC: a Roussanne, or a bone-dry Chenin Blanc with a nutty side. And with a burger? Cinsaut or Pinot Noir. A dry Riesling with lamb and hummus wrap. Or a calamari salad. "

Jean-Vincent Ridon, Signal Hill Winery

BEST BRAAIED LAMB CHOPS

Winemakers can be touchier about their braai (barbecue) skills than their wines. So we will doubtless offend multitudes by asserting that the best chops in the Cape are cooked by Thelema's Gyles Webb…No fancy marinades. (Though have Thelema Cabernet handy for lubrication while tending the fire.) Here's how.

Have the chops cut at least 25mm thick with a good bit of fat on them. Crunch some coarse black pepper on both sides. We use an old oil drum as a braai and wingerdstokkies for fuel. Make a reasonably big fire and when there are suitable coals scrape some to the side and cook the chops fat-side down over low heat until the fat is crisp. Some rosemary twigs on the coals add a nice flavour. Then move the chops to higher heat and cook quickly, adding salt to taste. The outside should be well-cooked, and the inside still pink – just a few minutes on each side.

"I get a real kick out of opening a posh bottle of wine and enjoying it with the simplest of meals."

Rozy Gunn, of Iona Vineyards

CURRY AFVAL

Swartland revolutionary Adi Badenhorst says: "My dad and I eat loads of this. I learned to cook it from my grandmother." He uses sheep's trotters and cow's stomach (tripe). "Sheep stomach is way too thin and has very little fat." Afval is the Afrikaans word for offal.

The base is chopped onions and garlic (whole pieces) fried up until soft. Use the masala/curry powder of your choice and add this to the onions. Add a half-cup cup of brown vinegar, then all the afval. Just cover with water. I now season with white pepper powder, whole black peppercorns and good salt. And adjust again later if necessary. Simmer slowly all day – or for at least 4 hrs, adding more water if needed. You can also put the pot straight into the oven for 4 hrs at 165c. Serve with rice..

STINCO BRASATO AL VINO ROSSO

Translation: Braised Beef Shin with Red Wine, a favourite of both father Giorgio and son George Dalla Cia. Sometimes, if you are lucky, it is on the daily-changing chalkboard menu at Pane E Vino, the family's rustic food and wine bar in Stellenbosch, prepared by owner, cook, accountant and manager Elena Dalla Cia. To whom George is fortunate to be married. It is superb with the sort of Cape super-Tuscan blend that Giorgio is making. Elena serves with mash or polenta on a nice old silver or pewter platter. And says: "Do not send the bone back to the kitchen until you have dug into the marrow with the help of some long, thin tool!" One shin yields 4-6 servings.

1 whole beef shin

Marinade
1 bottle of barrel-aged red wine
2 carrots, chopped
2 onions, sliced
1 celery long stick, chopped
Sage (1 small bunch)
Rosemary (2 sprigs)
Salt
1 tsp black peppercorns
Put shin and marinade in a bowl in fridge, leave overnight

To prepare next day
40g butter
3 Tbsp extra virgin olive oil
Salt to taste
2 Tbsp tomato concentrate
Ground black pepper
Light beef stock

Drain and pat dry meat. Put butter and oil in a big enough casserole, heat on stove. When nice and hot add meat, sear on all sides. The oil must stay very hot throughout.
Once meat is nice and browned, add tomato concentrate, pepper, and the marinade. Move casserole to oven. Cook at 160-170c for about 2 hrs or until the meat is soft (a fork must go through without holding the meat) and the sauce has thickened. Keep spooning juices over the meat while it is cooking. If it starts drying out, add some light stock. If the sauce is too liquid but the meat is ready, remove the meat, let the sauce thicken on top of the stove and then pour it over the meat when ready. During the whole cooking process in the oven the meat must be kept moist by pouring over it some of the juices every little while.

A DELICIOUS VEGETABLE DISH OR SIDE

Substantial enough to stand on its own, with a tomato salad and some leaves, this Tian also shines in company - with roast chicken, say. And lamb chops. As her husband braais them. This is a recipe from Barbara Webb of Thelema. If served as a vegetarian main, team with something like the charming Sutherland Viognier-Roussanne blend. If a side, with lamb chops, Thelema Cabernet.

150 g rice
2 onions, grated
4 Tbsp olive oil
2 large cloves garlic, finely chopped
1 kg courgettes, grated
2 Tbsp flour

1 chicken stock cube
500 ml milk
80 g Parmesan cheese (or strong Cheddar)
Salt and pepper
1,5l baking dish
2 Tbsp olive oil

Boil rice in water for 5 mins. Drain. Fry onions in oil for about 10 mins. Add garlic, grated courgettes. Toss for 5 mins. Add flour and stock cube, cook 2 mins. Add milk, cook 2 mins. Then add rice and 2Tbsp cheese. Blend, cook 2 mins. Season to taste. Put in a buttered baking dish. Spread rest of cheese on top. Drip last 2 Tbsp oil over. Bake in the upper third of your oven at 220c for about 30 mins or until the cheese bubbles on top.

CHEESE OR PUD?

Ending a meal with cheese and fruit, so far so traditional. But with garlic and red wine, too… is this a step too far, this dish from Kerry Kilpin, executive chef of Bistro Sixteen82 at Steenberg Estate? Gorgonzola fritters with wine-poached pears, kumquats and garlic confit? Absolutely not. She is a shining star at pairing food and wine; spent years learning from the reigning king of this sort of thing, Franck Dangereux, at The Food Barn. She uses the estate's Nebbiolo in her recipe; it works like a dream. Good drinking partner, too. Serves 6.

Fritter
150g Gorgonzola cheese
150g grated mozzarella
200g flour
200g bread crumbs
3 eggs, whisked
Pinch salt
1l sunflower oil

Combine cheeses and pinch salt in a food processor to bind. Roll into 6 balls. Refrigerate for 30min to set.

Place flour, eggs and crumbs in 3 separate bowls. Dip cheese balls in flour, then eggs, lastly bread crumbs. Repeat, so cheese balls are double-crumbed. Set aside.

Heat oil, fry balls until they become nice golden fritters.

Poached pears
2 pears peeled, cut into 6 slices each
300ml Nebbiolo wine
150g sugar
10g butter

Place pears, sugar and wine in a pot. Slowly bring to the simmer, poach for about 10mins or until cooked through but not soft. Cool pear in the liquid, before removing. Bring liquid to the boil, reduce to syrupy consistency (down to about 50ml). Whisk in butter. Cool.

Garlic Confit
12 garlic cloves
100ml sunflower oil

Place garlic cloves in a pot on the stove over very low heat. Allow the garlic to confit (stew, soften) gently in the oil for about 15mins. The garlic must become very soft but retain its white colour. Cool.

To serve
100g baby salad leaves
6 preserved kumquats, halved

Arrange salad leaves in the centre of a large platter or individual plates. Alternate pears, garlic and kumquats around the leaves (Kerry makes a star shape). Place cheese fritter on top of leaves. Drizzle leaves and plate with Nebbiolo syrup.

FIGS, HONEY, NUTS, CHOCOLATE PLUS

*This beautiful sweet is from Klein Constantia's award-winning food book **Vin de Constance with Michel Roux Jnr**. It features recipes dreamed up by this distinguished contemporary chef, of Le Gavroche in London, to partner the legendary Cape dessert wine. He advises: "Use the best chocolate possible… it really makes a difference!" Serves 4.*

100ml milk
Finely grated zest of ¼ of an orange
3 cardamom pods, crushed
1 Tbsp maple syrup
100g milk chocolate, chopped
4 Tbsp pistachios, peeled
2 Tbsp icing sugar, sifted
8 slightly under-ripe figs
1 Tbsp olive oil
2 Tbsp honey

Bring milk to boil in small saucepan. Add zest, cardamom and syrup, cover, set aside off the stove to steep for 15 mins. While still hot, pour through sieve onto chocolate in a bowl. Stir until melted.

Scatter pistachios on baking tray, dust with icing sugar, bake at 180c, shaking tray every now and then, until they start to caramelise. Watch carefully, this happens quickly. They should be slightly brown with a tinge of green. Remove from oven, leave to cool. They will become crunchy after 4-5 mins.

Slice figs into three, discarding the tip. Heat a large non-stick frying pan intil very hot. Pour in olive oil, then immediately follow with fig slices. After 20 secs flip over to cook other side. Add honey, cook another 30 secs. Remove from heat, gently remove figs to a warm plate.

Toss pistachios in remaining honey and pan juices, add to plate.

Drizzle with chocolate, orange and cardamom sauce. Serve immediately.

BRILLIANT BREAD
TO SERVE WITH CHEESE

Eric Bulpitt, chef of The Restaurant at Newton Johnson in the Hemel en Aarde Valley, a South African Top Tenner, is renowned for his use of local, seasonal and foraged produce. And for attention to detail from start to finish of his menu. This is the bread he makes to serve with local cheeses. It is great made into melba toast, too.

150g flour
150g nutty wheat flour
20g bran
50g oats
10g salt
7,5g instant yeast
50g poppy seeds
50g sesame seeds

50g pumpkin seeds
50g linseed
50g sunflower seeds
50g oil
500 ml water
37,5g honey
100g raisins or sultanas, optional

Mix all dry ingredients. Mix oil, water and honey, add to dry ingredients. Place in loaf tin, allow to raise in a warm place. Bake for 90 mins at 180c. Cool. Slice thinly when cold.

AND A SNIFTER...

After a long wine evening, at home, and with apologies to my Cape Vintage (port) friends the Nels, whose exploits in the South African answer to the Douro, Calitzdorp, are admirable (and will feature in my next book), I sometimes like a bedtime nip. In which case it has to be Upland. A brandy, not another wine.

You come to this farm, just outside Wellington – if you can find it, I usually take a couple of wrong turns - for an original take on brandy and grappa, which they call Grapé, and leave overcome by the magic of this hidden gem, and marvelling at the cocoon of charmingly unkempt, organic self-sufficiency Edmund and Elsie Oettlé have woven around themselves. She is an engineer, he an Onderstepoort vet who invented a unique dye that's now used worldwide in invitro-fertilization. They were the first estate producers to achieve official organic status - way back in 1994. About a decade ahead of the pack. Their slogan: 'Our wines don't cost the Earth'. Fertilizer, pest controls and protections against erosion are nature-driven. The fat ducks and arrogant African prototype cockerels, resplendent in coppers, reds and blacks, all seem part of the profusion of indigenous grasses in the vineyards – Pinot Noir, Cabernet, Chenin - that inhibit excessive yields and define character.

I've always marvelled at the home-made, copper potstill – a feat in itself – not only because it produces fine brandy but because its 'waste' hot water is channelled into steam baths so the family can enjoy sumptuous saunas. Rustic independence is evinced perfectly too by Elsie; on our last visit, when the discussion turned to dispassionate wine assessment, she said, "You know, if the guy who makes the wine pisses me off, however good, why would I drink it?"

Since our last visit, Guinevere, a regal Canadian-bred raptor whose job it was to nobble yellow-billed duck and other wild protein around the district for the Oettlés' table, had passed on. She is due to be replaced.

There's a small range of individual organic still wines, and the Grapé spirit has the expected thrust, earthy, heathery and faintly husks-and-berry-flavoured, sometimes from Cabernet, sometimes from Pinot. And there's a Chenin-based Pure Potstill Brandy – also cleanly powerful, touch smoky. But I am unable to resist **Upland Organic Estate** - The Undiluted Cask Strength – 65% alc. – **Potstill Brandy**. A magnificent blast of grand wild essences and perfumes, to be taken in minute sips.

"Just wet the lips now and again," advises Oettlé.

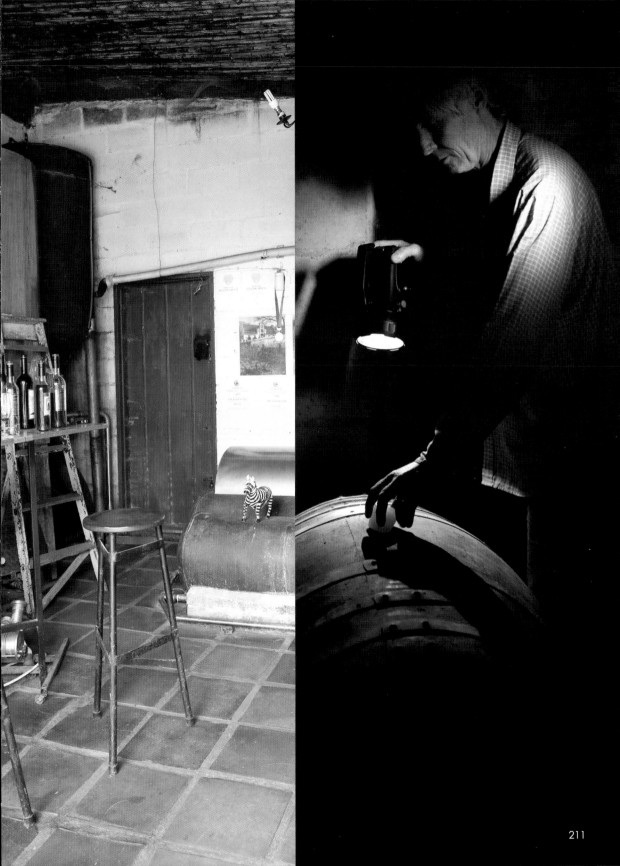

INDEX

WINES

82 Meerlust
78 Newton Johnson Family Vineyard,
    WindandSea, Mrs M, Block 6
81 Radford Dale Freedom
86 Storm Moya's
86 The Drift There Are Still Mysteries

87 RED BLENDS
94 Anthonij Rupert
92 AA Badenhorst Family
96 Dalla Cia Teano
100 David & Nadia Sadie Elpidios
100 De Trafford Elevation 393
100 Fairview Extrano
101 Hartenberg The Mackenzie
101 Jordan Cobblers Hill
101 Kanonkop Paul Sauer
99 Keet First Verse
98 Ken Forrester Three Halves, Renegade
101 Klein Constantia Estate Red
101 La Motte Pierneef Collection Shiraz-Viognier
101/2 Marvelous Blue, Red
102 Meerlust Rubicon
102 Meinert Synchronicity
102 Miles Mossop Max
100 MR de Compostella
102 Nederburg Edelrood
102 Paserene Marathon
102 Rall Red
102 Rupert & Rothschild Baron Edmond
88 Sadie Family Columella
102/3 Savage Red, Follow the Line
103 Sjinn Flagship Field Blend, Low Profile
103 Steytler Pentagon
103 Swerwer
103 The Blacksmith
97 Tokara Director's Reserve
90 Vilafonté C, M
95 Waterford The Jem
103 Webb Ellis

104 RIESLING
107 Eendevanger
106 Paul Cluver Close Encounter (2)
105 Spioenkop
107 Jordan The Real McCoy
107 Nitida

108 ROSÉ
109 De Toren La Jeunesse (light red)
109 Eendevanger Pinot Gris

109 Felicité
109 FRAM Grenache Gris
108 Graham Beck Gorgeous
109 Ken Forrester Grenache
109 Klein Constantia
109 Sutherland Grenache
109 Tokara Siberia Grenache

109 ROUSSANNE
109 Joostenberg

110 SAUVIGNON BLANC
114 Buitenverwachting Hussey's Vlei
111 Cederberg Private Cellar, Longhavi,
    Ghost Corner Wild Ferment
114 Delaire Graff Coastal Cuvée
114 Iona
113 Klein Constantia, Metis, Block 382
114 La Motte Pierneef
114 Reyneke Reserve
114 Sophie Te'Blanche (Iona)
114 Springfield Life from Stone
114 Steenberg Black Swan
114 Tokara Reserve
114 Vergelegen Schaapenberg
114 Villiera Bush Vine

115 SEMILLON
115 Thorne and Daughters Tin Soldier

116 SYRAH-SHIRAZ
128 Boekenhoutskloof
128 Craven
128 De Trafford
129 Intellego Kolbroek
128 Jordan The Prospector
122/3 Hartenberg Gravel Hill, The Stork,
    Doorkeeper
128 Keermont Steepside, Topside
129 Kleine Zalze Family Reserve
118 Mullineux Granite, Schist
120 Porseleinberg
124 Reyneke Reserve
129 Richard Kershaw Elgin
126 Signal Hill Clos d'Orange
129 Stark-Condé Three Pines
129 Terra Cura Kasteelberg
129 Tokara Director's Reserve
129 Vondeling Erica
129 Waterford Kevin Arnold
129 Wine Cellar Syran
128 Winery of Good Hope Nudity

WINE COUNTRY FOOD

WINE PEOPLE

ACKNOWLEDGEMENTS

To everyone who shared their wines and stories to make this book, a big thank you.

Many others have fabulous stories and great wines too. Regrets. Next time, please.

Image-maker - Clinton "The Eye" Friedman
Editor - Erica "The Chief Whip" Platter
Palate - John "A Drop More Please" Platter

No sponsors and no advertising were sought nor offered in preparing My Kind of Wine; no commercial ties exist between the authors and any labels or names mentioned and no other considerations, beyond the customary wine samples, were accepted, save in the case of four long-standing old friends, the Webbs of Thelema, the Newton-Johnsons, of Newton-Johnson, the Brownes of Hartenberg, and Pieter Ferreira of Graham Beck, who had us to stay overnight. No commercial ties have existed with the Platter Wine Guide for many years.

My Kind of Wine

PawPaw Publishing (pawpawpublishing.co.za)
First edition 2015
Author: John Platter
Concept, editing, marketing: Erica Platter (platter@wol.co.za)
Photography, design, production: Clinton Friedman (clintonfriedman.com)
End papers: Cameron Platter (cameronplatter.com)

ISBN: 978-0-620-66361-8

Printed and bound by TWP Sdn. Bhd. Malaysia